ALTERNATIVE MODELS OF
SPORTS DEVELOPMENT
IN AMERICA

Alex —

Enjoy The Book!

Doc K

Ohio University Sport Management Series

Dr. Norm O'Reilly, Series Editor

20 Secrets to Success for NCAA Student-Athletes Who Won't Go Pro, by Rick Burton, Jake Hirshman, Norm O'Reilly, Andy Dolich, and Heather Lawrence

Alternative Models of Sports Development in America: Solutions to a Crisis in Education and Public Health, by B. David Ridpath

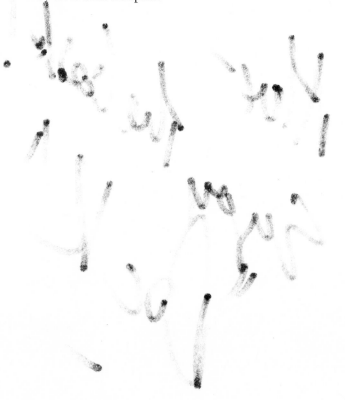

Alternative Models of Sports Development in America

SOLUTIONS TO A CRISIS IN EDUCATION AND PUBLIC HEALTH

B. David Ridpath

Foreword by Tom Farrey

OHIO UNIVERSITY PRESS • ATHENS

Ohio University Press, Athens, Ohio 45701
ohioswallow.com
© 2018 by Ohio University Press

To obtain permission to quote, reprint, or otherwise reproduce or distribute material
from Ohio University Press publications, please contact our rights and permissions
department at (740) 593-1154 or (740) 593-4536 (fax).

Printed in the United States of America
Ohio University Press books are printed on acid-free paper ⊗ ™

28 27 26 25 24 23 22 21 20 19 18   5 4 3 2 1

Library of Congress Cataloging-in-Publication Data

Names: Ridpath, B. David, author.
Title: Alternative models of sports development in America : solutions to a
  crisis in education and public health / B. David Ridpath ; foreword by Tom
  Farrey.
Description: Athens, Ohio : Ohio University Press, 2017. | Series: Ohio
  University sport management series | Includes bibliographical references
  and index.
Identifiers: LCCN 2017053673| ISBN 9780821422908 (hardback) | ISBN
  9780821422915 (pb) | ISBN 9780821446140 (pdf)
Subjects: LCSH: Physical education and training--United States. | College
  sports--United States. | School sports--United States. | Sports--Health
  aspects--United States. | College athletes--Education--United States. |
  Athletes--Education--United States. | Public health--United States. |
  BISAC: SPORTS & RECREATION / General. | EDUCATION / Physical Educa-
  tion. |
  MEDICAL / Public Health.
Classification: LCC GV223 .R54 2014 | DDC 613.70973--dc23
LC record available at https://lccn.loc.gov/2017053673

This book is dedicated to
Jacqueline, Chiara,
and Bradley II

Contents

Foreword

Let's start with the end in mind, with a vision of the communities that we as Americans want to live in, based on human needs and shared values. Imagine, if you will, towns and municipalities where people want to get out of their homes because life is richer out there, full of parks and balls, dogs and laughter, old friends and new. Imagine places that offer a rich array of recreational options, where citizens and schools and industry demand those options because they appreciate the myriad benefits that flow to those whose bodies are in motion.

How do we get there?

It's a question that has guided much of my work at The Aspen Institute, where we convene leaders around the important challenges of our time, help them find common ground, and inspire solutions that aim to deliver the greatest good for the greatest number. My focus is on how sport, broadly defined, can serve the public interest, starting with the building of healthy communities.

This book makes a great contribution to that dialogue. David Ridpath recognizes the essential role that sport plays in the vitality of the nation and its people, then asks whether the sport system we have in place, drawn up more than a hundred years ago as a tool of nation-building, is serving the needs of Americans in the twenty-first century. Better yet, with research and courage, he identifies several potential paths forward.

We should not be afraid to explore systems-level change in the development and delivery of sport programs in the United States, but rather understand it as an opportunity to respond to the marketplace.

Consider: More than four out of five parents of youth under age eighteen say it's "very important" or "somewhat important" that their child play sports, and a full 96 percent see some value, according to household surveys conducted in 2017 for our Aspen Institute program, Project Play, a multistage initiative to provide stakeholders with tools to build what we call "Sport for All, Play for Life" communities. Americans *get* sports, and not just as spectators. It's a physical expression of the spirit, and a site of self-learning and social connection. No one wants their kid stuck on the couch, glued to a screen, all but thumbs inert.

Yet today, as early as first grade in some communities, the structure of our sport system begins to push aside kids. We create tryout-based travel teams, sorting the weak from the strong well before children grow into their bodies, minds, and true interests. Those who don't make the cut, or don't receive the playing time, get the message that they are not a priority and begin checking out of the system. Meanwhile, the kids at the center of the system—those told they are the next generation of athlete-entertainers—are increasingly encouraged to train year-round. They often play too many games for their developing bodies, risking overuse injuries, unnecessary concussions, and burnout.

For each of the past five years, the number of youth who are "active to a healthy level" through sports has fallen, according to the Sports & Fitness Industry Association. Only 24.8 percent of kids ages six to twelve, and 38.4 percent of youth thirteen to seventeen, play at least three days a week. Further, only 27.1 percent are physically active one hour daily, as recommended by the Centers for Disease Control & Prevention, even as participation on high school teams has held steady at about half of all students.

To date, Project Play has been focused on ages twelve and under, given the mountain of research on the physical, mental, social-emotional and educational benefits that flow to physically active kids. Getting them moving early unleashes a virtuous cycle—they go on to college more often, stay active into adulthood more often, make higher incomes in the workplace, enjoy lower health care costs, and are twice as likely to have active children. As a society, we must make quality, regular sport activity accessible to every child, regardless of zip code or ability.

At the same time, we recognize that the landscape of youth sports has been transformed over the past generation by the priorities of the two institutions that Ridpath explores in this book—school sports and college sports. NCAA member institutions today offer $3 billion in athletic aid, up from $250 million in the early 1990s, according to the NCAA. That's a lot of chum tossed into the sea of youth sports. Even for the well-positioned, it's rarely a meal, as full-ride athletic scholarships are confined to just a few sports; rather, it's just enough to induce a feeding frenzy among parents, terrified about how they one day must pay hefty college tuitions. So they invest, at ever-earlier ages for kids, in private trainers, traveling club teams, and $300 cleats or bats.

If they can.

They seek return on investment, even if it's just playing time for their kid on the high school team. Not an easy thing to come by today. Intramurals are largely a thing of the past, as is regular PE past middle school. At large, public high schools, eighty kids might try out for the varsity basketball team. Thirteen might make the team, with eight or nine seeing real minutes in games. It's hardly a recipe for broad-based provision of the health and other benefits that sports participation can provide.

In places, school-based sports works beautifully. Go to just about any prep school. They usually create as many teams in a sport as necessary to accommodate the kids in the school who want to play that sport—an A, B, C, and D team if necessary. They allow the supply of sport opportunities to meet the demand. And they ask that every student participate in that economy, by playing at least one sport. Often, sports are not extracurricular but cocurricular, in recognition of the educational value they can provide.

Write me if you think that's an awful model, one that leaves US students less prepared to compete in a global economy. I'm guessing that my inbox isn't about to explode.

So, to me, the question becomes: Can that model be adapted to high schools with larger student bodies and/or smaller budgets? If so, how? This is where the conversation that Ridpath seeds gets very interesting—and promising, if we allow it. Given schools' responsibility to serve all students, can they work more effectively with local clubs to identify participation opportunities for students? Can they allow them to use campus facilities more readily, if clubs embrace policies and practices that are inclusive and model best practices? Can the role of the athletic director or PE teacher be reimagined, making it less a provider of sport opportunities and more a connector to community programs?

One level up is the hard question to ask: Do NCAA Division I member universities need to continue to position themselves as the pathway to the pros? To fill their stadiums and arenas, do they need the very best emerging athletes—or should they turn over the training of the top 1 percent of the major sport pipelines to leagues like the NBA starting at age sixteen or even fourteen? And, if the model adjusts in that direction, could the NCAA amend its rules to make room for prospects who, after spending time with such a club, realize college is likely their best option?

What's clear to me, having studied our sports system as an author and journalist for thirty years, is that the day will come when the role of sports in schools gets reappraised and updated by its key stakeholders.

This day could come suddenly, and from any of several angles. The catalyst could be a legal ruling, changing the economic relationship between universities and athletes. It could be a legislative action, akin to Title IX, which with a stroke of a pen in 1972 opened up sports opportunities for one disenfranchised group, women. It could be an administrative action, a meatier version of the Dear Colleague letter issued by the Obama administration prohibiting discrimination of disabled students in school sports. It could be a unilateral industry action, such as the NBA embracing a version of the European club model described above. It could be a collective industry action—a serious push to legalize and tax sports betting, with a cut dedicated to investments in parks and other recreation infrastructure.

When that day comes, you will hear doomsday scenarios about the end of sports as we know it, and maybe the loss of American values. Sports participation is too easily conflated with participation trophies, which no one outside the trophy industry is really all that big a fan of but have become a great tool anyway to grouse about millennials and liberals. It's ironic, given that the original vision of school sports in America, by its founders more than a century ago, was of mass participation, of sport as a tool of public health and educational achievement.

The way you can support renewal of this vision is to be open to new ideas. Do not buy the theory that if change is made, our games will go away. The sports entertainment industry will be just fine; the market demands that Alabama play Auburn on one Saturday each fall. Nor is anyone going to start tearing down the gyms and fields attached to schools; the physical infrastructure of sports in our country remains.

What is in play is the software side of sports—how the operating system works, who gets to use it, how its assets can best be deployed and services scaled.

Do not marinate in nostalgia. Do not idealize the way we used to do it, because, while for many of us there was much to like about our childhood experiences, there was not much room on playing fields for girls and almost none for kids with disabilities until the '80s. The next great sport development and delivery system that we embrace will be the first great sport development and delivery system that we have.

Do not forget that most kids do not play sports regularly today.

Scan your network of friends and family, and think about who is left out of our de facto sport system. Picture their faces . . .

The nephew who is slow to grow into his body.

The niece with a chronic condition, like asthma.

The coworker's kid who is overweight.

The neighbor's kid who can't play football anymore because of concussions.

Think about how we can help them, how we need them, to become their best selves. And think too about the role that you know sport can play in that process.

Tom Farrey

Executive Director,
Sports & Society Program

The Aspen Institute

Preface

The title of this book may seem radical; frankly, that is by intent. However, it has an important premise and, dare I say, even promise, in proposing needed changes to a long-standing, popular, but ultimately fragmented sports delivery and entertainment system that is in desperate need of change. Proposing that the United States change its deeply imbedded, educationally based sports system is akin to changing the health-care marketplace in America or proposing new gun control measures, and one does not have to look too far to see the challenges both of those issues present. Is it any wonder that this, too, is a difficult proposition? The United States' primary way of delivering sports while concurrently developing athletes of all skills is under immense pressure as to how it fits within the funding-starved public education system. Yet, educationally based sports in America remain incredibly popular overall, despite this tenuous relationship. School-based competitive sports have long been touted, in many ways correctly, as a source of community pride, an effective strategy for school branding, and a way to develop skilled athletes, while presenting many other intrinsic and tangible values. Still, this does not mean that we as citizens should not look at ways to potentially change the status quo of sports development and delivery, for the potential betterment of the country and our entire sports development system.

There are many direct and indirect comparisons when it comes to attempting to change existing, deeply embedded systems, regardless of what they may be. This applies even if the need for improvement is highly evident, as I feel it is with how we do sports in America. Change is hard for many, especially when money and control are involved. Resistance to change in most any walk of life will always be there, by those who are comfortable and/or fear change for whatever reason. For example, it is arguably critical to the health and economy of the United States to have better access to health care for all, which in turn might increase competition, lower costs, and provide health and wellness benefits. This sounds great in theory and may ultimately be accurate, but it certainly does not mean there will not be resistance to any change in the American health-care system, since the current system does benefit certain segments of society and those populations do not want to abandon the status quo. We see arguments about this subject almost every day in the news.

One can also debate the current state of sports delivery and sports development in the United States, both as it compares to other countries around the world and as to whether the primary education-based model should be revised, if not changed completely. Sports development and sports delivery are broad terms that need to be defined. Essentially, there are several definitions, and in this country there are no standard definitions for overall sports development and sports delivery processes. Empirically, elite sports development has been defined as "the skill development of talented athletes in the continuum of elite athlete 'production'" (Hogan and Norton 2000, 215–16). Sports development can also be described as a delivery system of sports in a certain context, such as how sports are delivered to and accessed by groups and individual citizens of a certain country. In America, sports development and sports delivery are rather fragmented, in that the United States does not have a centralized national sports policy or a governmental sports ministry to provide a governance framework, as is the case in many other countries. What we have is a mishmash of several organizations that are educational, public, and private, which provide sports and exercise opportunities throughout the country. For the purposes of this book, "sports development" is an umbrella term for all sports delivery options that currently exist in the United States, whether scholastic, public, private, professional, or amateur.

This book proposes various options to potentially assist in creating better and more centralized sports development systems in order to offer more alternatives for athletes, coaches, administrators, and others, beyond the current educationally based system in America. Despite the availability of other options, competitive and recreational sports opportunities in America are still primarily available only in schools. According to the United States Olympic Committee, educationally based athletics encompass over 80 percent of all sports delivery and sports development options in the United States. Access for all participants in sports beyond the schools is often restrictive and limited because of cost and a dearth of offerings. Meanwhile, most schools are focusing more on elite sports development and delivery than on mass participation and exercise. We are becoming a nation mostly of spectators and the systematic development of elite athletes rather than a nation with a system or systems that provide access for all. Sadly, even most of the primary and secondary public schools in the United States are charging additional, often high participation fees for athletes just to play in sports that are ostensibly already funded by public taxes, thus making it even tougher for individuals to participate and exercise in what might be one of the only available sports development options.[1]

Scholars have debated and analyzed the issues and problems with educationally based sports development for over a century. Somewhat ironically, this is about the same time period that organized sports gained a foothold in our education system. I have been part of this debate for well over a decade, following a long career in intercollegiate athletics as a coach and administrator in which I passionately defended the very system this book proposes to change. I am intensely cognizant of what this book is suggesting, and absolutely understand that dramatic change will not be quick or easy, but that does not negate the need to create, analyze, and modify different approaches that can ultimately provide real and meaningful change before it is too late. These are not short-term options. Any potential solution must present generational changes and proposals, but significant alteration of sports development and sports delivery in America can and should be done.

I do not think it is either quixotic or wishful thinking to propose dramatic changes to the way we do sports in America. There is almost universal agreement among scholars, coaches, university presidents, secondary school teachers, and even athletes themselves that the present commercialized, economic, and academic foundation of educationally based sports is on very shaky ground and its future is certainly in doubt. Thus, many conclude that it is not a question of whether economics, legal challenges, and athlete's rights movements and other forces will change the current system, but only a matter of when.[2] Even some of the most jaded supporters of the education-based model are raising questions and looking toward the future. Big Ten Conference Commissioner Jim Delany, one of the most powerful people in National Collegiate Athletic Association (NCAA) Division I athletics, recently said, "Anybody who thinks that we're in a good place or that what we have is totally sustainable—I would suggest, is not really reading the tea leaves, because of the federal litigation, the federal interest in Congress, and the public's skepticism, and even the media's skepticism. We're not in 1965; we're in 2015. We think it's time for a good, full, broad, national discussion on where education fits in the system" (Planos 2015).

The United States of America is basically the only country (with some exceptions, such as a limited system by comparison in Canada and limited educationally based extramural sports opportunities elsewhere) whose primary avenue of sports development and delivery for most of its citizens lies within the structures of primary, secondary, and higher education. On the surface, this may appear to be a mutually beneficial arrangement and even a noble effort to combine the shared aspects and goals of education and sports development. Education, maturity, and growth have consistently been discussed in terms of the effort to foster a sound mind and sound body in developing a total person as part of the educational process. Ostensibly, gaining a valuable education while participating and competing in sports, even at an elite, hypercompetitive level, can seem to be an effective and promising combination. This meshing of sports and education is not unique, in the sense that most educational systems in the world include some type of physical education and sports component. Most young people in countries other than the United States actually get their first exposure to sports in school through broad-based sports participation opportunities, while more specialized and competitive development continues in local and regional sports clubs.[3] The main difference between the United States and other countries is in the prominent place sports has in education and the academic eligibility requirements to be able to practice and compete.

Interscholastic and intercollegiate athletic competition in America is not only hugely popular and at times profitable, it is also the primary avenue for mass participation as well as elite sports development and competition. That is where any similarity between the United States and other countries with regard to sports and education begins and ends. As mentioned previously, it is estimated that over 80 percent of sports development and delivery in the United States is done through educational systems. Approximately 65 percent of the US Olympic team at the 2012 London Summer Olympic Games had participated in university-based sports programs (Forde 2015). This does not even include the numerous athletes from foreign countries who come to the United States not only for an education, but also to hone their athletic skills within its higher education system. In the 2016 Summer Olympic Games in Brazil, 1,018 athletes, representing many nations, were either current, incoming, or former American college athletes, including the 430 athletes in the US delegation (Martinez 2016). This in itself can cause numerous issues, not the least of which is that the primary American sports development system is providing training opportunities for elite foreign athletes who may take away opportunities from potential US athletes.[4] There is nothing inherently wrong with this, but it is another reason why more opportunities should be available to all athletes, beyond the education system, to play and participate in sports in America. In countries such as those in Europe that are a primary focus of this book, the major avenue of sports development and delivery is outside the educational system, embedded in separate nonprofit sports club systems. The details, benefits, and weaknesses of this model, when compared to the current educational sports model in America, are discussed in greater depth as the book progresses.

Despite the existence of empirical research and popular discussion regarding issues and problems with the American sports development and sports delivery models, there has been a dearth of discussion regarding potential changes to the status quo. Ironically, very little of the research has discussed the mechanisms, concepts, or theories for change, even though there is almost universal agreement that change must occur. In 2015, an outstanding empirically based book, *Sport Development in the United States: High Performance and Mass Participation,* by Peter Smolianov, Dwight H. Zakus, and John Gallo, put forth a practical, theory-based process for potential changes to the current US model and began to drive serious discussion about needed changes to the way this country conducts sports and develops athletes.[5] Candidly, that book is a primary inspiration for this work, and I strongly feel that both sets of proposals are needed to add to the debate and the body of knowledge regarding future sports development models and changes in the United States. Many of the ideas presented in their work are similar to mine. Although there are significant overlaps and synergies in potential applications, this work is based more on conceptual models of change, including modification of the current educationally based model.

This book analyzes historical aspects of interscholastic and intercollegiate sports development in the United States as well as reasons for the parallel development of the non-education-based model found in European countries. The final chapters discuss the why and how of reviewing, analyzing, and ultimately proposing new models of sports development and delivery for the United States both inside and outside the existing educational system. Some of my proposed changes to the existing American model draw upon the European sports club system as one of the potential templates. The overarching analysis points to the inevitable unsustainability of a primary sports development and sports delivery model being part of all levels of education in the United States. The "why" concerns the challenges to the system via legal and legislative structures, as the NCAA's Jim Delany mentioned, and also those arising within the system itself. The primary thrust of this work is one of extreme caution or even outright worry. An overwhelming percentage of all participation in sports in the United States, whether elite or mass, is grounded in education, and the potential for loss of many of these opportunities (outside the special cases of football and men's basketball) within the educational system is very real. There is also very real potential for the continued and worsening loss of external opportunities in a number of sports that are not available or are out of reach for many because of the costs involved. The ability of America to be competitive internationally in many of those sports in the future could also be dramatically impacted. The loss of these opportunities within the American education system is already happening, bearing negatively on public health in the United States due to decreased exercise and sports options. The lack of mass sports participation and physical education opportunities is a significant contributor to the epidemics of poor health and obesity facing America today. If we continue on our current path of chiefly supporting only commercially viable sports that can rake in television, sponsorship, and ticket revenue, opportunities in other sports, and the health benefits that come with them, will eventually be reduced or even evaporate.

My personal sports background, while fairly broad based, was mainly in wrestling. As checkered as my competitive and coaching careers were, my participation and competition in sports was a defining, largely positive element in my life, and one I was fortunate to have access to throughout my formative years. Sadly, sports like wrestling, swimming, gymnastics, and track and field are being downsized at all levels of the US education spectrum, if not outright eliminated, in the face of increased costs, budget reductions, and a desire to field more competitive teams in football, men's basketball, and other largely male-dominated, entertainment-centric sports. It cannot be discounted that other extra-curricular offerings at the scholastic level, such as music programs and other nonathletic options, are also being downsized and eliminated to save costs.[6] While these other issues are not within the scope of this book, there are very real dangers to not providing broad-based educational and nonathletic life-skill opportunities for American students. In the critically acclaimed 1995 movie, *Mr. Holland's Opus*, starring Richard Dreyfuss as the title character and longtime high school music teacher, Mr. Holland reacts to his music program being eliminated by saying, "The day they cut the football budget in this state, that will be the end of Western civilization as we know it!"

I am not promoting the end of Western civilization by advocating the end of sports as we know them in America. To the contrary, I am actually advocating massive expansion of low-cost sports- and health-related options for all Americans, most notably our youth. We must as a country begin to explore alternatives and determine the best role for sports and physical activity to play within and outside the educational system. Our goal must be to establish options that improve health, physical fitness, access to sports, and competition. It is time, after more than a hundred years of a primarily education-based sports development model, to explore structures that will not only grow sports opportunities for people of all ages, but also keep the United States a premier player in the competitive international sports world. This can be done, and must be done, by taking at least some of the sports delivery stress away from the educational system, developing alternatives that are both publicly and privately financed.

My main goal here is to help move the discussion and frame the inevitable changes that are both already occurring and on their way in sports and sports development in America. The United States is a leader in the world in arenas ranging far beyond those of sports. It is important for it to understand and accept the responsibility of being (or becoming) a leader in this sphere, too, by pushing for the adoption of improved international sports development and sports governance systems. I hope that this book also adds to that needed conversation.

Acknowledgments

It would be difficult to thank everyone who assisted with and inspired this project, but there are some very important people I need to mention. Writing a book is not easy, and for me that certainly applies. No project of this magnitude can come to completion without the assistance of many people who often are nearly as invested as the writer in seeing it accomplished. First, I must thank my family, which has been an inspiration and a source of motivation for me over the years as I worked on various projects that often took me away from the house and the more important things in life, such as being a husband and father. My wife Jacqueline has been the glue holding our family together, and my kids Chiara and Bradley continue to amaze me with their accomplishments and by being the wonderful people they have grown into.

The German-American Fulbright Commission was a major resource which gave me the ability to travel and live overseas with my family while working on this project for fifteen months in 2014–15. I specifically want to thank Reiner Rohr and Catharina Hansch of the Fulbright office in Berlin for all of their assistance. I also thank my German graduate students at the University of Bayreuth—Daniel Tunessen, Kim Wolf, Max Mueller, Steven Moore, Carolin Frei, David Buss, Judith Stiegelmayr, Manuel Jakob, Martin Leidtke, Natasha Reitz, Steffan Hein, and Simon Von Schwedler—who through their bachelor & master's theses and other research helped me compile several resources needed for this book, as well as providing strong writing and editorial assistance. Their hard work and writing assistance is reflected throughout the manuscript and I could not have accomplished this without them. I cannot thank enough my University of Bayreuth colleagues and the University of Bayreuth International Office, led by Ami Saini, for all of the support given to me and my family during our time in Europe. I want to especially thank Drs. Herbert Woratschek, Tim Strobel, Arnim Heinemann, Bastian Popp, Christian Meyer, Christian Durcholtz, Johanna Muhlbeyer, Michael Stadlemann, Christian Gamelmann, Markus Buser, and Markus Seufurt, and their wonderful administrative associate, Carmen Back, for everything they did for me and my family. It is not easy to completely relocate as we did and we could not have done it without your help. Thank you for letting me be part of a tremendous university and faculty, but, most of all, it is an honor to be your friend.

My friends in the Netherlands at the Hogeschool van Amsterdam, Frank Kolsteeg, Dr. Jaap Van Hulten, and Dr. Remco Koopemeiers, were critical in assisting me with regard to research on the operation of sports clubs in Europe, especially AFC Ajax Amsterdam. There are many others to thank who gave me encouragement and help along the way, both in America and Europe, including Amy Perko, Ben Bendrich, Chris Chaney, Christian Papay, Todd Kearns, Aaron Chapius, Sonny and Pam Vaccaro, Dr. Richard Vedder, Dan Beebe, Dr. Richard Southall, Dr. Katie Otto, Dr. Jason Lanter, Dr. Lawrence Chalip, Dr. Ellen Staurowsky, Dr. Jay Coakley, and Dr. John Gerdy. I must also thank my anonymous reviewers and the editorial team at Ohio University Press/ Swallow Books, including editor Gillian Berchowitz, Nancy Basmajian and Susan Welch, along with members of the editorial review board. Other primary influencers for this book include Terry Holland, Dale Brown, Dr. Ming Li, Dr. Michael Cross, Oliver Luck, and Tom Farrey. I also thank my crack graduate assistants at Ohio University, Ali Speck and Alec Koondel, who spent hours helping me revise and enhance the manuscript.

I want to recognize and deeply thank my colleagues in the Department of Sports Administration at Ohio University's College of Business, who are some of the finest teachers, scholars, and people I know. It is an honor to work with the best sports management faculty in the world. Drs. Michael Pfahl, Norm O'Reilly, John Nadeau, Charles "Doc" Higgins, Andy Kreutzer, Heather Lawrence, and Greg Sullivan, plus Bob Boland, Louis Iglesias, Jim Kahler, Annie Brackley, Christina Wright, Luke Sayers, Aaron Wright, and Teresa Tedrow, are colleagues and friends who certainly keep me motivated and excited to come to work each day. All of the The Drake Group members deserve praise and thanks, but I want to specifically thank Mary Willingham, Sally Dear-Healey, Dr. Jay Smith, Dr. Gerald Gurney, Dr. Allen Sack, Dr. Donna Lopiano, Jayma Meyer, Dr. Brenda Reimer, Dr. Fritz Polite, Dr. Michael Malec, Brian Porto, and Dr. Andy Zimbalist for their support and counsel over the years. Special thanks to the AFC Ajax soccer club in Amsterdam, FSV Bayreuth, Hertha BSC Berlin, and the world headquarters of Puma and Adidas in Herzogenaurach, Germany, especially Matthias Fischer of the Adidas Group, for all of their assistance and help.

Finally, none of this would have been possible without the support of Dr. Kahandas Nandola, Professor Emeritus of Ohio University. Dr. Nandola sadly passed away in September 2017, but his legacy continues on through a generous endowed professorship and professorial stipend that I have been privileged to hold since 2012. It has been an honor. I strive every day to uphold his ideals, passion, and achievements, so that I may be a worthy holder of the title that bears his name.

Why America Needs Alternative Models of Sports Development and Delivery

Sport is part of every man and woman's heritage and its absence can never be compensated for.

—Pierre de Coubertin, founder of the modern Olympic Movement

THE ESSENCE OF SPORTS

The phenomenon of sports throughout history has been a consistent subject of empirical and popular inquiry. Arguably, there is not a better quote than the one above to describe the importance of sports and sports participation in the world. As de Coubertin stated, sports are ubiquitous and will always be a part of our lives in some form. The former president of the International Olympic Committee, Juan Antonio Samaranch, once placed sports and sports development among the most important social phenomena of the twentieth century. He added that "sport has confirmed itself as a means of education, source of health and improved quality of life, an element of recreation and leisure occupation, first-rate entertainment, [and] factor of social communication" (quoted in Thoma and Chalip 2003, xi). As a researcher of sports and social phenomena in sports, as well as a lifelong participant and fan,

I wholeheartedly agree with the pronouncements of de Coubertin and Samaranch. However, we also have to recognize that sports delivery and sports development are changing and, like anything else, need to evolve to keep up with shifts in the industry and with the current time. Sports development and delivery worldwide has changed dramatically with the availability of new technology, including fantasy and e-sports activities. Variations in sports participation and the subsequent impact on public health, in access to sports and recreation opportunities, along with the increasing financial cost of participation, to name a few issues, have also changed how we consume and participate in sports in ways we could never have imagined. The real questions now are how we are to understand the ways in which sports affect our lives, positively or negatively, and how we are to manage the future of sports and sports development in a rapidly changing world.

While the positives of sports and sports participation are many, it is clear that the system in which they take place is undergoing a significant evolution, specifically in the United States. As indicated in empirical and popular literature over the past century, sports occur in the context of large, complex organizations and processes that have constantly evolved into what Thoma and Chalip called, two decades ago, "this new world of international sport" (2003, 1). Today, this new world of sports involves globalization, television and other rights, licensing, sponsorships, and an increased flow of traditional and nontraditional content, such as e-sports, with all of this and more leading to unprecedented changes in sports and sports development as we know it. However, there are numerous problems, many of which this book defines and offers potential solutions for. Several issues are pushing us to the point of seriously discussing how we evolve American sports development. Several current problems and challenges in the American sports system are discussed in forthcoming chapters along with proposed solutions. There are obviously many issues that can be addressed, but for the purposes of this book, the problems addressed are primarily focused on economic issues, public health problems, education, and access to sports and recreation. Specific problems discussed include elite and competitive athletics within the educational space, a growing athletes' rights movement that is even focusing on labor relations at the intercollegiate sports level, changes to the status and competitive level of primary and secondary school sports, legal challenges, legislative and other potential government intervention, public health issues, greater access to sports and recreational activities, and where to put "other" less commercially viable sports that are losing teams and opportunities as more money and resources are directed toward football and basketball.

Even with these many issues and problems that need to be corrected, numerous benefits and positives regarding sports and sports development continue to exist in the United States. At their core, some things regarding sports and even the sports industry have remained fairly constant through their history (more fully discussed in chapter 2). Whether it is a matter of elite, mass-participation, or recreational sports, it remains possible (and, if done correctly, even probable) that, through sports, one can learn how to move, use, and know one's body, and that participation in sports can be a vital part of an active and healthy lifestyle. Sports can help one develop needed social and personal skills like discipline, confidence, leadership, teamwork, and organization. They can teach one to respect rules and authority and gain core values like tolerance, respect, and fair play. Additionally, organized sports can be a valuable augmentation to the educational and maturation processes. Learning how to cope with defeat as well as victory is an important life skill for both young and old to master. All of these life skills and more can be learned and enhanced via active sports participation throughout life.

To ensure the development of these skills and values, and to strengthen the understanding of a healthy lifestyle, it is of paramount importance for every member of society to have the ability to participate in sporting activities by way of widespread and ready access to sports facilities and sports participation. For many people, that means being able to play their favorite sports and exercise at the lowest price possible, regardless of their age, skills, and social background (Stiegelmayr 2015). Exploring how different countries use sports and provide access to sports participation, ostensibly to benefit society and the country at large, is a major focus of this book.

SPORTS DELIVERY AND SPORTS DEVELOPMENT MODELS AROUND THE WORLD

Throughout modern history and up to the present day, each country and/or culture has had its own systems and organizations for sports and sports development, whether in mass-participation, recreational, or elite sports. Two of the most popular and widespread sports development models are the European sports club model and the American model. Sports in European countries are largely organized through nonprofit, mainly local and grassroots clubs. This is in sharp contrast with most sports development in the United States, as its typical participants are either primary or secondary school athletes, along with those competing in college- and university-based sports.

Comparing and contrasting the European sports club model and the American education-based model, we can begin to ascertain whether other models might be developed in conjunction with or separate from our current way of governing sports. I do not propose in any way saving the almost exclusively education-based system we have in the United States. My argument starts from a baseline belief that the current model does not work and must be changed. Frankly, we should no longer entertain any debate that is grounded in saving the system. It is, I will say again, only a question of *how*. In other words, we must first recognize and admit that we have a problem; only then can this society finally and fully address the need for reform. I am not here to advocate killing off educationally based sports in America. Educationally housed sports can certainly be part of new approaches toward the evolution of sports governance and sports delivery in America. However, the stress on our education system with regard to sports participation and finance must be relieved, and soon.

As a nation, the United States must address such problems before the situation deteriorates beyond repair. If we want to continue to provide and enhance plentiful opportunities for as many people as possible in a wide variety of organized sports and recreational pursuits, preserving educational primacy along with improving public health, then I believe we simply must change how we do sports in this country. If we want to continue to develop elite athletes at local, regional, and national levels—in many sports, not just football and men's basketball—who will excel at home and abroad, then we must change. The United States seems to be stuck in the past on this. Meanwhile, for its citizens, opportunities for better health and the personal growth that can be gained from sports are vanishing.

This book examines four potential and dramatic alternatives to the current model, including consideration of adopting portions of the sports club systems prevalent in Western and Eastern European countries, with a focus on Germany and the Netherlands. I spent fifteen months in Europe conducting research for this project as a Fulbright teaching and research scholar at the University of Bayreuth, Germany, in 2014–15. The research consisted of immersing myself in the system via empirical research, site visits, interviews, and focus groups to learn as much as possible about the European sports model and to ascertain if a similar model could be developed in part or in whole in the United States. I also had a front-row seat, figuratively and literally, observing how a local European sports club operates as my son Bradley competed for FSV (Fussball Sport Verband) Bayreuth on its C-level (under-sixteen) soccer team. Since most European sports club systems are similar, I made the choice to focus on Germany and the Netherlands, as they were the two countries I spent the most time in during my research sabbatical. As more fully discussed in chapter 5, most countries in the European Union have a basically similar approach to sports governance, delivery, and development.

This book also focuses on other potential models for elite, mass-participation, and recreational sports development in the United States. As sports choices decrease in a funding-challenged American educational system, and recreational opportunities outside that system become more expensive, it is increasingly apparent that more sports opportunities need to be developed outside the educational system for competitive, mass-participation, and general recreational exercise. The United States is not only suffering from an education funding crisis, made worse by its way of too frequently prioritizing sports over education. It is also suffering under the strain of its citizens becoming primarily sports spectators while maintaining very unhealthy and mostly inactive lifestyles, in turn impacting health care and the federal and state budgets devoted to it.

Where would the money and infrastructure come from for a dramatic shift in sports development in America? It's a fair question, but one with realistic and measurable answers. This book covers the potential positive impact that an extreme paradigm shift, including a shift to models such as the ones being proposed, can have on public health in the United States. Any reorganization of how we do sports in the United States must take into account the overall health benefits to the population, not just competitive and commercial benefits. Other countries are outdoing America in offering widespread options in sports, whether it be for mass participation or elite development. Many scholars agree that opportunities in the United States are dwindling and that we should learn from countries like Germany, with its "Sports for All" movement, or Canada, where the government is promoting physical activity to enhance all of its citizens' well-being.[1] Sports clubs around the world are supported in several ways, including through government subsidies (via taxes), membership dues, revenue from ticket sales and ancillary businesses, sponsorships, and donations. Some countries, such as the United Kingdom and Australia, also draw on lottery and gambling proceeds to help fund their sports club systems.[2]

While proposing any tax increase may seem foolhardy and a non-starter in the United States, as a country we can actually save money by promoting and achieving better public health through increased access to and participation in sports. This means paying it forward and focusing on prevention, with benefits more on the back end, but it is critical for everyone to have skin in the game, including the government. A tax subsidy could be something the public gets behind, if it can reduce overall health-care costs and save money in the long run. Combining this with entrepreneurial spirit, public and private partnerships, and good old American ingenuity and creativity, we can enable and sustain the funding and infrastructure for newer, more accessible models of sports development and delivery.

THE ORGANIZATION OF SPORTS

Sports have been a part of society for most of the history of human civilization. People all over the world have been engaging in physical exercise for millennia, mostly through work but also through games and athletic events. In the Western tradition, organized competitive sports date back to 776 BCE, when the first Olympic Games were held in Olympia, Greece. Some twenty-five hundred years later, as the Industrial Revolution took hold in the late eighteenth and early nineteenth centuries, games that had been largely unsupervised and unregulated were recognized as being beneficial for members of the working class (Gerdy 2002, xiii–xiv). From their origins in unstructured play and loosely organized events based in communities and schools, increasingly organized sports competitions were gradually established via host organizations, schools, or rudimentary sports clubs in a variety of countries. Throughout this period and into the early twentieth century, several sports spread across the globe, often introduced by young participants who had learned of the games in other countries (especially England) or who made up rules on their own. In general, this type of recreation was viewed as a healthy outlet for students, while being a needed respite from the rigors of academics. It was also a healthy physical and recreational outlet for workers, one that could potentially enable higher productivity in the rigorous and demanding factory jobs that dominated this time period (Gerdy 2002; Coakley 2014; Frei 2015).

AMATEURISM AND PROFESSIONALISM IN EARLY SPORTS DEVELOPMENT

In the early days of sports development in the United States, the difference between a professional athlete and a nonprofessional athlete was not as obvious at it may seem, but it was determined to be an important distinction for those participating in school-based sports and later helped define the separation of education and professionalism. In the early stages of college sports contests in America, it was not unusual for nonstudents to be allowed to participate in college sports contests. This use of "ringers" to gain a competitive advantage was frowned upon by university hierarchies, and to university administrators a different definition was needed to ensure that games were played only between actual enrolled students (Crowley 2006; Falla 1981; Gaul 2015). The primary role of a school-based athlete, at least in theory, was being a student first and foremost. Those athletes were not allowed to receive any compensation or anything that would resemble a tangible benefit for their efforts lest they become less focused on their studies and no different from the ringers and nonstudents that institutions were attempting to eliminate. Sports in the schools were designed to be an avocation and not a vocation. One could play professionally and earn money for one's sports skills, but school-based sports and most international competitions clung to the notion of amateurism and playing for the love of the game.

The term "amateurism" was not initially established as a mechanism to have athletes participate in sports for no compensation, but actually was developed to separate the working class from the upper class and maintain that social separation in all areas of life, including recreation. In short, the rich wanted to play their own games, separate from the working class, and due to this segregation of participation different sports began to develop within the different social and economic classes. Sports such as tennis, golf, and polo were "white-collar games," while the blue-collar working set participated in sports that did not require much if any money or upper social class status to play, like baseball and football which would later become more commercialized and monetarily beneficial.[3] In 1916, the National Collegiate Athletic Association (NCAA) defined an amateur as "one who participates in competitive physical sports only for the pleasure, and the physical, mental, moral and social benefits derived therefrom" (Sack and Zimbalist 2013, 3). This was the beginning of the definition of amateurism moving away from the original British intent and fully separating school-based sports from professional sports in the United States. Bylaw 12.01.1 in the NCAA manual states that "only an amateur student-athlete is eligible for intercollegiate athletics participation in a particular sport" (NCAA 2014, 57). This requirement has really not changed for over a hundred years, but the sports development model we now see in America has changed exponentially. The same tenet of amateurism still applies to scholastic sports, for the most part— indeed, the concept of amateurism has remained fairly stagnant—but the environment and status of sports in America have changed drastically.

In simple terms, amateurism in sports means participation as an avocation rather than a profession, and not getting compensation for playing a sport or using one's "athletics skill (directly or indirectly) for pay in any form in that sport."[4] This definition has been expanded over the years to include preventing athletes from capitalizing on their commercial utility, such as endorsement opportunities, to the level of receiving any benefit, no matter how small, such as a free meal, as a violation of their amateur status. Amateurism eventually evolved into an ideal that many supported as a way to separate educationally based sports and Olympic sports from the perceived scourge of money and professionalism.

In this sense, amateurism's last stand is taking place in the sports development educational model of the United States, as it really does not exist anywhere else in the world. The Olympic Games long ago dropped the façade of amateurism in its competitions starting in 1988, against immense resistance.[5] Many thought that bringing in professional athletes to the Olympics would stain their purity and even that they would eventually cease to exist, yet it is virtually nondebatable that the Olympic Games are now as popular as ever, even while using overtly and well-compensated professional athletes. The feared demise of the games did not happen, and television rights and sponsorship fees are at record highs (Zimbalist 1999).

As a society, we continue to cling to the notion of playing for the love of the game in American educationally based sports, but ultimately it does not seem that the public would mind if college athletes became overtly professional, as they just want to watch the games.[6] That might be an inaccurate view on my part, but it doesn't seem to be, as the games themselves are what attract the fans specifically at colleges, universities, and primary and secondary schools. We are cheering for the names on the front of the jersey—the institutions—and for the names on the back of the jerseys chiefly as representatives of the institutions that hold our loyalty. Consequently, if we were watching sports where the participants were real students, competing as an avocation, we would likely be just as happy and cheer the same way as we do under the quasi-professional athletic model that exists today in the upper reaches of the American educational system. Regardless of where we end up with sports development in America, it is clear that this "educational ideal" is dying, because we simply are not doing what we claim and are often not providing athletes the education that is cited as being so valuable to them. Meanwhile, college athletes—and, to a lesser extent, other amateur athletes—are restricted, in many ways unlike any other American citizens, from monetizing their economic utility when it is at its peak earning potential. I predict that, if so many continue to profit from college athletics, but not the athlete labor themselves, the current model in America will ultimately cease to exist in theory or practice.

EDUCATION

The United States is often touted as having the best education system in the world, yet the facts tell a surprisingly different story. This is especially clear when it comes to America's rank as opposed to other countries in STEM (science, technology, engineering, and math) education. STEM jobs are growing at a faster rate than non-STEM jobs in America, but the US education system is not producing a sufficient number of graduates in the field (Rosen 2013). American students are far below many of their foreign counterparts in math and science performance. Losing in this important education race cannot be entirely blamed on the overemphasis of athletics and their place within the US educational model, but the athletic-centric model does have an impact, and its role in undermining education at all levels can no longer be ignored.

In their groundbreaking book *The Game of Life*, Shulman and Bowen (2001) found that college athletes participating in all types of sports tend to underperform academically and that this is even more pronounced in higher-profile sports like football, basketball, and ice hockey, most notably in the NCAA's lower divisions. While the more notorious academic issues are usually at the top Division I level, this study showed that even the more participatory and allegedly less athletically competitive levels in college sports also show numerous academic deficiencies. Meanwhile, this has not changed in the top division, as the most recently reported NCAA trends show lower graduation rates in high-profile sports: consistently, high-profile academic scandals almost always involve high-profile sports.[7]

The cost of increased spending on athletic programs at all levels of education in America has put severe stress on many institutions in their efforts to deliver effective academics. America's overall health and well-being are dependent on educational leadership that can help promote an educated and skilled citizenry. Can removing or reducing the stress on our academic infrastructure caused by an emphasis on competitive athletics increase academic primacy and effectiveness? This book offers that it can and will, but in order to remove or reduce that stress we must provide sports development opportunities outside the educational system.

HOW DIFFERENT SPORTS DEVELOPMENT AND SPORTS DELIVERY SYSTEMS WORK FOR THE ELITE ATHLETE

Both the US and European systems can produce elite athletes who go on to very prominent athletic careers. How athletes navigate through the two systems is different, yet many of the outcomes are the same. For example, Dennis Schröder and Jabari Parker are young, talented basketball players who each ultimately made it to the National Basketball Association (NBA), for the Atlanta Hawks and Milwaukee Bucks, respectively, but came from entirely different sports development and educational backgrounds.[8] Schröder started his career in the German sports club system, whereas Parker was a product of the American educationally based model.

Parker played basketball at all levels of the education system in Chicago, Illinois, most notably at Simeon Career Academy, a public high school in the city's South Side neighborhood that has long been noted for its ability to produce elite basketball talents such as Parker, Nick Anderson, Ben Wilson, and Derrick Rose, to name a few.[9] Parker only played one year of college basketball as what is now commonly called a "one and done" player—usually a highly elite prospect who will play college basketball for one year to make it to nineteen, the minimum age to declare for the NBA draft. This minimum was instituted in 2005, ostensibly to prevent high school players going directly to the NBA, as was increasingly being done by influential young superstars like Kobe Bryant and LeBron James. The thought behind the rule was allegedly to encourage, if not mandate, that elite basketball athletes go to college even if only for one year, in order to have some exposure to higher education before jumping to the NBA. What cannot be ignored is that this is also a prime year of athletic development and maturity for many athletes. Theoretically, this NBA rule was governed by the most recent collective bargaining agreement between the National Basketball Players Association (the NBA players' union) and the owners. While that is technically correct, it is hard not to notice the monetary and competitive benefits for both the NCAA and NBA to having a rule like this. The NCAA gets superstars, if only for a year, and the NBA gets players one year older and one year better after playing in a very good and competitive development system.

Incidentally, this basketball development system is both cost-free to the NBA and a massive revenue source for the NCAA, considering that almost 96 percent of the NCAA's national office budget comes from television and corporate sponsorship revenues generated from the hugely popular NCAA Division I men's basketball tournament, also known as "March Madness."[10] How the absurdity of a rule like this impacts elite sports development and what little integrity may remain in American educationally based sports, while at the same time preventing an athlete like Parker from being able to maximize his earning potential, is discussed more fully in later chapters. In my opinion, rules like this are a major example of why our current systems need to be changed, to evolve, and to provide more choices for both the elite athlete and our citizenry.

Schröder, on the other hand, developed his skills through the German club sports system, not in his local school system, on a path similar to what is offered elsewhere in Europe and in other countries. Identified as a potential elite athlete shortly after taking up basketball at a young age, he moved from the mass-participation sports clubs in the area around his hometown of Braunschweig, Germany, to the elite developmental basketball teams that serve as feeders for the top divisions of Bundesliga basketball. As an elite athlete he was able to focus on basketball at a time when his skills were at their peak. He still attended school while working his way up through the feeder clubs, and advanced schooling was often provided on-site at his clubs (a very common arrangement in Europe for higher-level clubs). Thus, education was still an important part of his total development package. For Schröder, the main difference from the US model was that he was not constrained by arbitrary academic standards that could have limited his ability to compete, or that could have led him into a substandard educational experience just to maintain his eligibility. In European systems, success (or failure) in academics is really up to the individual. There is no motivation on the part of either players or teams to violate academic standards because academic eligibility is not a requirement—nor is it needed, as the bulk of the sports development system lies completely outside formal educational borders.

Schröder eventually played his way to the top club basketball team in Braunschweig, the Bundesliga first division Phantoms, before being drafted in the first round of the 2013 NBA draft, the same as Parker. While Schröder did not attend college in the United States or university in Europe, he was still able to reach the highest level of professional basketball competition in the NBA. If Schröder wants to attend college at some point in his life, he can certainly do it after his playing career is over. In the meantime, the separation of club sports from the German secondary school and university systems was not an inhibitor to his education.

These two players present similar outcomes for two elite players from two different systems, with this one specific difference: one sports development system is embedded in the education system, with specific academic requirements needed to compete, and the other is separate and distinct from the educational model. Both systems have their benefits along with their negative points. In many ways, it is difficult to say which model is better for producing elite athletes or for presenting athletic, exercise, and entertainment opportunities to the masses.

There could be a healthy debate, if one were forced to make an absolute choice between one or the other, but that is not the focus of this book. Instead, I intend to explore several alternative sports delivery models for both elite athletes and citizens in the United States, both inside and outside the current educationally based model.

LACK OF OPTIONS

Currently, American sports development is essentially governed by an educational system that is highly restrictive for the athlete but beneficial to many others. Many athletes, most notably in football and men's basketball, are virtually forced into this model to maximize their development and potential advancement to the big-money world of professional sports. While there are some alternative paths in other sports, such as baseball and hockey, educationally based sports are still the primary "feeder" system for participation at higher levels. This has helped create a situation where a few organizations and people—highly paid coaches, conference offices, television networks, corporate partners— control the narrative for many athletes in the United States, keeping them essentially powerless and limited as to the best choices for their own academic and athletic future. If, instead, more sports development options were available, it would expose higher education to the market forces of choice and competition. This could initiate a revolution driven by the needs of the athlete, who would be able to decide what option is better for him or her, just as the needs of consumers drive the progress of every other industry in a free-market economy. It would also allow colleges to pull back from the insanity of the ongoing facilities and personnel "arms race" we have under the current intercollegiate athletic system, at the expense of educational primacy.

Parker and Schröder are just two of the thousands of examples that demonstrate that both systems can produce elite athletes. The difference lies in the degree of direct connection to education, and how we define, at various levels, academic eligibility to compete in sports. In theory, the American system, with its combination of participating in sports while getting an education, sounds like a perfect match. Unfortunately, the academic component has been abused and often outright ignored at all levels of our education-based sports system virtually since its inception (Falla 1981; Ridpath 2002). In short, the goals of scholastic sports often do not mesh with the goals of academia, most notably when substandard academic performance might keep superstar athletes off the court and field. When those two worlds collide, it is often sports priorities that win out—but it does not have to be that way. There is room for both sets of priorities in a new world of American sports development. The current stress our education system is under from an ever-growing and increasingly expensive athletic-industrial complex cannot and does not need to go on. There are better ways to define sports development in America while preserving educational primacy.

VANISHING SPORTS AND PARTICIPATION OPPORTUNITIES

Both elite athletes and nonelite sports participants need more choices, because opportunities for both are deteriorating under the current model. For example, opportunities for mass participation in sports have been dwindling at many levels of our education system. Wrestling, men's gymnastics, and swimming have been hit especially hard as revenue and energy are focused on the more commercially popular sports, which seem to be more valued from the youth level all the way to university campuses. A survey conducted by the Sports and Fitness Industry Association in 2014 found that 26 million children ages 6 to 17 played team sports, a 4 percent drop from 2009. Recognizing the somewhat disturbing trend of sports specialization by many athletes who are focused more and more on one sport year round, the total number of different sports played within the same age group had plunged by nearly 10 percent (Rosenwald 2015).

It is time for a dramatic change in how we do sports in America. Although some European clubs are pointing to issues such as financial problems that could threaten their survival, the American college model has many more acute issues and is drowning in scandals and debt, while the primary and secondary levels of education are being squeezed financially and are dropping opportunities for sports and physical education. It is imperative that all these systems be analyzed more closely to see if there might be a better way to maintain sports as an integral part of the culture without losing the benefits.

IS IT REALLY ABOUT EDUCATION?

The current athletic model in the United States is often justified because of the perception that it provides access to education and even an impetus to continue one's education at a college or university. Social mobility through the combination of sports and education is often mentioned as a primary benefit for minorities and other disadvantaged groups. In other words, it can be argued somewhat successfully that athletics can allow potentially significant access to educational opportunity for some who may have not had that opportunity without participating in sports. The ultimate vehicle for social mobility is education, but while using athletics as a way to attain that educational promise sounds appealing on paper, it does not always provide the social mobility and brighter future that are promised. It is a truism that, first and foremost, individuals have to take personal responsibility for their own education. However, many athletes find their educational options limited and/or controlled in order to ensure their academic eligibility, with an emphasis on more time for training rather than access to a bona fide education. This becomes a trap: athletes know they have to be eligible to compete and that others may be counting on them, not just to win games but even to be a family's potential lottery ticket out of poverty should they make it into the professional ranks—as unlikely as that is.[11]

These scenarios are damaging the academic primacy of our educational system. For example, it is easy to deduce that if a school's major football star is needed to compete in a very important game, but he is not academically eligible under standards set by the governing organization (e.g., a state high school activities association or an intercollegiate athletics governing body such as the NCAA), things may be done to "game the system" to ensure that the star player is able to play, at the expense of educational integrity. Sadly, I can say that I did this myself during my time as an athletic administrator and coach at several NCAA Division I universities. I tried to rationalize any effort I made to keep an athlete eligible by saying that this young man or woman would go back to a very dark place, and that we were doing them a great favor by keeping them on the field or court. In reality, I was doing the school and fans a favor. I was not helping the athlete develop as a person nor was I doing anything to assist in his or her actual social mobility. I was only concerned about the here and now: we needed that player to give us a better chance to win. Now I realize the error of my ways, and it is a major motivation for writing this book.

The conflict between sports and academics is very real, and it is only getting worse. The NCAA's vice president for enforcement, Jon

Duncan, announced in early 2015 that the governing body was investigating twenty serious cases of academic fraud (Wolverton 2015). This came on the heels of a major scandal at a premier public institution, the University of North Carolina, where it was uncovered by the *Raleigh News and Observer* and some impressive reporting by investigative reporter Dan Kane that a high percentage of men's basketball and football athletes were kept academically eligible through a series of bogus, almost nonexistent classes in its Department of African and Afro-American Studies. Other details showed direct knowledge and involvement of athletic department personnel, faculty, and staff in grade changes, plagiarism, and the covering up of the scandal for up to eighteen years.[12] This is one of our public ivies and an institution which prided itself on doing things "the right way." If North Carolina is doing this to keep its athletic machine afloat, it does make one wonder what others schools may or may not be doing to keep their athletes on the field.

Academic scandals and improprieties regarding athletic eligibility are not just the domain of intercollegiate athletics. Unfortunately, this has been happening not only at the commercialized level of NCAA Division I sports, but at the high school and youth sports levels. Middle and high schools are not immune to the desire to keep athletes on the field no matter what the cost, and scandals have damaged school-based sports in America for many years. A recent example is the private, football powerhouse Bellevue High School in a suburb of Seattle, Washington. It was alleged that the remarkable success of the school's football program, considered one of the nation's elite high school programs, having produced several NCAA Division I players, depended on players who weren't actually Bellevue High students. As strange as that may sound, according to the *Seattle Times* it appears that up to seventeen of the athletes became eligible to play "by traveling to a Bellevue office park for classes at an obscure, 40-student private school: The Academic Institute, Inc.," which many Bellevue faculty stated did not adhere to basic educational standards. The high tuition to this storefront school was often picked up by the coaching staff or wealthy boosters (Liebeskind and Baker 2015). This is just one of many examples of high school programs rivaling their college counterparts as to how far some institutions of learning will go in abandoning their educational mission to gain a few wins.

THE IMPORTANCE OF CHANGE

Father Theodore Hesburgh, the well-respected former president of the University of Notre Dame, summed it up very well when discussing what the United States is up against concerning its educationally based sports development model, specifically in higher education. He stated, "Many have concluded that little can be done to rein in the arms race or to curb the rampant excesses of the market. As we stated in the 2001 Knight Commission Report: 'Worse, some predict that failure to reform from within will lead to a collapse of the current intercollegiate athletics system'" (Splitt 2003, vii).[13]

I agree with Father Hesburgh and I will even take it further. If the intercollegiate athletics system as we know it does collapse, and we are not prepared for the change or a change occurs that we as passionate followers of college sports do not want, it will dramatically impact what happens in primary and secondary school sports, along with other currently available youth sports options. It is my hope that the alternative models and concepts outlined in the ensuing chapters can be built upon to prevent such a disaster, and to preserve and enhance sporting opportunities at all levels in America.

2 Interscholastic and Intercollegiate Athletics Development in the United States

IT IS important when suggesting new models or reform of any long-standing and accepted system to review where we are and how we got to where we are. This chapter provides a historical review of the American sports development system in an attempt to answer a very interesting question: Why is the United States the only country that has its primary vehicle of sports development and opportunity within its various educational borders? The European model, covered in chapter 5, essentially manifested itself in the same way but now has a much different and inclusive structure in comparison to the United States, most notably how the system is separate and distinct from the educational space. How did two systems that developed at virtually the same time, for many of the same reasons, end up creating drastically different governance and development models? It is a great question and one that must be discussed via a historical overview of how both systems developed.

AMERICAN SPORTS DEVELOPMENT AND EDUCATION

Few issues in sports have captivated Americans as much as intercollegiate and interscholastic athletics. The passion, the pomp and circumstance, the rivalries, and the unique American flavor of it all make them a significant part of the social fabric. I begin with the development of college sports in the United States because they provided the main impetus to those sports manifesting themselves at the primary and secondary levels of education.

College and other educationally based sports in the United States, while hugely popular and embedded in the cultural framework of the nation, have been the subject of significant concern and empirical inquiry for over a hundred years. Millions of fans attend games between athletes who are advertised as students first and athletes second. These "student-athletes," as they are commonly referred to, provide fans with entertainment and possess the ability to bring communities together, while ostensibly gaining valuable life experience and access or potential access to a college education, with a financial package to help pay for it. Proponents of college sports, and to a lesser extent high school sports, point to other potential benefits that sound promising, but may not in reality be consistent residual effects of having athletics on campus. This includes such often-cited positive attributes as increasing a school's visibility on a national level, which can lead to enhanced fund-raising, marketing opportunities, and applications for enrollment. In addition, sports participation is touted as a vehicle to provide educational opportunities for athletes to develop leadership, teamwork, and other beneficial social skills (Dosh 2013; Litan, Orszag, and Orszag 2003; Miracle and Rees 1994). Some critics have argued, with or without empirical research, that coaches and sports administrators will often denigrate academics and overemphasize the importance of sports to an institution, while gaining power to influence the academic primacy and moral compass of the institution (Splitt 2003).

INTERCOLLEGIATE ATHLETICS

Educationally embedded sports, throughout their history, show both similarities and differences with regard to other models of sports development and governance. The unique relationship of education and sports, forming the primary sports development model in America, essentially happened by accident. It began with American university students seeking recreational opportunities outside the few intramural activities available within their particular institution by organizing sporting events with other colleges, presumably to test their athletic prowess, manhood, and superiority in various events. By the mid-to-late nineteenth century, student bodies and even administrations at prominent universities were progressively more determined to win in these rudimentary, student-organized intercollegiate sports, sometimes at any cost. While football was the main focus, other sports were also rising to sufficient importance in colleges' profiles that certain institutions began to turn a blind eye to academic requirements just to get athletes onto the field. Professional baseball pitchers were becoming campus stars, playing college baseball under pseudonyms. Coaches were inserting themselves and nonstudents into football games.

In the early days of American higher education, faculties and administrators had never planned for anything as frivolous as organized athletics. The concentration was to be solely on academics. But students increasingly clamored for recreational activities that would offer a respite from the daily rigors of academic life (Chu, Segrave, and Becker 1985). Many faculty members recognized that this was actually beneficial to the academic progress and success of the students (Falla 1981). Whether it was a rowing regatta between Harvard and Yale in 1852, or the first "football game" between Rutgers and Princeton in 1869, these relatively little-noticed, social, yet oftentimes very competitive events were the precursors to today's nationally popular, multibillion-dollar industry of intercollegiate athletics (Staurowsky and Abney 2011).

While the concept of a sports development model being primarily embedded within higher education might seem somewhat strange to observers who are not native to the United States, intercollegiate athletics have been a part of higher education and university life even outside the United States since the early eighteenth century, when athletics were made part of the curriculum at the Rugby School in Warwickshire, England. Intercollegiate competition in the United States is traced back to before the first recognized intercollegiate athletic rowing event in Boston in 1852, to as early as the 1820s, with no-holds-barred football and rugby games between Ivy League schools like Harvard, Yale, and Princeton. These "informal" events predate most organized athletics in America, scholastic or professional, including baseball (Ridpath 2002; Falla 1981; Howard-Hamilton and Watt 2001; Zimbalist 1999).

After the first official organized football game, pitting Rutgers against Princeton in 1869, proved to be very popular among the students and alumni as a social event, the faculties of the two schools canceled the following year's contest because they feared an overemphasis on athletics as opposed to academics (Funk 1991; Zimbalist 1999). This strong faculty intervention might be one of the few times, if not the last, that university faculty exercised such control over the growth and power of college sports. Later, and to the disgust of the faculty, representatives of athletic interests (commonly known today as "boosters") from both schools tried to leverage the very popular contest to raise funds to acquire property to build their own football fields. The 1883 game, played at the Polo Grounds in New York City, drew more than ten thousand fans and generated the money for the boosters to pay for the new fields. For the first time, intercollegiate sports were beginning to dictate university policy and conflict with academia in ways not even imagined (Zimbalist 1999).

New sports such as baseball and track and field were beginning to be established on college campuses across America. Contests were popular, but, as mentioned previously, many of the athletes were not even registered students at competing universities and colleges. There were even early reports of pay-for-play and recruitment of high-level athletes, mostly nonstudents, to play at certain schools. There was not a national or even regional governing body to harness what was becoming a burgeoning industry within the hallowed halls of academia, but it became apparent that governance was needed.

THE NATIONAL COLLEGIATE ATHLETIC ASSOCIATION

Several attempts at organizing an intercollegiate athletics governing body were made before the eventual formation of the National Collegiate Athletic Association (NCAA) as the primary and best-known governing body over college sports. On January 11, 1895, there was a historic meeting of the Intercollegiate Conference of Faculty Representatives, which later became the Big Ten Conference (Byers 1995). This was the first intercollegiate athletic conference on record that made regulations regarding student-athletes' eligibility and participation (Chu, Segrave, and Becker 1985; Wilson and Brondfield 1967). Academic eligibility and participation rules began to spread across the country at other campuses, but many abuses of academic requirements still existed, and more needed to be done to keep the growing beast of athletics under the academic tent. There were many attempts at reasonable compliance, but manipulations of academic standards and what is referred to today by the NCAA and its member institutions as competitive equity standards needed to be addressed collectively by all higher-education institutions at a national level, before the enterprise became too big to control. Regulation and effective governance needed to start with what was as popular a sport then as it is now, the behemoth known as college football (Falla 1981).

In 1905, a nationwide call for college football reform led to the first steps toward creating a governing body for intercollegiate athletics. Collaboration among institutions was initiated not to address academic, booster, or even recruiting abuses, but to regulate college football on the playing field and reduce the numerous injuries and lack of consistency in the rules (Grimes and Chressanthis 1994). The call for reform in the rules of the game came from President Theodore Roosevelt himself. In the eyes of many, college football, with its mass-momentum formations, few rules, and anything-goes philosophy, had reached an unacceptable level of violent play that resulted in several deaths. President Roosevelt used the prestige of his office to try to calm the fears of a majority of the public about the growing sense of lawlessness surrounding college football, including the abuse of institutional academic requirements now pervasive in intercollegiate athletics. Many colleges and universities, fearing overemphasis on sports and seeing the dangers of the game, eventually suspended football, including Columbia and Northwestern. Harvard president Charles Eliot threatened to totally abolish the game on his campus (Grimes and Chressanthis 1994; Zimbalist 1999).

According to Falla (1981), there was a sense that something needed to be done at the highest levels to regulate intercollegiate athletics, as society clamored for the college game to adopt stricter rules. The response to this public outcry brought about the initial meeting in 1906 that eventually led in subsequent meetings to the formation of the Intercollegiate Athletic Association of the United States (IAAUS), the forerunner of the NCAA (Watt and Moore 2001; Zimbalist 1999). Although most of the concerns about college athletics focused on excessive violence, questions regarding the relationship of academics and athletics received almost as much attention from the first meeting onward (Funk 1991; Sack and Staurowsky 1998). In 1910, the IAAUS adopted a new name: the National Collegiate Athletic Association. In the words of one of the founding fathers, later the first president of the NCAA, Captain Palmer Pierce of the United States Military Academy at West Point, the association would be forever known as "the voice of college sports" (Falla 1981).

THE GROWTH OF SPORTS WITHIN HIGHER EDUCATION

By the 1920s and 1930s, almost all higher-education institutions had physical education requirements in the curriculum. This, combined with an increased emphasis on intercollegiate athletics, made physical education and competitive sports popular and, effectively, big business. In the 1920s, intercollegiate athletic competition grew exponentially across the nation, making it a "golden age" of college sports. Students had new freedoms, new drives, and new desires for emotional and physical outlets. College sports seemed to provide the one common denominator (Wilson and Brondfield 1967). Colleges and universities were adding sports and building formidable athletic programs in the process. The NCAA held its first championship in track and field in 1921 (Byers 1995; Falla 1981).

The post–World War II era brought forth significant rules and regulations that were later adopted by NCAA member institutions as a whole. The postwar NCAA also returned to the business of attempting to restore and maintain integrity in intercollegiate athletics. At the first NCAA convention (actually called the "Conference of Conferences"), in July 1946, the participants drafted a statement outlining "Principles for the Conduct of Intercollegiate Athletics" (Brown 1999; Sack and Staurowsky 1998).

The principles concerned adhering to the definition of amateurism that existed at the time. This included not allowing professional athletes to compete, holding student-athletes to the same academic standards as the rest of the student body, awarding financial aid without consideration of athletic ability, and developing a policy of recruiting that basically prohibited a coach or anyone representing a member school from recruiting any prospective student-athlete with the offer of financial aid or any equivalent inducement. These principles collectively became known as the "Sanity Code," or Article III of the NCAA constitution when it was first presented in 1947. This code was initially developed to help colleges and universities deal with the growing levels of abuse and violations in intercollegiate athletics, especially football and men's basketball. The code was a tortured, yet in some ways brilliant effort to reconcile a number of disparate interests and philosophies concerning intercollegiate athletics (Falla 1981; Sack and Staurowsky 1998; Sperber 1990; Zimbalist 1999). At the time of the development of the Sanity Code, values in intercollegiate athletics remained skewed toward winning and athletic success, rather than academic achievement and graduation.

Intercollegiate athletics in the first half of the twentieth century faced other issues similar to those that colleges and universities still deal with today. These included amateurism, academic integrity, financial aid to athletes, and recruiting restrictions and violations. The birth of the NCAA brought the once shockingly high death rate of football players prior to 1910 to an almost nonexistent low by having somewhat consistent rules and regulations to make the game safer, while to some extent keeping academic cheating and pay-for-play under control. Even though rule problems both off and on the field were minimized, as the competition grew nationwide, the exploitation of academic requirements became tougher for the NCAA membership to control (Byers 1995).

Back in 1910, the first NCAA constitution, like the Sanity Code put in place in the 1947 NCAA constitution, had many provisions that are applicable today in the areas of initial athletic eligibility and satisfactory academic progress. These led to the reform of intercollegiate athletics and the restructuring of academic eligibility standards for athletes. Article 2 stated, "Its [i.e., the organization's] object shall be the regulation and supervision of college athletics throughout the United States in order that the athletic activities in the colleges and universities may be maintained on an ethical plane in keeping with the dignity and high purpose of education." Article 8 went on to address the area of intercollegiate athletic and academic eligibility, stating that the "Colleges and Universities in the Association severally agree to take control of student athletic sports as far as may be necessary to maintain in them a high standard of personal honor, eligibility and fair play and to remedy whatever abuses may exist" (Falla 1981, 134–35). These goals are still supposed to drive the governance of educationally based sports in America today.

However, problems arising from the drift away from academic primacy were exacerbated by four major changes in the latter half of the twentieth century. The first step toward actual professionalization of college sports happened in 1956 when the core definition of amateurism, concerning not receiving any remuneration for athletic competition, was modified to allow athletic scholarships that paid for tuition, books, and course-related fees as an "educational award" for college athletes. This was done in an attempt to curb prohibited payments and other benefits to college athletes. Athletes were also given a stipend of $15 per month as laundry money, until that became impermissible in the early seventies.[1] At the time of this redefinition, athletic scholarships were guaranteed for four years and could only be taken away for extraordinary, college-based reasons, such as not meeting academic standards, and not for athletic reasons, in an attempt to keep education at the forefront and preserve athletics as a true extracurricular activity. Athletes were still able to keep their athletic awards even if they quit the team voluntarily.

The second step toward professionalism came less than a decade later, when many universities expressed frustration at that last provision, that an athlete could quit a team, but keep his or her athletic scholarship. This early version of guaranteed scholarship had also planted the seeds for an athletes' rights movement, mostly by African American athletes who began demanding equal rights and treatment parallel to civil rights demands and protests that were happening elsewhere in the United States. Coaches and administrators grew frustrated with what they felt were challenges to their authority and a growing lack of control over athletes. In response to the concerns of many athletic departments, the NCAA determined in 1967 that scholarships could be canceled if an athlete quit a team. In 1973, the athletic scholarship was made a one-year award that could be taken away for virtually any reason at the end of the period of the award, even for athletic reasons. It essentially became a yearly pay-for-play contract, with coaches given immense authority over whether an athlete would remain on scholarship (Strauss 2014).[2]

The third and arguably the biggest challenge to college sports' being an integral part of education was the growth of television and other media in the latter half of the twentieth century. It is difficult to fathom today that as recently as the mid-eighties one could only watch one college football game per weekend, or potentially another regional game, if lucky. If Ohio State was playing Michigan in football, one of the greatest rivalries in college sports history, it had to be selected by the NCAA for national TV coverage or it would not be available for the general public, unless, of course, you had a ticket to the game. The logic behind this was multipronged. There was a belief that television, despite the potential mass marketability, would dramatically affect the home-gate revenue of participants in a negative way. However, the potential for television revenue drove several schools, most notably the University of Oklahoma and the University of Georgia, to challenge the NCAA's authority to control television broadcasts in a landmark legal case, *NCAA v. Board of Regents of the University of Oklahoma*, which went all the way to the US Supreme Court in 1984.[3] The NCAA lost in a 5–4 decision that forever altered the landscape of intercollegiate athletics and moved the collegiate system even further away from a primary focus on the academic mission in regard to athletes. The NCAA wanted desperately to control broadcasts and revenue, not just to protect the live gate, but also in an attempt to provide a level playing field among competitors. The fear was, if schools and conferences negotiated their own television and other media contracts, it would lead to a system of haves and have-nots, along with damaging the live gate. This could influence schools to have a "do whatever it takes" mentality to get star players and star teams on the field or court, in order to make more revenue via television and, by extension, corporate sponsorship rights (Byers 1995).[4] While it can be argued that a system of haves and have-nots has existed anyway, since the beginning of college sports, it is true that this decision opened up unprecedented amounts of revenue for some schools in the more high-profile conferences. This in some ways forced smaller schools to overspend and overextend in a desperate attempt to keep up with the major institutions, often trumping educational priorities in the name of athletic success, or face the prospect of dropping out of Division I football altogether. Some, like Drake University, decided to downgrade to a lower, non-scholarship division; others to this day are trying to keep up in a race they cannot win.[5]

The last of these steps toward professionalization was letting freshmen compete in varsity athletics and not requiring a year in residence if they had met minimal academic standards in high school, measured by grade point average and/or standardized admission test scores. Freshman athletes were ineligible for varsity competition until 1973. The purpose of the one-year residency requirement was to allow an academic transition to college without the distraction of ultracompetitive sports. Many schools had freshman teams that played lighter schedules, therefore limiting practice, travel, and emphasis on competition in order to minimize the impact on academics. Doing away with the mandatory year of residence before varsity play continued to solidify, for many, the impression that college athletics was no longer "education-based" in any meaningful sense, but had become more about winning and revenue generation.[6]

The debate about intercollegiate athletics, and, by extension, American sports development grounded primarily within the existing educational system at all levels, has been growing for over a century. It is exacerbated by an inability to fully quantify its costs and benefits within an educational model. Thelin refers to college and university athletics as "American higher education's 'peculiar institution.' Their presence is pervasive, yet their proper balance with academics remains puzzling" (Thelin 1994, 1). According to Sperber (1990), intercollegiate athletics participation and competition have been scarred by abuse of academic requirements for athletic eligibility almost since their very beginnings in the early nineteenth century. Abuse of academic requirements in intercollegiate athletics has had a long and sordid history (Ryan 1989; Sperber 1990).

THE PROBLEM OF SHAM AMATEURISM

In America, the United States Olympic Committee and/or other sports national governing bodies (NGBs) could actually act as the broker for the athlete, and bargain for an educational opportunity outside of directly competing for the school. The US government could also adopt ideas used in Europe and provide educational credits or grants to assist athletes of national and international caliber to maximize their opportunities in both athletics and education. Let's not forget capitalism, either. If individuals and/or corporations want to sponsor athletes either solely or in conjunction with the government to further their athletic development and educational opportunities, then that should be encouraged and formalized. Considering that the USOC is the only privately funded Olympic committee in the world, it is not a huge leap to believe that the private sector could be involved on behalf of elite American athletes in a more flexible model such as this. It's conceivable that private individuals and companies could directly assist athletes and help finance their educational goals. Currently, arrangements like this would run afoul of archaic NCAA rules prohibiting direct assistance as not aligned with the tenets of amateur athletics. Even though individuals can donate to university foundations for athletic scholarships, at this point in time any direct payment to an athlete would be a violation and cause the institution to be sanctioned.[7] But this raises the whole issue of amateurism in American sports, an issue that we need to revisit in this society.

A repulsive example of how current eligibility and amateurism rules can detrimentally affect an elite athlete is the story of former dual-sport athlete Jeremy Bloom. Bloom was a noted professional skier, world champion in moguls skiing, and a member of the US Ski Team from the age of fifteen. He represented the United States in the 2002 Olympic Games in Salt Lake City and became the youngest person and only the third American ever to win the World Grand Prix title. Bloom was also blessed with the ability and in some ways the misfortune to be a highly successful athlete in two sports, one of which happened to be part of the American intercollegiate athletics system. He enrolled at the University of Colorado in the fall of 2002 and excelled as a Division I football player, gaining a number of receiving, punt return, and kick return records and earning freshman All-American and Big XII honors in 2003. Later that year, he won a world championship gold medal in mogul skiing. In 2004, despite Bloom being an outstanding student, the NCAA declared him ineligible due to the compensation he was receiving as a professional skier, and he lost the last two years of his football eligibility.

Note that the problem here is with definitions of amateurism in intercollegiate sports specifically. The US Olympic model at least allows athletes, even college athletes, to earn outside income through endorsements, sponsorships, and employment, often actually brokered by the USOC and/or a particular sport's NGB. While not receiving a straight salary, Olympic athletes can provide themselves a good living, depending on their marketability, along with receiving funds or in-kind support for training. Under USOC rules, Bloom was allowed to earn outside monies as a professional skier.

As a football player, Bloom did everything he was supposed to as an amateur athlete. He did not receive any impermissible income based on his marketing utility as a college football player. In fact, even under then-existing NCAA rules he would be allowed to receive income as a professional skier—that is, as a professional in a sport other than football—without sacrificing his amateur status. Many athletes have done exactly this over the years, including such luminaries as John Elway, who was paid six figures by the New York Yankees organization as a Minor League Baseball player while he was quarterback at Stanford during the early 1980s. Other prominent college stars who were also simultaneously amateur and professional athletes include Kirk Gibson at Michigan State University (football in college and Minor League Baseball), Trajan Langdon at Duke University (basketball in college and Minor League Baseball), Danny Ainge at Brigham Young University (basketball in college and Major League Baseball with the Toronto Blue Jays), and Tim Dwight at the University of Iowa (indoor track in college and NFL football), to name just a few.

Bloom, however, in a shocking departure from NCAA precedent, was ruled to be receiving impermissible benefits via endorsement income as Jeremy Bloom the college football player—even though those endorsements were contracted with Jeremy Bloom the professional skier. Bloom fought the NCAA in the courts, but to no avail, due to the potential for further sanctions against the University of Colorado. In the end, he was forced to abandon his final year of college football so he could continue to earn compensation as a skier.[8]

It's particularly troubling to me that, even as Bloom was pursuing his legal case against the NCAA, it was revealed during a congressional hearing that Tim Dwight had received endorsement income as a member of the NFL's Atlanta Falcons, but was able to continue at Iowa as an amateur athlete in indoor track and field without penalty. In a 2004 hearing before the House Judiciary Committee's Subcommittee on the Constitution (in which Bloom and I both testified), an NCAA representative, Jennifer Strawley, pressed by Indiana congressman John Hostettler to explain the "substantive differences" between the situations and NCAA treatment of Bloom and Dwight, stated that Dwight had asked for forgiveness after the fact, whereas Bloom had asked for permission prior to competing as a skier.[9] There are many cases of inconsistency and unfairness in critical NCAA decisions, and people like Bloom have suffered for it.

The point here is that it can be quite normal for a professional athlete to attend college (or high school, for that matter) and make money playing a sport, or receive outside income as a result of being involved in a sport, without impacting their education. No one can say that John Elway was not a viable student at Stanford while he was earning a significant amount of money as a minor league baseball player, and the same holds for the other examples presented. Meanwhile, no one seems to mind when the Olsen twins are making millions as child stars, or Natalie Portman or Jodie Foster continue to work as actresses while enrolled in college. Did it make them bad students? Did it take away from their education? The answer is an unequivocal "no." The same can be true for many athletes—if adjustments are made.

Earning money for being an athlete doesn't in itself make someone a worse student. Forcing student-athletes to make unreasonable commitments of time, while those around them manipulate the system of academic eligibility against their best interests, certainly can. It is time for us to end what is essentially a sham regarding amateur athletics in America. This model will enable that, while still keeping some aspects of school-based sports that we seem to value as a country.

The main argument for student-athlete amateurism in the United States is that these athletes should play sports as an avocation and not a vocation, with an educational opportunity as the payoff. Earning market value for playing an educationally based sport has long been thought of as a perversion of amateurism that would taint the sports themselves—and make them less marketable, since school-based sports are supposedly popular because of their amateur aspect and would suffer commercially without it. This is central to the NCAA's argument in the O'Bannon case.[10] If the NCAA were to win on these grounds, it would essentially mean that it could prohibit wages and other compensation for college athletes (including outside income from use of a player's name, image, and likeness) precisely because allowing such compensation would make colleges sports themselves less marketable. It is easy to refute this. We heard the same arguments regarding the Olympic Games when an end was put to the requirement that competitors be "amateur" athletes, and it is nondebatable that the Olympic Games are more popular than ever. These types of restrictions also exist, of course, at levels below intercollegiate athletics, where athletes are also prohibited from participating in sports aligned with educational institutions if they receive outside compensation. LeBron James, the standout All-Star NBA forward for the Cleveland Cavaliers, once had to miss two games for receiving an extra benefit in high school.[11]

It is my belief that athletes should be allowed to receive financial support in any way that can maximize both their educational and athletic access and success. As noted, there are many ways this is being done in Europe. If we want to continue to have restrictive amateurism rules in educationally based sports in America, then we can. But we can also have a parallel alternative system that would allow athletes to profit from their athletic ability and compete at the highest level during the time in life when they are most able to do so.

It is debatable in the twenty-first century whether lofty ideals of amateurism from the mid-twentieth century have ever been close to being achieved. Many of the same problems that existed during the first hundred years of intercollegiate athletics, such as recruiting improprieties, the changing definition of amateurism, and excess commercialism, are still happening today, but they are more frequent and much more publicized. Despite the stated mission of intercollegiate athletics as being about education first, it is challenging to justify the system in its current state as being an education-first model, as opposed to an athletic-development model. The inherent flaws of the NCAA, and why the system should be modified to a more education-centric model, are examined more closely in later chapters.

INTERSCHOLASTIC SPORTS IN EUROPE AND THE UNITED STATES

During the same period in the twentieth century, public and private school systems began to copy their higher-education counterparts, installing extracurricular activities, specifically sports, outside the existing curriculum but still within the confines of the school. Previously, primary and secondary school students, like college students, had organized clubs to engage in all kinds of activities, including sports, outside school hours as a way to have a needed break from the academic rigor of studying and classes. School officials recognized that some of these extracurricular activities were difficult to control, and many experienced discipline problems. As a consequence, sports clubs were incorporated into the primary and secondary educational systems so that schools could have control over the activities, with one intent being to keep them from conflicting with the educational mission (Pot and van Hilvoorde 2013). Although colleges and universities wanted control of activities in order to prevent injuries, while also gaining the benefits of competition with other schools, having control was also a major reason to not let athletics flourish outside the primary and secondary education systems.

In contrast, school systems in Europe were primarily reserved for academics. Extracurricular activity would take place outside the school doors, allowing for greater integration and participation in sports by members of all socioeconomic classes and academic backgrounds via a community-based club system. Throughout the eighteenth and nineteenth centuries, in various European countries it was the student body that established sports clubs outside the schools and independent of school officials, but that is where many of the similarities end. Unlike in the United States, European school officials felt no need to place such student clubs under their supervision, as the students and parents typically cooperated with school authorities and for the most part kept the activities separate and did not let them become a distraction from education. Another and more compelling reason for student clubs, including athletics clubs, not being under the supervision of school authorities is that throughout the bulk of the European education system separate high schools existed and still exist for students of different social and academic classes. This makes populations in most European schools rather homogeneous as compared to the American system, at least in public schools, which in the United States are typically more diverse. Due to this homogeneity, students and parents felt no need or obligation to further associate with the same people from their schools in extracurricular clubs or in interscholastic athletics, but certainly there was a desire to associate, through sports and other activities, with others in their central community whom children might not interact with during the school day (Stokvis 2009).

Like university sports, virtually all youth sports in the United States were integrated within the educational system and have remained, with few exceptions, embedded in this system ever since. Primary and secondary schools in the United States are similar to their university counterparts in that they often have both elite and mass sports facilities on campus and numerous teams that participate in interscholastic competition and tournaments locally, regionally, and even nationally. These interscholastic events are frequently characterized, through their strong emphasis on competition, as effective enhancements to education, and are often very selective in nature. As with colleges and universities, achievements in these interscholastic events are viewed as important for the status and brand identity of both students and schools, even though the effect of this connection is often disputed by empirical research (R. Mandell 1984; Frank 2004; Orszag and Orszag 2005; Orszag and Israel 2009).

Another main reason why competitive sports morphed into the club system rather than being based in schools in countries like the Netherlands, Germany, Austria, and Sweden, specifically, was a heavy resistance against sports within the educational system by academic officials for its un-pedagogical elements such as competition, selection of athletes, and a strong focus on winning. Many authorities considered competitive sports to be dangerous, unhealthy, or even immoral (van Hilvoorde, Vorstenbosch, and Devisch 2010; Pot and van Hilvoorde 2013). However, this does not mean that some form of school-based sports programming does not exist in Europe. As in the United States, having at least some form of physical education in schools in Europe was intended to compensate for sedentary behavior and promote a healthy lifestyle for students, apart from the pressure of competition sometimes found at certain levels in the sports club system (Stokvis 2009).

In the United States, interscholastic sports are organized in a way similar to colleges and universities in which the best athletes from schools compete against each other. These interscholastic school sports are mostly selective in nature and highly competitive (Park 2007). The competitive characteristic of interscholastic sports is considered important for the social functioning of American schools. For instance, being selected as part of a school team is deemed important for the status of athletes within the school and local community. Conversely, it can be socially and psychologically devastating when one does not make a team or is demoted to a lower level of competition, but this can also provide a teachable moment on how to deal with adversity and challenging situations (Miller 2009). The competitiveness of US educationally based school sports is further illustrated by the rituals and symbols that surround interscholastic matches. As in intercollegiate athletics, these rituals and traditions run deep. Things like intense rivalries, mascots, bonfires, and championship playoffs, while smaller in scale, are just as intense and popular. These rituals, traditions, and symbols at both the high school and intercollegiate level can serve to enhance competitiveness and the importance of beating the opponent, not just for the competitors, but also for the students and other stakeholders such as parents and alumni (Stokvis 2009).

While sports competitiveness is important in almost any culture, it is often amplified in the United States because sports within the education system form a separate social sphere in which competition and rivalry are more accepted (Pot and Van Hilvoorde 2013; Curry and Weiss 1989). The social network that interscholastic and intercollegiate sports can provide in the United States is present instead in the European club system, and is perhaps even farther-ranging. In Europe, the desire for competitiveness and socialization is mainly fulfilled in the sports club system, while what rudimentary forms of interscholastic competition as exist are characterized by a focus on physical wellness. Taks (2011) notes that community-based sports clubs are primarily voluntary, led by boards of directors and requiring cooperation among all of the stakeholders. Sports clubs in Europe were further solidified by the Sports for All movement, which began in 1966 and was designed to promote participation in sporting and fitness activities by children, teens, and adults. The Sports for All movement opened the doors for greater development of the sports club system as national, regional, and local governments started to provide direct and indirect support to the voluntary infrastructure and keep the physical activity and social aspects of the clubs going (Pot and van Hilvoorde 2013; Curry and Weiss 1989; Taks 2011). This European sports-for-all ideology is partly related to the nonselective nature of interscholastic school sports that initially existed in America, but which has mostly given way to an emphasis on competitive excellence rather than non-elite participation and wellness.

Several other factors differentiate the educational sports model in the United States from the European sports club system and what exists as far as school sports in Europe. One factor is the intensity of the competition itself. In the United States, high school sports involve weekly (or more frequent, in some sports) competition in which school teams play against other schools in regional, state, or even nationwide events. At most schools, these competitions are taken very seriously and the athletes practice numerous times a week, even outside the season. Conversely, interscholastic sports outside the sports club systems in Europe vary, but usually require very little time in comparison, and may range from one to five days per week at various times throughout the year. This comparatively low intensity can be explained by the dominance of club sports, but it is not uncommon for even a very competitive sports club to have a more relaxed competition and practice schedule in comparison to US educationally based sports (Pot and van Hilvoorde 2013).

This is likely the result of the dominance of club sports and the less competitive relationship between the educational and sports club systems found in Europe. As Pot and van Hilvoorde note, in their comparison of school sports in the Netherlands with those in the United States, "one of the main goals of interscholastic school sports in the

Netherlands is to increase sports participation rates among children, excluding children by means of selection and competition is not a desired effect. In addition, competitiveness in Dutch interscholastic school sports is not stimulated, as performances in school sports have little or no influence on the status of either the school or the students involved. Therefore, rituals and symbols that provoke (and are provoked by) competitiveness are absent in most schools" (ibid., 1168).

Interscholastic sports in America, by comparison, seem to be clearly more important to the athletes, coaches, and local community. In local newspapers (city or town), school sports can take up pages. Local stations and regional networks report results of what has become a dominant weekend activity not just for local people attending games, but, through the media, for anyone (Miracle and Rees 1994; Stokvis 2009). Schools use this media exposure to distinguish themselves and use the achievements of their student-athletes to promote their institutions. From a marketing perspective, prestige can be gained from interscholastic school sports in the United States. In Europe, schools by and large do not use their interscholastic school sports results in their marketing strategies, because the prevailing wisdom is that people do not associate the school's athletic performance with the educational value of the school. While interscholastic sports achievements typically do not gain any media coverage, that void is filled by the local sports club or clubs, all the more so due to the different levels of participation in terms of age, gender, and skill. Meanwhile, in the United States, school-based athletes have a higher status and are often viewed as more prominent than other students.[12] This higher status influences the connection that student-athletes feel to the school, since their status depends on their relationship to the school community (Fredricks and Eccles 2006; Hintsanen et al. 2010; Marsh and Kleitman 2002). The status of the sports club athlete may not be as pronounced as that of the school athlete in the United States because of the lack of affiliation with an institution, but successes are known and celebrated by members of the club and local residents.

One of the other and arguably most significant differences between US school-based sports participation and the European sports club system is the connection or lack thereof between academic results and athletic eligibility (Barber, Eccles, and Stone 2001; Broh 2002; Marsh and Kleitman 2002). In the United States, essentially, students are not eligible to participate in interscholastic and intercollegiate sports if they do not meet academic eligibility criteria, usually by maintaining a certain grade point average.[13] As noted previously with regard to intercollegiate athletics, the tie-in with academic eligibility is both a blessing and a curse. It creates numerous issues that call into question the entire concept or model of educationally based sports. The idea behind these eligibility criteria in the United States is maintaining a balance, even with trade-offs, between academic work and school athletics. Although negative effects are indeed observed by some—including myself, on many points—it can be argued that these eligibility criteria can intensify the interest of athletes in their own academic achievement, since they will be unable to play if they neglect their academic priorities (Coleman 1961; Marsh and Kleitman 2002; Stokvis 2009). On the other hand, eligibility requirements have led to many academic scandals in interscholastic and intercollegiate athletics over the years, when decisions were made to keep top athletes eligible to compete, no matter what damage was done to the value of educational primacy. The constant tension between academics and athletics in sports development in the United States has been an increasing concern, recently illustrated by a massive academic scandal at one of the finest public universities in the United States, the University of North Carolina. This particular scandal involved a curriculum being developed for athletes that involved no-show classes and classes that required very little work, just to ensure athletic eligibility.[14]

In Europe, participating in a local sports club or even in school sports is open to all students who desire to compete, regardless of their grades. While education is stressed (and study time is even provided for athletes at many local sports clubs in Europe), absolute academic criteria for practice and competition in sports clubs are rarely, if ever, in place or, if in place, enforced. In my time researching in Europe, I found no sports club in Germany or the Netherlands that enforced an academic policy or eligibility standard. However, clubs allowed for study time, many even offered opportunities to study at the club, and students were able to miss practice and/or games to study or attend class. It is primarily left up to the parents to decide if any penalty should be applied for not meeting academic expectations. Given the absence of eligibility criteria and the disconnection of sports and school in Europe, it would be difficult to determine by comparison whether the

American interscholastic sports system prepares participants better than the European club sports system does. One could draw inferences from academic performance levels, US-based university college board exam scores of American and European prospective college students, and other criteria, but it is difficult to say one system is better educationally that the other because of a lack of hard data. However, I hypothesize there is a potential correlation between academic performance and the presence or absence of highly competitive sports and elite development within the two systems that needs to be examined via future research.

The differences between the United States and Europe in the competitiveness, intensity, and prestige of interscholastic sports provide an interesting basis for discussion and empirical inquiry as to whether the current US model of educationally based sports development is the best choice going forward. Does the use of eligibility criteria enhance the educational *and* athletic experience of the young American athlete? Is it better at doing so, when compared to the experience of the young European athlete? While some elements of the American model of interscholastic sports, in its organizational structure and social impact, may work to improve academic performance and self-esteem, it can be argued that the European sports club system promotes many of the same intrinsic values.

3

The European Sports Club and Sports Delivery Systems

THE COMPARISON of other sports development approaches around the world with the current American system is an important exercise, and can be used to examine potential ways to improve not just our but any system. However, there is not much existing empirical research comparing the American system with other ones. In current empirical literature, sports systems are mostly described in themselves rather than compared. There has been research and discussion on the structural changes within sports models in Germany, France, Great Britain, and elsewhere, chiefly regarding governance aspects, sports clubs and national and European politics, and the organization of sports in several European countries (European Commission 1999; European Commission 2014; Hartmann-Tews 1996; Heinemann and Schubert 1999; Jütting 1999; Scheerder et al. 2011; Wegener 1992). Part of the reason Germany is highlighted in this book is that specific empirical studies concerning the German sports club system are more plentiful and provide a good base of study. The history of German sports clubs has been discussed in several papers, mostly regarding governance aspects and sports development in general (Krüger 1993; Krüger 2013; Kurscheidt and Deitersen-Wieber 2011; Nagel 2006; Miège 2011).

Some sports scholars and sociologists claim that while there are some similarities among sports development systems in the world, there are also some significant differences that are the main focus of this book and inspiration for potential changes. According to Fort (2000), the main differences between the European and American sports development systems are in three areas: the fans, the sports organizations themselves, and the team objectives. European fans are primarily concerned with winning international competitions, while American fans are more concerned with what are essentially regional or national titles, or, in the case of interscholastic sports, city, county, or state championships. Organizationally, the differences in European and American sports governance are dictated essentially by what the fans of the sports want to see "their teams" accomplish. Since European sports are primarily both national and international in scope, different organizations oversee them. This is similar to how American sports governance is structured with regard to different governing organizations for national and international competitions. The teams themselves obviously want to win, but in Europe the major focus is preparing for national and international competitions, whereas in America the main focus is on educationally based sports as a pathway to competing in the professional ranks. Another glaring difference on the team side is that the United States does not have a system of relegation and promotion of teams, in either professional or education-based sports, like the one under which most European club teams play, both in first-level leagues and lower divisions.[1] In addition, Fort notes that there is not the same level of funding for teams via sponsorships and television in Europe, albeit with some notable exceptions such as Bundesliga soccer and the English Premier League.

HISTORICAL AND SOCIAL DEVELOPMENT OF THE EUROPEAN SPORTS CLUB

The local sports club is at the core of European sports development. Sports clubs and sports development in Europe are an exercise in social development, longevity, importance, and persistence. Previous research into the historical beginnings of sports clubs in Europe has described them primarily as social clubs organized for "casual exertion and sociability," along with the development of social networks (Holt and Mason 2000). In many communities in Europe, the local sports club provides a venue for community activities, politics, and events, in addition to being the hub of most local sports activity. Regarding this social context, MacLean (2013) notes that, as with today's local sports clubs, there were, historically, many clubs that were similarly central to organizing everyday life in villages. This included sponsoring sports like football (soccer), but also offering programs in gardening, sheepdog training, or sewing, or serving as the location of the annual village carnival. These clubs and their development highlighted the social aspect of sports and the blending of various other activities, similar to what you may see in many American recreational and community centers today, although arguably not structured and task organized as their European counterparts. Sports clubs in Europe are essential to sociability, providing an important addition to the bonds based in friendship, family, and common background and language.

Originally, the concept of sports in Europe was focused around discipline and the will to strengthen young people whose fitness would be beneficial in the case of war. While formal games and sports were played, the sports themselves were organized by students and workers, often morphing into what some educators called "mob games," which were for a long while deemed not to have a place within an educational environment (Miracle and Rees 1994). This, of course, was different than American sports being primarily developed along an education-based path, as American educators felt the need to gain control of rapidly developing student-organized sports. Still, during the Industrial Revolution, primarily private and boarding schools in England took the same approach toward emerging sports development initially, as they wanted to control their students and ensure that the games had rules and that those rules were written down and enforced. In the nineteenth century, this institutionalization of sports was brought about under the banner of Muscular Christianity.[2] Later in the twentieth century, in England as in other European countries, other sport development options and elite development fell primarily outside the educational system.

Many in Europe, especially faculty, did not want direct control of sports by the school, and adamantly wanted sports kept separate from academics. Since European students were often assigned to particular schools based on their individual academic achievement, it was not unusual for neighbors to be attending different schools.[3] Consequently, many students and workers wanted to play and interact with friends from the same neighborhood, because they might be separated during the day by occupation or placement in different schools. Since the schools did not provide this organized outlet, the sports club solidified itself as the primary way to conduct local competitive sports activity and allow for such interaction within the community.

THE START OF AN EXTERNAL CLUB SYSTEM THROUGHOUT EUROPE

In the nineteenth century, Belgium, Czechoslovakia, France, Germany, Italy, Poland, and Switzerland established gymnastics and shooting societies that focused on cultivating a patriotic spirit, much like the concept of Muscular Christianity that was found in England. In fact, England influenced sports development worldwide, and specifically the development of German and other European sports clubs. In England, there was a greater focus in athletics on competition between individuals or teams in sports like tennis, soccer, or rugby. Sports like these and others manifested themselves in most European countries during a similar period in the nineteenth century as more traditionally English sports gained popularity and expanded rapidly. Along with the gymnastics and shooting associations, other organized sports clubs were established throughout Europe (Miège 2011).

By the end of the nineteenth century, English sports like tennis, sailing, golf, and rowing had been exported to Germany and other countries, primarily by traders. Due to often expensive equipment and time demands, these sports were generally restricted to the upper class, similar to the experience in the United States, which eventually led to the creation of a code of amateurism. While amateurism in America primarily means playing sports for an avocation and not a vocation, initially it was used as a way to separate the upper class from the lower classes, just as in day-to-day life. Nevertheless, both types of clubs, for the upper and lower economic classes, combined physical activity with the social, community aspect and gained popularity. The exclusive, upper-crust amateurism aspect of English sports waned as soccer became extremely popular between 1890 and 1910 and spread virtually throughout the whole country, from small villages to big cities. English sports slowly became more inclusive and popular with other social classes as the government (including the royal family) started to promote physical activity, seeing benefits for industrialized workers. Germany and other European countries followed England's example of industrialization and modernization in many ways, including in the growth and development of sports (Frei 2015).

As the nineteenth century ended, gymnastics and English-style sports were no longer mutually exclusive, as they were combined within several clubs throughout Europe. Gymnastics became more competitive due to organized championships, and the traditional gymnastics-only clubs began to offer more sports and started to call themselves "gymnastic and sports clubs." The original ideals of the gymnastics clubs were transferred to the adopted English sports, and this combination of German gymnastics and English sports led to a new concept of sports clubs as offering participation in various disciplines (Heinemann and Schubert 1999, 149). World War I temporarily stopped the spread of sports and gymnastics, but soon after the war ended sport became a mass phenomenon in Europe. People of all classes of society participated in clubs, and even teenagers and women took advantage of being allowed to participate (Nagel 2006). It became essential to organize and provide better and more extensive governance of club-based sports.

GERMAN HISTORY OF ORGANIZED SPORT

The history of organized sports in Germany, as in other European countries, starts roughly at the beginning of the nineteenth century with gymnastics (*Turnen*). Friedrich Ludwig Jahn is noted for initiating this type of cooperative activity at a place called Hasenheide, near Berlin, in 1811. It was there, in this picturesque outdoor park, that the very first gymnastics *Turnplatz* (open-air gymnasium) was founded. The Hasenheide Turnplatz then became the model for future gymnastic demonstrations and clubs in Germany (Krüger 1993, 39–40). This was in the midst of the Napoleonic Wars of the early nineteenth century (1799–1815). Many gymnasts fought in the wars, and, after the wars finally ended, gymnasts and gymnastics became very popular in Germany. The particularly high level of fitness of these soldiers was looked at as a very positive contribution to the successful war effort and led to increased respect for and interest in gymnastics. Consequently, the first organized clubs were founded around 1816 (Krüger 1993, 48–49; Nagel, Conzelmann, and Gabler 2004, 7). Gymnastics clubs were not only about gymnastics but also about running, jumping, throwing, climbing, and playing games. It was the spirit of the sport which was new. Gymnastics was a lifestyle, now free from duty and allowing for personal development, but, as noted previously, also focusing on discipline and physical preparation in case of war.

Yet, just as quickly as gymnastics gained popularity, political issues within Germany led to the prohibition of gymnastics in 1820. When it was eventually allowed again in 1842, a second generation of clubs was founded at an even more rapid rate. Groups of athletes formed clubs with the goal of practicing together and creating a social environment. Gymnastics clubs saw themselves as educational and democratic, but also as political associations rooted in self-discipline and self-education, where values were shared and friendships were established (Nagel, Conzelmann, and Gabler 2004, 78).

Eventually, two different commissions represented the sports movement—the German Empire Commission for Physical Exercise (Deutscher Reichsausschuss für Leibesübungen) and the Central Commission for Workers' Sport and Hygiene (Zentralkommission für Arbeitersport und Körperpflege)—but in 1923 all sports-related civic associations were united under the Deutscher Reichsausschuss für Leibesübungen. At that time, this reformed umbrella organization totaled around four million members in twenty-nine thousand clubs. With the unification of sports governance came a reorientation in which clubs turned from the original gymnastic ideals (physical activity for military strength) to a focus on sports for every citizen and improving public health and wellness (Hartmann-Tews 1996, 65–66). That change was supported by an award called the "sport badge" (*Sportabzeichen*) that still is given today to amateur athletes who meet specific physical exercise criteria. In 1931, sports and gymnastics clubs received tax relief in the form of exemption from the amusement tax, which assisted the development of operations and infrastructure tremendously (Heinemann and Schubert 1999, 67).

The Third Reich had a major influence on the organization and growth of sports in Germany. Before the Nazi Party took power in 1933, sport was separated from political influence and the government. After the National Socialist assumption of power, middle-class clubs had to integrate into the German League of the Reich for Physical Exercise (Deutscher Reichsbund für Leibesübungen). Clubs lost their democratic principles as officers were not elected anymore, but chosen according to what was called the "authorities leader principle." The clubs' goals were now about maximizing the working capacity and fighting strength of the population. However, as noted prominently in histories of the era, the Third Reich felt that sports could and should lead to a glorious representation of the country. Through the 1936 Olympic Games in Berlin, the National Socialists won more public confidence in the country and managed to hide preparations for the upcoming war (Kurscheidt and Deitersen-Wieber 2011, 261; Heinemann and Schubert 1999, 150–51). During Hitler's reign, sports were partially integrated into universities because physical education (*Leibesübungen*) was said to be part of the thorough education of students (Bernett 1973, 89). Still, these sports activities remained intramural, based in physical education, and did not expand to interuniversity competition.

At the end of World War II, the infrastructure of Germany was essentially destroyed. Thus, the entire sport structure in Germany, and in other European countries deeply affected by years of war, had to be revolutionized again. Due to strong relationships between members, traditional clubs were able to maintain internal communication during the war, and many members met to reorganize and reconstitute the clubs right after the war ended. The Allied forces also influenced organized sports in postwar Germany and elsewhere in Europe. They allowed volunteer and nonmilitary associations and created the position of "sport adviser," a middleman between athletes and the military government whose main responsibility was the development of a democratic sports system. The Allied forces also founded sports clubs that offered a variety of sports for everyone. Later, German athletes advocated for a sports system that was structured in national associations. By the fall of 1948, the occupation zones under the Western powers had created a system with several associations, but based on the club system. The dual structure, horizontal and vertical, which is still typical for the sports system in Germany today, emerged. Vertically, sports clubs in various disciplines formed local, regional, and national federations (*Fachverband*). Horizontally, all sports clubs of a particular geographical jurisdiction created federations (*Sportbund*). Both structures moved toward being united under a single umbrella, leading to the creation of the German Sports Federation (Deutscher Sportbund, DSB) in 1950, shortly after the Federal Republic of Germany was founded in 1949. After Germany was reunited in 1990, the sports federations of East Germany also joined the DSB, which still exists today (Hartmann-Tews 1996; Kurscheidt and Deitersen-Wieber 2011, 288).

Like today, the early sports clubs in Germany and elsewhere in Europe were primarily funded by member fees and run by volunteers.

Similar to early sports development in America, they were open only to men (Krüger 1993, 80; Nagel 2006, 34–35). Many factors supported the rapid expansion of clubs during that time, including industrialization, which led to mass urbanization throughout Europe. Another reason stemmed from students wanting to blow off steam after hours of lectures and studying. Sports clubs helped students and workers fight isolation and avoid losing their identity in the increasingly fast-paced modern lifestyle.

To this day, sports club names reflect some of these longstanding but still strongly held values. Words like *Eintracht* (harmony) and *Union* signaled the social meaning of clubs and can still be found today in club names like Eintracht Frankfurt or FC Union Berlin. Another reason for the popularity and growth of sports clubs was that members of the middle and lower classes were not allowed to play a significant role in politics for much of this period. Alternatives outside politics were needed, and established, to satisfy the desire of the middle and lower classes to influence their own environment. Clubs turned from being only about sports to being multifunctional and focusing on other aspects of leisure time and culture. Essentially, membership no longer required physical activity, but provided access to many community-based recreation options such as card games, nonphysical play, unstructured play, restaurants, *Stammtisch* (a regular meeting of friends), and other gatherings. All of these are still an appealing and important part of the European sports club system at the grassroots level today (Heinemann and Schubert 1999, 147–48).

CURRENT EUROPEAN SPORTS CLUB GOVERNANCE MODELS

The tip of the European sports system is formed by international organizations that represent all disciplines at a global level as regulatory and directory bodies. The European sports development model is based mostly on independent local sports clubs ("grassroots clubs"), with a pyramidal structure and availability of numerous sports. These local clubs are the basis of sports initiation for most citizens and also provide amateur and professional sports entertainment for the population. An international federation governs all regional and national federations, which unite local clubs and regional sports structures under one umbrella. Each sporting discipline within a specific country is promoted and organized by the national federation, which oversees the organization and governance of regional federations and local clubs, as well as providing representation at the international level. The national federations are responsible for setting up national competitions and managing all official awards and championships. Moreover, they regulate the sports club system through an enforcement process that applies needed disciplinary measures toward its members (see fig. 1).

In most European countries, as noted, sports clubs follow similar basic principles and mostly function due to the volunteerism of local citizens and teams. The type of voluntary work depends on the country, according to tradition and culture (Sobry 2011, 21). The leadership structure also depends primarily on voluntary governance, based on members' input, and most of these clubs are set up as nonprofit organizations. In order to offer a wide range of disciplines to the public, German sports clubs, like most clubs throughout Europe, deploy volunteers as well as employees to maintain club operations.

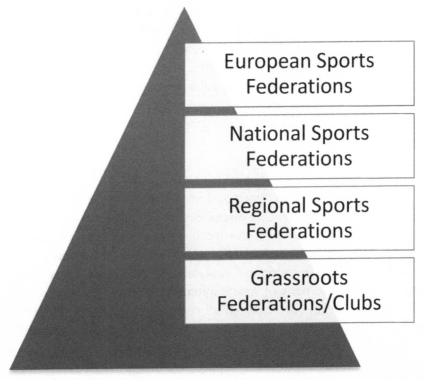

FIGURE 1. The organization of sport in Europe —the pyramid model.

HOW A EUROPEAN SPORTS CLUB OPERATES

Athletes perform on club teams in different leagues at different levels. Teams can reach higher leagues or can be relegated to lower levels based on their finishing position the year before. Theoretically, an amateur club can progress to the highest professional division, as the soccer club HFC Haarlem did in the Netherlands. It is unlikely that an amateur team can beat top-tier professional teams, but it is not impossible. This open system of promotion and relegation is a notable characteristic of European sports and instills motivation not only to advance as a team but also to avoid demotion to a lower division, which can cause players to leave and hurt the team and club's brand (Fort 2000; Miège 2011; Noll 2002). This system can encourage teams to compete hard for an entire season and not "tank" like so many American professional teams in search of a better draft pick or player in the following season.[4]

It is important to note that, despite all of the similarities among sports clubs in Europe, there is a difference between the northern and southern countries with regard to sports organization and governance. The northern European countries are generally marked by little governmental influence on sports associations, whereas the southern countries are, by and large, characterized by stronger intervention of the state. There are exceptions, such as Italy, the pattern of which is similar to those in Germany, Sweden, Norway, and the United Kingdom. In such countries, the task of government and public authorities is viewed as guaranteeing proper conditions for sports development through providing subsidies for sports facilities and equipment and support for research and training. Southern countries like Portugal, Spain, and France have their governments more directly control the development and promotion of sports, as they are seen as a form of public utility (Miège 2011, 27).

As the countries' national sports federations encompass most of the lower-level domestic federations, they also represent the sports movement to the government, similar to the role of certain national governing bodies in the United States. This is important, since the implementation of public policies might otherwise be more difficult due to the number of sports organizations and their variety of ideas and interests. In some European countries, this role is taken up by the national Olympic Committee, in addition to its responsibility for representing the Olympic movement and qualifying participants for the

Olympic Games. Countries that operate in this manner include Belgium, France, Greece, Ireland, Luxembourg, and Portugal. In other, mainly northern European countries, the confederation role is kept separate from the national Olympic Committee. Examples are Austria, Denmark, Spain, Sweden, and the United Kingdom. Specific characteristics of the national systems differ from country to country. For instance, sports confederations have quasi-governmental status in the United Kingdom and Spain. In Germany, Italy, and the Netherlands, the national Olympic Committees and domestic sports confederations are combined into one organization (Sobry 2011, 36–43).

A TYPICAL ELITE ATHLETE'S JOURNEY THROUGH THE EUROPEAN SPORTS CLUB SYSTEM IN COMPARISON TO THE AMERICAN SYSTEM

The typical process whereby an American athlete progresses to professional status in a given sport is usually via school-based sports, with the possibility of training and competition in elite camps, local tournaments, and independent clubs, then through college/university play, developmental leagues, and ultimately being drafted into the professional ranks. In the five main professional team sports in the United States—football, baseball, basketball, ice hockey, and soccer—it is very rare to find an athlete who did not spend at least some time in educationally based sports. While elite soccer players are now moving more and more through elite academies, and even away from intercollegiate competition, most of those athletes still spent significant time in school sports. In contrast, the steps of a typical career in the European sports club system, regardless of elite status, includes the following phases:

1.   Exposure in school

2.   Entry

3.   Membership

4.   Multiple Memberships

5.   Fluctuation

6.   Exit

It should be noted that all of the phases consist of diverse elements. Not all athletes progress the same way through the sports club system, or pass through particular phases in the same way, but this is a fairly typical form of advancement. Entry into a sports club is a process of gaining early exposure to a sport or sports through existing programs in the local school system (mostly intramural and limited extramural) or a club, then learning more about a sports club, showing interest, pondering joining, trying it out, and deciding to join. The social environment also influences the decision. If a teenager has siblings doing sports, or friends in the immediate neighborhood, there is a higher chance of him or her joining a sports club. The transition from entry to membership is also a fluid one, as it is connected to the expectations and cumulative experiences of the teenager, which affect the bonding of the athlete to the club. If expectations are met and the experience is mostly positive, there is a higher chance of bonding. Again, the social environment is an important factor. If the teenager likes his coaches or other members he will have a more positive attitude.

It is possible, in the progress of a sports career, that a person will be a member of several clubs at the same time. There are many reasons for this, as people experience growing commitment and widening interest through participating in multiple sports at the same time. While clubs in Europe typically offer several sports, particular sports are also distributed throughout other clubs in the community or surrounding communities. It can be that a child plays soccer in one club and tennis in another. An athlete might pursue one endeavor for elite competition and the other for recreation and enjoyment. Mass participation and nonelite options for youth are available in the clubs as well, though most recreational sport and physical education are done through the school system. This will be addressed further below, as potential avenues for new models in America are discussed in subsequent chapters.

Children and youth (under 18) in Europe have the ability to fluctuate by moving from one club to another or participating at multiple clubs. It is more challenging, logistically and financially, for a student in the United States to do this, even if they have interest in a sport that is not offered at their school. In Europe, the process does not need to be linear. The option exists to enter a new club prior to exiting an old club, and there are no transfer, academic, or other restrictions such as the ones American students may face when they switch schools or institutions. Ending membership in a club could mean the end of participating in sports altogether, or only for a period of time. The basis for this action may be negative experiences, changing motivations, or a change in the young athlete's environment or situation (e.g., switching or graduating from school, or the family moving to another place). Again, this flexibility is not always available to students in America, who are often bound by geographical and other governing limitations regarding transferring. Stopping a sport in school, seen as quitting, is highly discouraged in America—as it should be, to an extent—but often those athletes are not encouraged to come back or not even given the chance to return.

The career of former German national football (soccer) team captain and current FC Bayern München standout Philipp Lahm represents a typical European progression from childhood to professional status.[5] As with almost every other sports professional, Lahm started on his path from an early age. The first time he went to a soccer practice was with a kindergarten friend at the age of five. He started playing for a small local club called, for short, FT Gern (Freie Turnerschaft München-Gern), a "free gymnastics club" in Gern, a suburb of Munich. One typical reason for Lahm joining this particular soccer club was his family's history with it: his father played there, his grandfather played there, and his mother even worked for the club. This parallels in some ways the family ties to a local school system in America and the pull they might exert on an athlete to compete at a certain school.

Already at that young an age, others started to notice both Lahm's athletic talent and his extreme ambition. At the age of ten he was approached for the first time by one of the many youth scouts to be found in Germany. Scouts are made aware of potential youth talent via distributed statistics, word of mouth, and simply going out to find it—similar to recruiting that we see in the States, although perhaps not so often at the age of ten. The scout asked him if he would like to play for "1860 Munich" (Turn- und Sportverein München von 1860), a sports club that fields a professional-level soccer team and is oriented toward the development of young talent. While there are mass participation opportunities available through such clubs, athletes like Lahm are sought after for their potential to succeed at a high level. Lahm allegedly refused because he did not like the 1860 facility. This is an example of choices provided to athletes that are not as prevalent or available in America, or at least not readily affordable. A year later he was approached by an FC Bayern Munich scout and was asked to participate in a trial practice. At this practice he immediately found a friend and thus decided to change teams. Lahm noticed at once the difference between his old and his new club. At Bayern Munich he had practice three times a week. He realized the meaning of good organization and playing at a high level. At the age of seventeen Lahm was invited to join the under 17 (U17) national team and started dreaming of becoming a professional soccer player for the first time.

Nevertheless, he had a backup plan of becoming a bank clerk like his grandfather and uncle. At this age not everyone is allowed to stay with Bayern Munich, but each following year Lahm achieved the next team level. Instead of having practice (now five times a week) and matches on the weekend, his friends enjoyed going swimming, talking to girls, and going clubbing. Many young soccer players quit at this age because of these distractions. Lahm was different: his ambition and love for the sport drove him to stick with soccer and he was able to do this without his participation being theoretically tethered to education, as for most young athletes in America.

Later, Lahm played at the European Soccer Championship with the U19 national team. This allowed him to be promoted to the amateur team, which played in what is today called 3rd Bundesliga (3rd National League). Occasionally, he was also asked to play with the 1st Bundesliga (Premier National League) team during practice. The leap from amateur to professional is particularly difficult, especially with an organization like Bayern Munich. Teams such as this not only have talented recruits from within their clubs, but also sign players on the national and international trade market in a much more open way, in comparison to our college draft and player trade systems. This was why Lahm agreed to be lent out to VfB Stuttgart (Verein für Bewegungsspiele Stuttgart 1893 e. V.) to play 1st Bundesliga and become a professional soccer player prior to being able to join Bayern as a starter.

EUROPEAN CLUB ATHLETES AND ACCESS TO EDUCATION

The club system itself does not, as in America, directly support athletes in academic pursuits per se, as that is primarily the function of the school system, but it does encourage education and even sponsors educational opportunities within the club. Sports in Europe are not based upon a system of academic eligibility for competition, but that does not mean education is not important. To the contrary, recognizing that combining education and athletics can be beneficial, some extensions to the club system exist for top athletes in Europe regarding the possibility of

their obtaining a university education, while still competing and training at the highest levels in their sport—without, of course, an arbitrary
academic eligibility metric. While European countries do not have an
embedded, educationally based sports development system, as in America, they do have an extended system of sport-specific schools that are
put in place for academic and athletic advancement without the requirement of meeting minimal academic metrics and being registered
as a full-time student.

In Germany, there are around ninety partner universities of top
sports (Partnerhochschule des Spitzensports). Similar to America, elite
athletes can benefit from lower academic entry criteria, flexible schedules, alternative ways to meet course requirements, help through personal tutors, and, sometimes, financial compensation and scholarships
provided by sports federations or foundations (Henry 2013, 7). Additionally, the German Sports Aid Foundation (Stiftung deutsche Sporthilfe) supports an athlete's academic career and future through financial
aid as well as through preparation for career entry by training for job
interviews. It also cooperates with particular companies that support
athletes through employment or internships. Some of these partners
even have particular employees in their human resources department
who are responsible for top athletes.

It needs to be acknowledged that in Europe, as in America, there
are problems for young athletes in coordinating their sports and their
academic responsibilities. Trying to be successful in sports while also
trying to succeed at school creates a double burden for these young
athletes. The older the athletes become, the more time they are required to invest in their sport, leaving less time for other areas of their
life. This means family, friends, and school drift into the background,
especially when school requires a lot of attention in order to graduate.
Consequently, practice, matches, and tournaments compete against
classes, exams, and studying time. Many elite athletes in Europe are
trapped in a dilemma similar to that of their American counterparts.
The big question is, How can one handle this dilemma? How does the
German sports system assist young athletes to handle and succeed in
their dual duties?

One approach taken by the Deutscher Olympischer Sportbund
(DOSB), Germany's Olympic committee, to avoid this issue is the establishment of what are known as elite sport schools (Eliteschule des

Sports, hereafter "Sport Schools") governed by the DOSB. They support young and talented students under the guideline "Become a world champion and graduate from high school." It is their assignment to allow students to pursue education and competitive sports at the same time. School and practice are well coordinated by the Olympic committee and the Sport Schools. There is also the possibility for students to live at an "Olympic Base Camp" nearby, similar to a boarding school. Base Camps are an essential part of the control system of competitive sports for the DOSB, aiming to provide athletes with an ideal environment to have a successful career in sports. Olympic Base Camps are facilities for supervising and serving all-state team athletes and their coaches. They ensure premium medical, social, psychological, and athletic care. This is especially true in preparation for the Olympic Games. Base Camps have access to the structures of Olympic sports federations, regional sports federations, and local sports clubs, which have the overall goal of training and building up national- and international-caliber athletes. Currently there are nineteen Olympic Base Camps in Germany.

The privilege to be called a Sport School is granted by the DOSB for a four-year period, after which the respective school has to be reaccredited. Today in Germany, there are 41 Sport Schools, of which 27 specialize in summer sports, 6 in winter sports, and the remaining 8 in both. All German Sport Schools combined support over 11,500 athletes and compile about 300,000 hours of special practice and 450,000 hours of additional individual lessons per year. Of the 392 members of the 2012 German Summer Olympics team, 104 attended and/or were supported in training by a Sport School. The Sport Schools play a major role in the promotion of up-and-coming athletes. They give the student-athletes the opportunity to pursue a career in sports but also graduate from high school. In doing so, the Sport Schools follow three objectives:

- Long-term success in competitive sports
- Qualifying for high school graduation
- Development of a mature personality

To do so, the German Sport School system must achieve the following conditions:

1. The Sport School, Olympic Base Camp, and training facilities should be in the same area. Time management is very

important and the student should not lose time by traveling long distances.

2. The sport type of the student should match the profile of the Sport School and the Olympic Base Camp. For example, it makes sense that a downhill ski racer attend a Sport School and Olympic Base Camp in the Alps.

3. The Olympic and regional sports federations assist in the selection of students. To be allowed to visit a Sport School, the students have to qualify for competitive sports and educational support. This is typically decided once the athlete turns sixteen and has been identified as a potential elite athlete.[6]

4. Sport and school duties should be reasonably coordinated and balanced accordingly. Athletic and educational development should go side by side. The training schedule and class schedule should be well synchronized.

5. Support should be offered by local sports clubs through providing competent, skilled coaches and appropriate training facilities.

6. Sport Schools should offer a good education and the chance of graduation. They should offer at least one class exclusively with athletes as students.

The purpose of the Sport Schools is to provide efficient conditions for an athletic education and training. Conditions like high-performance training groups, premium and flexible training facilities, skilled coaches, and sports scientists are required. As mentioned before, time management plays a major role in fulfilling the multiple demands on a student-athlete. Practice, competitions, and class and study time have to be balanced, but are balanced differently than in America, as there are no minimum eligibility criteria and the primary focus is on elite athletic development.

Sport Schools have to meet the following basic arrangements: school, training facilities, and living quarters have to be within a short distance from one another. Both the overall course of an individual's school career and his or her particular class schedules should be flexible. The student-athlete should be able to be excused from class for practice or competition and provided the opportunity to make up missed exams and to receive individual lessons outside designated class time. Every talented athlete throughout Germany should have the chance to attend a Sport School. All athletes face the same eligibility criteria to be chosen, based on elite athletic ability and not academic performance. Athletes who come from another part of Germany than where a particular Sport School is situated have the same chance to attend that Sport School as athletes who come from nearby. Every Sport School should be a fixed part of the regional sports federation. Schools and federations together organize and manage the operation of the Sport Schools. They also have to consult with the governmental Department of Education and Sports, which takes care of communication, coordination, and decisional matters.

Sport Schools should be institutions that stand for both educational and athletic success. The idea of fair play and the development of mature athletes are of great importance. Successful graduation from high school, evolution into being a mature adult, and social competence have the same value as athletic development. The goal is to teach young athletes self-reliance, solidarity, and teamwork. It is also important to point out that the Sport Schools offer regular antidoping presentations and education, since athletes should learn right from the start of their careers about the risks and illegality of doping, should they desire to compete in elite sports. Additionally, Sport Schools and Olympic Base Camps offer counseling about future job perspectives for the athletes.

Certainly, all this support and promotion of the student-athletes should lead to something. Therefore, the Sport Schools are evaluated in part by the athletic success of their students, as expressed by nominations to the national teams and achievements earned in international tournaments. In addition, the fluctuation in the number of student-athletes is monitored, as measured by how many students leave these schools and how many new ones join them throughout their schooling. Finally, the number of successful high school graduations is also part of the Sport School rating system. Although academics are not the primary focus, a Sport School will not be able to continue if it is not guiding many of these students toward graduation. The state government determines whether a school can keep its title as Sport School or a new school earns the privilege to call itself one. Interviews with stakeholders of the schools, including teachers, coaches, and students, form part of the evaluation process.

Both the Sport Schools and the club system offer additional competitive opportunities. There are tournaments between regional schools and at the national level. The best-known tournaments are the Stadtschulmeisterschaften (city championships) and Jugend trainiert für Olympia (Youth Training for the Olympics), which mirror the limited extramural athletics that are available within all schools in Germany. Stadtschulmeisterschaften are held annually in every common sport, such as soccer, basketball, track and field, and volleyball, to name only a few. The annual Jugend trainiert für Olympia events are first held on a regional level, with the best athletes and teams advancing to national level. The sports teachers of each school decide which students are eligible for participation in these tournaments. Again, this is an excellent way of combining school and sports without the inherent issues and problems that are present within American school-based sports.

Another feature in Germany that mirrors the American educational system is the acknowledgment that few athletes will actually be able to make a living through their sports activity, and even less so after their career ends. That is why the Olympic Base Camps are obligated to try to prevent future social hardship for student-athletes. This includes employing a counselor whose job it is to help athletes balance and coordinate their preparation for a career through both sports and education activities. The counselor keeps in touch with athletes and their families, coaches, teachers, and employers, developing an individual career plan for each athlete and clarifying it with parents, coaches, and the athlete. The first aspect of this counseling is about school and job issues. Depending on the age of the athlete, choices have to be made about what type of school (Gymnasium, Realschule, Hauptschule) she or he would like to attend or what kind of further education (university or education through work) she or he wants to pursue. In the case of further education, counselors help the athletes with applications and discovering what kind of studies or jobs would suit them. They also assist with preparation for job interviews or finding a new place to live. In addition, counselors communicate with schools, universities, the armed forces, and companies. The goal is to build up partnerships with these contacts in order to provide athletes the opportunity of jobs, internships, or studies. Also, counselors are the liaisons for the Sport Schools. Meanwhile, they are in charge of managing schedules and exams with the athletes. It is important to note that not only active athletes are taken care of, but also former or injured athletes. Additionally, the counselor can advise athletes to apply for financial support, for example through Stiftung deutsche Sporthilfe, mentioned above. The aim of this service is to ensure a dual career and to prevent impoverishment of athletes. The basic aim of all these services is to advise athletes to have a backup plan and help them follow it, so that they do not concentrate only on their athletic career.

THE ROLE OF THE GERMAN ARMED FORCES

Other avenues for elite sports development exist outside the educational system and the sports club systems. The German armed forces, like those of most other countries including the United States, support high-level athletes. These include about eight hundred athletes in fifteen "sports foster groups" (*Sportfördergruppen*). Additionally, there are forty posts for officers in charge, forty posts for military sports, and three posts for Paralympic athletes. These athletes are known as "sport soldiers." Responsibility for these foster groups in the armed forces is held by the Joint Support Service Command (Kommando Streitkräftebasis, or KdoSKB), which resides in Bonn. Support costs are about thirty million euros each year, of which the major part is for personnel salaries. The German armed forces play a key role in the German competitive sports system, and therefore the number of available support posts is verified by the DOSB.

The goal of this support system is to ensure German presence and competitiveness on an international level in competitive sports. In addition, it provides the athletes with the possibility of a dual career and job prospects after their athletic careers end. For preliminary competition and participation in international events, the armed forces provide more than 2,500 combined days of practice for their athletes each year. During the year preceding the Olympic Games, it even reaches up to 3,500 combined days of training. To underline the importance of the German armed forces it should be pointed out that 115 of the 392 German athletes at the 2012 Summer Olympic Games in London were sport soldiers. From 1991 to 2005, members of the German armed forces won 468 world championship, 416 European championship, and 2,489 German championship titles.

4 The Positive Gain for Public Health and the Citizenry of the United States

AN OVERARCHING theme of this book and one of the main reasons for proposing changes in the American sports system, despite the legitimate concerns regarding our current education-based sports system, is the broader impact on public health, life span, and health-related costs that a more proactive approach to health and wellness in America can have. By providing greater public access to sports and reframing our sports development and delivery options, we can achieve an immense positive impact on public health and health-care savings in this country.

As in the early twentieth century, the health and welfare of athletes are again a major focus of sports in America and worldwide today. The issue of athlete safety can actually enhance participation and recreational opportunities in sports other than a collision sport like football. The growing popularity of soccer in America is a case in point. Previously many of those kids may have played football. This is another reason why we need to have opportunities for competition and play in these sports in and/or outside the educational system. While it is clear that the issue of concussions must be addressed and the dangers of football participation must be resolved, there are other profound health dangers if we do not increase physical education and competitive opportunities at the scholastic and higher education levels.

The continued reduction and elimination of opportunities can also have negative lifelong health effects. Primary and secondary schools in the United States are dropping physical education at an alarming rate, and the poor health and obesity rates of Americans are skyrocketing. When I was growing up, most schools, public and private, had physical education classes every day up to junior high, and even then we had it at least three days per week. Even as a competing athlete in high school, I still had to participate in at least two years of P.E. As mentioned before, there were also many more competitive opportunities available in the form of extra varsity and subvarsity teams. Today, American schools are cutting back on physical education at all grade levels (Patterson 2013). While it is easy to conclude that it is not the responsibility of the education system to solve the problem of inactivity, it can, and in my view should, be a major channel for positive change. Proper nutrition and access to physical activity and other things many children take for granted are difficult for many American children to get if they are not available in school. Consequently, children likely will not have access to it anywhere else unless other options are made available either in conjunction with the school system or in a separate system entirely.

In 2013, the Institute of Medicine of the National Academies published a paper called "Educating the Student Body: Taking Physical Activity and Physical Education to School."[1] In this report it is noted that 44 percent of the nation's school administrators have cut significant amounts of time from physical education, arts, and recess. Daily or even intermittent PE classes such as two to three days a week declined "dramatically" from 2001 to 2006. One reason given is that more time was devoted to reading and mathematics since the passage of No Child Left Behind in 2001. While spending more time on academics should be considered an important endeavor, education should still be about educating the mind and body, and physical activity and sports participation at the primary and secondary levels of education are still vital. If opportunities cannot be increased or enhanced via the current educational system then we must develop other accessible and affordable options for our nation's youth. The motivation to get kids off the couch and participating in sports to gain the intrinsic values of sport, along with the associated health benefits, is decreasing. Alternative sports development models could be part of the solution inside and outside of education.

It is undebatable that exercise and participation in sports can improve an individual's health. Study after empirical study has proven this. Exercise, a balanced diet, and an otherwise healthy lifestyle contribute to a longer life span, fewer health problems, and an overall cost savings to the individual, the health-care system, and the country. While there are many variables to consider when discussing childhood and adult obesity, along with other diseases such as diabetes that a sedentary lifestyle contributes to and incubates, it is important to note that family, economic, social, and psychological factors can also worsen these epidemics, most acutely in the United States. I am going to focus more narrowly, on the physical fitness aspects rather than other variables, in discussing how increased sports participation can contribute to a better society. However, it is important to note that greater access to sports and physical recreation can have a net positive impact on these family, socioeconomic, and other contributors to poor health. Living a healthier lifestyle through sports and exercise can increase desire and motivation to overcome other issues such as diet and economic factors. Thus, new models of sports development and sports delivery should not only focus on the competitive and monetary benefits for the elite athlete. They must also focus on access and affordability for all citizens, of any age and skill level, who wish to make sports participation and related activity part of a lifelong healthy lifestyle.

More than one-third of the American population is obese and another third is considered overweight. This is the highest percentage of obesity in the world. Certainly, McDonald's, KFC, and other fast food providers, with their extra-large servings and their advertisements that suggest happiness is to be found via eating, are an important factor in our arriving at those numbers. As a country, we also need to recognize socioeconomic factors: it is difficult to maintain a healthy lifestyle in places where there are few alternatives for healthier food, where healthier food is expensive, and where there is a dearth of access to health and fitness facilities.

My focus here, though, is on physical activity, a lack of which is directly connected with the obesity epidemic and a host of other health problems in the United States. Rates of obesity could be drastically lowered if our citizens participated in the recommended amounts of sports and/or exercise. In turn, studies show a direct correlation between obesity and other illnesses and conditions like heart disease, diabetes, and cancer, with further negative impact on health-care costs for individuals and society. According to the Centers for Disease Control and Prevention, in 2014 over 610,000 people died in the United States due to heart disease, accounting for nearly one in four deaths.[2] Regular physical activity can lower the risk of heart disease, lower the number of people dying from this and other perhaps preventable diseases, lower health-care costs, and increase worker productivity and other positive social and economic impacts. Knowing all this, it seems strange that, despite everyone understanding the importance of sports and exercise, the number of physical education classes and sports activities in American schools has declined drastically over the past two decades (*Der Tagesspiegel* 2014a, 2014b; Gems and Pfister 2009).

Physical as well as mental and social well-being can emerge from doing sports. Evidence supporting this can be found in the average lifespan in the United States, which is currently around 76 years and stands lower than those in many other countries. This can stem from numerous factors, but certainly one reason is our low sports participation and lack of access to various and plentiful participation options. Contrasting this with the German experience shows multiple interesting factors. In particular, the higher sport participation rate is reflected in positive health data on the German population.[3] To begin with, they are living longer: the average lifespan in Germany in 2016, according to the *World Factbook* published by the Central Intelligence Agency of the United States (CIA), was 80.7 years, which was number 34 out of 224 countries. The United States was at number 42 with a 79-year life expectancy. Most of western Europe has a life expectancy of 80 years or more. Statistical analysis concludes that this could be partly due to higher sports participation by its citizens. It is estimated that around 16 percent of the German population is obese; an additional 50 percent is considered overweight. Those numbers have grown constantly since 1999, although the sports participation did not decline. Although the total for these two categories compares to that in the United States, noted above, we clearly skew much more strongly toward obesity. In 1999, the average Body Mass Index (BMI) in Germany was 25.2; by 2013 it had risen to 25.9.[4] In the United States the average BMI is 28.5, which is one of the highest in the world. The influence of physical activity on the cardiovascular system has also been shown to be positively correlated with better health metrics in Germany: as a result of high levels of participation in exercise and sports, only 8.2 percent of the adult population was diagnosed in 2011 with heart disease. This is compared with 11.5 percent in the United States, as measured in 2014.[5]

There are other benefits to be gained from improved sports development and delivery. For example, with a healthier and more active population, worker productivity can be greatly enhanced. This is one of the top reasons that a "Sports for All" movement and a focus on prevention in health care rather than a reactive approach work arguably much better in European countries than in the United States, with its unorganized approach toward sports and activity. Higher worker productivity and fewer sick days benefit organizations and save money. Investing in fitness and local sports clubs by corporations can aid in this effort. Avoiding obesity-related conditions and other diseases related to a passive, sedentary lifestyle can make people much more productive, which can provide savings for businesses and society while dramatically increasing citizens' life spans and mortality rates. Avoiding these and other conditions and diseases can also dramatically alter the course of American health care. When I attended the Project Play Summit in Washington, DC, in April 2016, organizations such as the Sports and Fitness Industry Association and Project Play clearly illuminated the benefits, not just for the individual but for the entire country. Using a worn-out sports analogy, these benefits are really part of a marathon, not a sprint, and need to be looked at as coming about through a long-term, multigenerational, positive change in American culture. While there are some immediate and short-term things that can be done, this must be a long-term effort.

Two primary factors that inhibit access in America to structured sports, recreational sports activity, and even unstructured play are the simple unavailability of facilities in many communities, and the cost of participation where facilities do exist. This is in contrast to most European countries, where opportunities and facilities are generally plentiful, affordable, and available to all citizens regardless of ability and age. It is also important to note that European school systems still put a premium on physical education courses and related activities within the existing education system, while communities also have widespread opportunities for competitive sports, physical recreation, and unstructured play via well-established and largely government-funded sports club systems.

After examining the US and German systems, as well as demographic and health data from both countries, it can be said that both systems have their positives and negatives with regard to sports delivery structure, governance, sports development, and competitive opportunities. One obvious positive in the European system is the overwhelming impact that a greater number of exercise and recreational sports offerings outside the educational system can have on public health and wellness. While children and adolescents do have a variety of sports offered in most educational institutions in America, these options, as previously noted, are dwindling. Meanwhile, the sports participation and recreational sports options available for people over the age of thirty are significantly fewer. Our educational sports system, which was intended to promote participation, wellness, and exercise now is focused on the commercial and other economic benefits of having winning athletic programs. At the primary and secondary levels, recess and gym class are more the exception than the rule, and young boys and girls are less and less likely to get the learning opportunities that can be gained from organizing themselves, using sports as a vehicle. Competitive sports on the secondary level are often focused on developing elite athletes who are chasing a college athletic scholarship, and slots on those teams go to the more talented athletes because of the competitive utility they may bring. In all these areas and at all these levels, we have moved toward being more spectators of sports than participators.

Meanwhile, many communities and school systems have become so desperate for public funding that what a community is able to procure via taxes goes to projects deemed more important than recreation, sports, and exercise. These communities have had to make hard choices in the short term, either without realizing or without being able to address the long-term damage that can come from having an unhealthy population and a community that is no longer interacting through sports and exercise activities. To put it in economic terms, there is more demand for sports opportunities than supply—and, due to less supply, fewer people are interested and that desire further decreases over generations.

No matter how you spin it, the United States of America is significantly unhealthier than many other developed nations. This is reflected in reports that obesity, heart disease, anxiety, and depression are more likely among US citizens, and this data can be linked to there being fewer sports offerings and lower sports participation when compared to similar demographics in European countries. The sports system in Germany has a different construct. You can find a sports club in nearly every city and town in Germany that offers a wide array of sports opportunities. If the sport you want is in the next town, it is very easy to get there to participate via public transportation or the ubiquitous bicycle. Consequently, the degree of participation in athletics by residents of Germany as well as by those in other European countries is rather high in comparison to the United States. It is just part of the culture in Europe, and we need to make it part of our everyday lives in this country.

Physical inactivity is identified as a major health risk worldwide. According to the World Health Organization, physical inactivity has been identified as the fourth leading risk factor for mortality, causing an estimated 3.2 million deaths globally each year. Short of death, statistics also indicate that physical inactivity can lead to poor health and increased risk of disease. Schlicht and Brand (2007, 9) found disturbing trends, such as that 16 percent of chest and bowel cancers as well as 22 percent of ischemic heart diseases can be causally affiliated to inactivity.

One prominent ongoing study conducted by the Global Obesity Prevention Center at Johns Hopkins University and presented at the 2016 Aspen Institute and Project Play Summit "simulated the physical activity behavior of youth during the years of 2010 to 2020. Included were scenarios where 50 percent, 75 percent, and 100 percent of the youth meet the standard of 'Active to a Healthy Level' (25 minutes of physical activity, three times a week) and 100 percent meet the Centers for Disease Control and Prevention (CDC) recommendation (one hour of physical activity daily), compared to current physical activity trends" (Aspen Institute 2016, 21). While the study is still ongoing, some interesting and disturbing trends have been noted and empirically tested.

This chart from that study shows how maintaining an active and healthy lifestyle at certain levels can directly affect health-related issues like obesity and diabetes, medical costs, worker productivity, and years added to the lives of American citizens, simply by increasing access to exercise, fitness, and sports participation options.[6]

Table 1. Virtual populations for obesity prevention (VPOP) simulation models

	Fewer overweight and obese youths	Direct medical costs saved	Productivity losses saved	Years of life saved
50% of youth maintain active to a healthy level	243,830	$20 billion	$32 billion	4 million
75% of youth maintain active to a healthy level	624,818	$22 billion	$38 billion	13 million
100% of youth maintain active to a healthy level	991,019	$26 billion	$43 billion	20 million
100% of youth maintain CDC physical activity recommendations	3,093,196	$35 billion	$57 billion	33 million

Source: Johns Hopkins Global Obesity Prevention Center, *A Systems Approach to Obesity.*

In this study, obesity was defined as being at or above the 85 percent mark in the BMI profile. If millions of youth under the age of sixteen had a reduced BMI, they would have a much smaller chance of developing chronic diseases and obesity-related health conditions later in life (e.g., stroke, cancer, heart disease, and diabetes). Other eye-popping findings from the report include the projection that thirty minutes a day of activity just three to four times per week could result in more than one million fewer kids being obese. The Centers for Disease Control advises that one hour of activity per day could result in over $35 billion of direct medical cost savings and untold billions in economic impact. Changing our paradigm of how we do sports development and delivery in this country would reduce direct and indirect insurance and medical costs relating to hospitalization, medication, and doctor's visits, including the billions spent on the uninsured in the United States. Extrapolate that same philosophy and approach to other age groups in America, and the cost savings can be billions more.

OVERTRAINING AND OVEREMPHASIS ON SPORTS ARE NOT NEEDED FOR A HEALTHY LIFESTYLE

In Europe, sports club training sessions normally take place two or three times a week, while competitive matches are mostly played during the weekend. Three to four sessions of physical activity take place per week in most of the typical sports, like soccer, basketball, volleyball, or tennis, just to name a few, for all ages and skill levels. In America, though, it seems we simply cannot find the proper balance. In this country we are either both overtraining and overspecializing or we are doing very little exercise and sports at all. We do not seem to have the equilibrium that makes sports and related activity a part of a normal lifestyle, instead of something that one gets burned out on because of overemphasis and overtraining. Nor do we present as many options in comparison to other countries. The sports offerings in America, especially for those fifty-five and older, are rather limited by comparison to Europe. Only around 35 percent of males and 25 percent of females between eighteen and twenty-nine years of age reach the recommended level of three hours of exercise a week. Those numbers decline further for older groups, for both males and females. According to the Bureau of Labor Statistics and the President's Council on Fitness, Sports & Nutrition, only one in three children are physically active every day and only one in three adults get the recommended amount of exercise per week. Only 5 percent of American adults exercise thirty or more minutes per day. Contrast these findings with the Johns Hopkins Global Obesity Prevention Center study mentioned above, and a pretty easy correlation can be inferred as well as some measurable solutions. More sports options and activity can and likely will lead to a healthier population. The return on investment from reframing our sports, recreation, and exercise options in the United States is potentially immense.

A reframing of the sports development and governance system in America does not guarantee better health care for the citizenry, lower insurance costs, fewer doctor visits, or a longer life span, but the research clearly suggests that it would have a major positive influence, and it is a primary reason to reassess what we are currently doing with sports development in America. Access for all in sports, recreation, and exercise needs to be expanded to address this serious area of concern in our country. Changing how we do sports development and offer sports delivery options in the United States can go a long way toward helping us solve the problems outlined here and bettering the country overall.

5

The Educational Conundrum and the Need for a Comprehensive National Sports Policy in the United States

I BELIEVE the scholastic and intercollegiate athletics-based sports development and delivery models in the United States are poised for their most wholesale change in the more than one hundred years the systems that shaped and are shaped by them have existed. This is due to the aforementioned external pressures, the focus on commercialism, and the growing disconnect with regard to the education and social development of student-athletes. In the continual conflict between the value of academic primacy and the pursuit of athletic success, athletics—and the often-stressed tangible and intangible benefits that supposedly come with commercially successful sports in an educational environment—typically win out. In this chapter the main goal is to further examine whether the educational sports development system in the United States is still viable. If not—if it ultimately doesn't work as intended—is it to be merely tweaked or overhauled, or is there a middle way? Where do we start in the overwhelming effort that will be needed to implement, in whole or in part, proposals such as those discussed in later chapters?

Compelling arguments do exist on all sides regarding the positives and negatives of educationally based sports in America. As covered in previous chapters, there are other systems we can look at for guidance as we consider alternatives. We could try to modify the system we have in the United States, or radically change it through establishing a national sports policy and structures similar to European sports councils and ministries. There is much room for debate. What is almost non-debatable, though, in my view, is that attempting to maintain the system as it stands is futile. It is time to ask ourselves if we can continue as virtually the only country in the world that has a primarily education-based sports development and delivery system.

In Europe, where the sports development model is so distinctly different from the American model of sports entrenched in education, it is still recognized that young athletes need access to a viable education and a life beyond competitive sports. I am not advocating kicking education to the curb in the United States to focus only on elite sports development, essentially for our entertainment. The exact opposite is true. I believe there are ways for an elite athlete to obtain and value a good education while still being very productive and successful as an athlete, in America and elsewhere. It is not unusual today to see elite American athletes inside and outside the educational system. The 2016 Olympic gold medalist in women's gymnastics, Simone Biles, was home schooled and took online classes to devote more time to her training and competitive goals. The swimmer Missy Franklin, also a winner of multiple Olympic gold medals, attended high school in Denver and the University of California, Berkeley, although she did step away from being a college student to train for the 2016 Rio Summer Olympics. These are just two examples of how elite athletes are using many existing structures to reach their goals. There can still be a place, even a prominent place, for educationally based sports in the United States, but as a primary driver of sports development and delivery its days are numbered, and they should be.

Meanwhile, the difficulties in changing direction in how sports and physical activity are managed in the United States are compounded by having few options for sports participation separate from education, and by many access problems involved with those options that are available. We do have an external club "system" for elite athlete development, sport specialization, and, to some extent, mass participation, but it is disjointed and socioeconomically elite, neither accessible to nor inclusive for all.

This chapter addresses many of the specific problems from previous chapters and details the risks involved in not having potential alternatives at least conceptually developed beyond the current educational model. These include risks to sports development itself in the United States. Many experts are predicting, for instance, that other sports opportunities will be lost in the education system due to the increased costs associated with the drive to compete in high-profile sports like football and men's basketball. We need a comprehensive national approach to kick-start and guide the reforms necessary to avoid such a disastrous outcome, among others.

THE NEED FOR A NATIONAL SPORTS POLICY TO GUIDE CHANGE

Even with compelling reasons, changing the current system or systems will be difficult, to say the least. There have to be, at a minimum, guiding principles as a basis for planning and implementing changes. Consequently, there is a strong argument for adopting a newly developed and comprehensive national sports policy that includes overall governance for all levels of sports in America by something similar to the sports ministry or council found in most European (and many other) countries. The United States is one of the few countries that does not have a national sports policy, commission, council, or even a director. What we do have are many organizations with different, competing agendas, with the lures of winning, revenue generation, and elite athlete development trumping what is likely better for the entire country, including greater sports and physical fitness access.

There has been little discussion or theory development concerning creating a national sports policy and sports ministry in America. The United States Olympic Committee, since its inception in 1961 and later in its redefined role after 1978 under the Amateur Sports Act, has had an unfunded mandate to govern amateur sports outside the educational system in America. As mentioned before, the USOC is the only national Olympic committee that is privately funded and receives no government support. In 1998, the Ted Stevens Olympic and Amateur Sports Act amended the original act, specifying in even greater detail such goals as maintaining competitive excellence for American athletes, male and female, able-bodied or disabled, along with developing interest and participation among the population (Sawyer, Bodey, and Judge 2008, 246–54).[1] As an unfunded mandate from the US government, these goals obviously cannot be achieved without using existing federal, state, and community support structures such as the education system, nonprofits like the YMCA, sports councils, sports foundations, and the private sector. It is time to bring these diverse sports delivery elements under a consistent and cohesive governance umbrella.

Publicly, important voices have brought up the need to reframe sports and its organization in America for the betterment of all citizens from a participatory perspective, and also to improve and regulate the competitive and entertainment options that sports provide. Ken Reed, the sports policy and communications director of the League of Fans, which was created by well-known consumer advocate Ralph Nader, recently stated as much in a 2016 *Huffington Post* article in which he detailed reasons the United States desperately needs a national sports policy to make a nation of spectators a nation of participants before it is too late.[2]

I wholeheartedly agree with most of the reasoning presented by Reed. A comprehensive, nationwide approach to sports via an overall organization or even organizations, whether public, private, or a combination of both, is critical to achieving any meaningful change in our sports development and sports delivery options. Reed highlights what much of sports has become in America: winning and profit for a few, at all costs, while most are losing opportunities to participate. This mentality has trickled down and negatively affects sports at all levels—all the more reason to have a national approach to guide sports policy. Others who have called for a national approach to sports governance include Project Play and the Aspen Institute, already mentioned above. Other important groups advocating for examination, discussion, and even implementation of a national sports policy include the YMCA, Special Olympics International, the American College of Sports Medicine, and the Robert Wood Johnson Foundation.

Enthusiasm about developing a national sports policy will likely be limited, at least at first, for several reasons. One is the perception that spending money and effort on sports and exercise is not the most important thing the country as a whole should be doing, considering the other issues facing the government and private organizations on a daily basis. While I understand that argument, I also know that having a national sports policy can actually contribute to positively dealing with and solving many other issues, most notably in regard to health and wellness. The net positive effects on so many things, including cost savings in health care, improved workplace productivity, and community enhancement, are almost immeasurable. In Canada and England, two countries with national sports ministries and policies, it is estimated that every dollar or pound spent on increasing access to sports and wellness correlates to at least five dollars or pounds in savings. The expense for related programs is considered to be an investment bringing about cultural changes that will benefit the entire country in multiple constructive ways that go far beyond developing elite athletes. Looked at this way, the cost of planning and implementing a national sports policy is a bargain, not wasted expense. There will almost always be a net financial gain, considering the potential cost savings.[3] As a country we need to get beyond that narrow mindset and realize how access for all to sports and physical activity can be leveraged to produce positive outcomes.

Second is the aversion to government control of anything. We do live in a capitalistic society and I am certainly not the biggest fan of government regulation, but in some cases it is necessary. This, I believe, is one of those situations where the federal government, in conjunction with states, communities, private organizations, and other existing sports development infrastructures, can beneficially regulate, control, and guide competitive, mass participation, and recreational sports and exercise. Federal, state, and local government being involved in a national sports policy gives credibility and importance to the goals and purpose. The private sector can certainly be part of the policy and governance structure: the government frequently works with both nongovernmental organizations and the private sector to accomplish goals in the domestic economy, international trade, education, and other issues of national interest. When it comes to a national sports policy, establishing a governmental division or even cabinet position would give the federal government and, by extension, state and local governments involvement in the game. It would enable development of a strategic plan, inherent leadership, and the ability to build the capacity and opportunity to actually change how we do sports in America. If the federal government were to seriously focus on the issue, just as when the Special Olympics were made a priority by John F. Kennedy and his sister Eunice Kennedy Shriver, other stakeholders would get involved to help start the reform process and see it through. While it will be a marathon, not a sprint, it can be done if all the stakeholders are motivated by a governmental edict of a national sports policy.

The United States needs a sports commission and a sports "czar," if you will, to bring together all the diverse entities in sports and sports governance that exist today. The purpose of this organizational approach would be identifying and implementing overall strategies and tactics for steering sports development and delivery toward being more accessible for all, as well as for better developing elite athletes outside the current educational model. An example of how this can be done, at least in theory, is the Department of Homeland Security, which was established after the September 11, 2001, terrorist attacks to oversee and coordinate a variety of efforts relating to threats to the country. While there is certainly ongoing argument as to how successful this security approach has been for America, it is a useful template for bringing together diverse organizations at the federal, state, local, and even private levels to better coordinate and streamline complementary operations.

Other templates concerning sports governance and national sports policies can be found in virtually every other country on the planet, and certainly in Europe. The United States can sample and assess different approaches to developing a national sports policy that could work even in our diverse republic. The German Olympic Sports Confederation (Deutscher Olympischer Sportbund, or DOSB), that country's national Olympic committee, is a salient example of how an effective national sports policy can work to benefit the entire country, beyond just elite sports competitiveness. The DOSB is actively involved in directing and promoting all aspects of sports development and delivery (Foster, O'Reilly, and Dávila 2016, 156–62), including not just elite sports but sporting and physical activity options for the entire population. In line with many national sports policies in Europe, it is also active in training and licensing coaches who work with almost 10 million children, its more than 28 million individual members, and ninety-thousand-plus sports clubs. The DOSB, like other national sports governing bodies throughout the world, receives substantial financial and logistical assistance from federal and state government, though financing also comes from other areas such as ticket sales, sponsorships, marketing licenses, and even lottery revenue (157). It is my view that sports federations and national sports policies cannot be as effective or inclusive as they should be without such direct financial support.

A national sports policy in the United States does not have to be overly regulated and bureaucratic. What it can do is unite and give direction to existing governmental, nonprofit, and for-profit entities while providing funding opportunities and governance at all levels.

This could be done from the top down at the federal government level, or even from the bottom up at the local level, where many successful public-private partnerships already exist and do a pretty solid job of providing access to health and wellness opportunities. The YMCA is a good example of a nongovernmental organization that can be an active participant in a national sports policy and also be itself enhanced and improved through a scaled, national approach to sports.

SPECIFIC REASONS WHY WE NEED TO CHANGE SPORTS NOW IN AMERICA

A national sports policy and a new approach to governing and managing how we do sports in America is not only needed, it is almost inevitable. There are six main reasons that will eventually, likely sooner rather than later, force the current educationally based sports development model to change, and a national approach to sports governance can best deal with these changes. Those six primary reasons have to do with (1) economics, (2) the athletes' rights movement, (3) legal challenges, (4) legislative action, (5) educational priorities, and (6) ensuring a viable "home" for other sports than the high-profile sports, particularly football and men's basketball.

Reason 1—Economics

While funding affects everything in education, many of the economic issues that educationally based sports force on schools and colleges are of their own making, based on what they choose to spend money on rather than not having enough funding, most notably in American higher education. This does not mean that budgetary limitations, specifically at the state and scholastic level, don't affect the economics of sports in America—but many of the problems that exist are due to the choices being made about how to spend budgeted amounts. Of course, the inability to control overall spending is another problem, especially in college sports.

At both the scholastic and collegiate levels, many other sports programs and additional physical activity options are either being eliminated or are in danger of being eliminated due to the cost and popularity of the marquee sports of football and men's basketball. Since the end of the twentieth century, sports like men's and women's gymnastics, skiing, and water polo have seen declines in educationally based opportunities. Wrestling, which I have a deep love for as a semi-elite competitor, coach, and official, has lost almost a third of its college teams since 1989, and that has made it easier to drop wrestling from scholastic programs. The same pattern can be seen in other sports.

The college years are also the peak development age for athletes, and that age range consistently provides the lion's share of US gold medal winners in the Olympic Games (Dure 2015). The most notable college sports for producing US gold medalists are swimming and diving, track and field, rowing, basketball, water polo, wrestling, and soccer. Yet many of these sports are the ones seeing dramatic reductions in educationally based participation opportunities, and the future of international sports excellence for the United States, in these and other sports, is in jeopardy. At the same time, there is a nationwide scarcity of sports and competitive opportunities outside the educational system. According to PlayyOn.com, "a discovery and management platform for sports, fitness, and clubs," youth participation in competitive and recreational sports is rapidly decreasing. Currently, 94 percent of high school graduates in the United States are faced with fewer options for participating in competitive sports after graduation.[4] This is dramatically different from what is available in other countries.

There are many examples of colleges and universities making an "investment" in football and men's basketball while dropping other athletic opportunities. My current employer, Ohio University, eliminated hugely successful men's programs in track and field and swimming, along with women's lacrosse, as a cost-cutting measure in 2007, but later announced massive infrastructure and facility improvements for the football program (Znidar 2007). In a personal conversation with former Ohio University athletic director Kirby Hocutt several years ago, he told me that eliminating the sports was an "investment for the university," and that athletes in the remaining sports could not be provided a Division I experience if Ohio University maintained the sports they had just eliminated.[5] I am not quite sure what a "Division I experience" means, nor has anyone explained it to me, but it appears to some that focusing on only a few sports that bring revenue and publicity will bring more to the university than broad-based participation and competitive opportunities for many college athletes rather than a privileged few. I disagreed with Hocutt then and disagree with him even more now. I do not feel that Ohio University has been improved overall as an institution by this "strategic investment." In fact, it has damaged the university more than it has helped, because it eliminated many opportunities for students—academically and athletically.

Educationally based sports are not supposed to be about only a few individuals enjoying an elite-athlete experience. They are supposed to be about creating opportunities for many to develop a sound mind and body. If an elite experience is the main goal, then that can and should be provided elsewhere. Clearly, in America, we have lost our way. Ohio University would have advanced to the same levels, educationally and athletically, that it has to the present date by keeping those other sports alive and preserving those opportunities. Eliminating those sports has not in any way made the university more desirable or better academically. It was simply done to try to compete at a higher level in the more commercially viable sports. Yet, given the landscape of college athletics in America, there is only a certain level of competitive excellence a mid-major NCAA Division I university like Ohio University can attain in the college athletics landscape when its total athletic budget is 100 million dollars less than some of its competitors. It is a colossal waste of resources for schools like Ohio University to attempt to compete at a level they will never attain, and it will only continue to limit broad-based participation opportunities.

Temple University in Philadelphia is an even more recent, glaring example. After years of on-field futility, the school had a very successful 2015 football season—but Temple's success on the gridiron was achieved at the expense of other athletes who had their sports programs cancelled in 2013, including baseball, softball, men's crew, women's rowing, men's gymnastics, and men's indoor/outdoor track and field (Petchesky 2013). One could argue that Temple is seeing success in football on a national scale, so maybe the strategy worked to an extent. That argument may currently seem strong on its face, but is it realistic? In the future, will the football program be sustainable, cost effective, and beneficial overall to the university? These cuts saved Temple only about three million dollars, but eliminated competitive and participatory opportunities for over 150 athletes each year, along with nine coaches. But what is the purpose of educationally based sports, if not student participation and health? Is it just to support commercially successful programs and elite athlete development, or is it to use sports as an impetus and augmentation to educational progress and overall development? We simply have not yet reconciled this in America, but we need to, or it will be reconciled for us, perhaps in a way we do not prefer.

Temple is in the majority of collegiate athletic programs that do not generate enough revenue to support not only football but other sports in the way some of the larger, more commercially successful programs do. One could easily argue that the demand for competitive athletics at a school like Temple is not as high as it might be made out to be. With that being said, I still feel the institution and even the student body should support the university's intercollegiate athletic programs through institutional subsidies and student fees, as they would in other areas of activity on campus. We all have an obligation, in my view, to support overall programming on campuses, even programs we may not like or actively engage in. The point here is the excessive amount of institutional subsidies, student fees, and tuition dollars going to increasingly costly, money-losing athletic programs that are providing fewer and fewer options for the student body at large.

There is significant evidence that student fees and institutional subsidies for intercollegiate athletics are rising at a rate much higher than tuition. At public institutions, the growth rate of expenditure on athletics is over 13 percent higher on average nationwide (Denhart and Vedder 2010). There is no sign that these costs are going down, as too many schools continually pump money into a race they likely cannot win—while others have to just drop sports to help meet a budget, and the rest manage to hang on, at least for now. It defies logic that with more money coming in, at least for college sports, participation opportunities are shrinking.

Some argue that Title IX, which requires equal treatment and opportunities for female athletes, based upon finances, treatment, and proportionality of enrollment, is a major reason for lost sports participation opportunities for males. The real root cause of those lost opportunities is money, and commercialism in particular.[6] I grew up in an era when many if not most people believed the common refrain that women were not supposed to play sports nor have the same access that men had. I can vividly remember female athletes essentially getting the worst of everything in terms of equipment, locker rooms, travel, media coverage, and more. The playing field was far from level. In time, I personally evolved to passionately advocating that women deserved access to the same benefits that male athletes were receiving. This was also later mandated by Title IX, and both federal law and sports in the United States are the better for it. The struggle continues, though, as male sports are still getting higher priority and most of the funding, despite the goal of balancing and even restricting spending on certain sports since equality was mandated by federal law. Any thought that Title IX would cause a "market correction" to balance spending between genders in public school and university sports has been proven to be unrealistic. It simply has not happened to the level the law intended.

The desire to fund commercially popular sports at even higher levels than in the early days of Title IX enforcement has reduced overall sports opportunities for everyone, both male and female. Ironically, Title IX has often been used as a means not to increase opportunity, but to limit it. As Carpenter and Acosta note, "Institutions who failed to meet any of the three prongs of the participation test [or other components of Title IX] all too often decided to manipulate numbers rather than expand opportunities . . . the manipulation of numbers typically included terminating the men's 'minor' sport teams (e.g., wrestling, gymnastics, and swimming) rather than, for example, curbing the excesses of football" (2005, 185). Jim Duderstadt, the former president of the University of Michigan, primarily blames insufficient presidential leadership at the university for allowing football and basketball to be engulfed by the entertainment industry and extensively commercialized and professionalized, leading to the corruption of college sports (Duderstadt 2000).

It is true that Title IX has changed the paradigm of sports development by providing the needed and correct change regarding female athletes' access to athletics at public institutions. Successes in female athletics at the scholastic, intercollegiate, and international levels of competition have been noteworthy for American girls and women. However, putting the blame on Title IX for reductions in participation opportunities for male athletes is highly misguided and contrary to existing empirical research. The loss of men's sports programs and opportunities is related more to institutional decisions, as Duderstadt noted, that focus on the perceived economic benefit from revenue-generating sports such as men's football and basketball, rather than on meeting Title IX requirements by reducing expenditures and unneeded and mostly unused playing spots. These economic decisions, arguably, are the root causes of sports outside football and basketball being eliminated and reducing competitive opportunities (Ridpath et al. 2008).

The same strategy has trickled down and is now being applied to scholastically based sports. As sports are dropped at the collegiate level, opportunities for all—elite and mass-participation athletes—are also being reduced at the lower levels. This is partly in response: when there are fewer and fewer opportunities to participate in a particular sport at the college level, more and more secondary schools will tend to follow suit. Primary and secondary schools in the United States are also bound by Title IX, but also have found themselves literally falling into an athletic trap based on belief that winning athletic programs will provide sustainable benefits like increased enrollment and fund-raising for the entire institution (Nixon 2014). Many have continued down the same road as other colleges and universities by maximizing resources for football and men's basketball at the expense of other sports and fitness opportunities. This is frequently driven by commercialism, which is too often also present at the high school level.

In 2007, the *Chronicle of Higher Education* predicted that "as financial pressures mount, more athletic departments [at the intercollegiate level] will eliminate sports" (Wolverton 2007). John Cheslock (2007) has encouraged research that would specifically examine reductions in men's sports teams in relationship to the arms race in athletic spending, and not Title IX, in the Football Bowl Championship Series subdivision. Current research supports Cheslock's challenge that the reduction in sports opportunities throughout the United States is grounded primarily in increased spending on a few sports, rather than following a broad-based plan to support many sports. In the 2005–6 academic year, long after the extension of Title IX to athletics, spending at the NCAA Division I level per male athlete averaged $58,000, while only $33,000 was spent on average for a female athlete (Lawrence and Li 2007). That gap has gotten even worse. According to NCAA statistics, while many male teams have been eliminated since the inception of Title IX, women still receive fewer sports opportunities and much lower spending per sport based upon enrollment figures at public institutions (Ridpath et al. 2008). While the situation for female athletes in America has improved, the increased spending on the commercially popular sports continues to affect opportunities for both male and female athletes. A 2013 white paper from the Women's Sports Foundation states, "Despite progress, . . . today the scales of opportunity in interscholastic and collegiate sports still tip unfairly toward a male advantage, and Title IX remains a legislative beacon and, sometimes, a legal bludgeon" (Sabo and Snyder 2013, 2).

There are other ways to keep education as an important component even if a sport is not part of the school system. Other sports models, such as in Europe, are open to all, are affordable, and provide athletes the opportunity to get noticed and/or at least compete, even if athletic ability is not at the elite level. Moreover, access for all improves community cohesiveness, work productivity, and overall health as it provides opportunities for lifetime participation in certain sports and greater benefits through physical activity (ibid., 15–16). Even though I am advocating for change in how we develop and create access for both elite and mass-participation sports in the United States, there can still likely be a place for a scholastic-based athlete in America, but under a very different model or models.

Reason 2—The Athletes' Rights Movement

If sports and sports development are really to change in America in the quickest way possible, a push for change has to come from the athletes themselves. For too long, scholastic and collegiate athletes have been not just controlled but used by coaches, administrators, boosters, and even the media. The days of the coach having total authority and control, with the athlete following in lockstep or else, are essentially over. Athletes, most notably at the intercollegiate level, are now making their voices heard at all levels of sports development in the United States, and they are demanding certain rights, addressing health and welfare issues and compensation and revenue sharing. This is not completely restricted to the intercollegiate level, although that is where athletes have been most active and public in standing up for their rights.

If these athletes were to decide they want changes regarding such things as being paid for play, being able to capitalize on marketing rights, the length of seasons, and, let's not forget, actual access to an education, those changes could happen tomorrow. The athlete has the power to enact tremendous change by simply refusing to play. One might think that if athletes did refuse to play they could just be replaced, or forced to play by a powerful coach. In theory, I suppose that is true, but if exercised I believe it would ultimately backfire. As seen in the past with player walkouts and strikes at the professional level, the fans want to see the best elite athletes compete, and the market would force administrators and management to eventually acquiesce to the players' demands in whole or in part.[7]

Recent events give some idea of the tremendous leverage that athletes could have in shaping the future of educationally based sports in the United States. At the University of Missouri in late 2015, over thirty African American members of the football team joined in solidarity with a growing number of students who were protesting over racial inequities on campus, including one now on hunger strike and many more participating in a student boycott. On November 8, right in the middle of the season, the players stated they would not participate in any football-related activities until university president Tim Wolfe resigned. Instead of threatening to withdraw scholarships, kick them off the team, or punish them in any way, the head football coach and athletic director made statements publicly supporting the athletes and their right to protest. Although pressure had been building throughout the semester, the football players' action certainly drew new outside attention and heightened concerns about the reaction of alumni, trustees, and other university stakeholders. President Wolfe resigned the next day (Belkin and Korn 2016). When athletes speak with a united voice, they have power, and they are realizing that more and more.

In 2013, the football team at Louisiana's Grambling State University actually refused to play a road game against Jackson State University over substandard facilities and burdensome practice and playing conditions, which had even included a bus trip of nearly twenty-four hours to another road game. The stance of the players forced the university to forfeit the game against JSU (ESPN 2013). After concessions including promises to improve the facilities and other conditions for the players, the boycott was ended a week later. The lesson is clear: as the Grambling players clearly demonstrated, even athletes at lower-tier schools have the power to enforce change by simply refusing to play.

College athletes have gotten some significant publicity and backing that have given this movement great power. Media commentators, scholars, and other prominent individuals such as former Duke basketball player Jay Bilas have come out strongly against the current model and for the rights of college athletes, including the right to be paid a salary for services rendered to the university. The National College Players Association (NCPA), led by former UCLA football player Ramogi Huma, has established itself as essentially the first broad-based advocacy organization for intercollegiate players, with over fourteen thousand current and former Division I athletes as members. While it is not yet a union, the NCPA has become a major force in the struggle for fair treatment of college athletes, and has succeeded in getting several NCAA rules changed.

A Unionization Effort. Since the NCAA was established in 1909, its role in higher education and its tenuous hold on the concept of amateurism have been endlessly debated, with relatively little change occurring. The premise that college sports are to be played by unpaid amateur athletes has been fairly consistent, even though the definition of amateurism has been a moving target over the years.[8] Meanwhile, the commercialization of and revenues from educationally embedded sports in America have dramatically increased with the advent of multibillion-dollar broadcast and merchandizing deals that have essentially eroded any notion that the participation and use of athletes in big-revenue sports have much to do with their education. The recent realignment of the most athletically powerful colleges into five conferences designed for maximum generation of capital has brought even more revenue into the picture. In current football and basketball broadcast deals alone, the NCAA and these Power Five conferences—Atlantic Coast, Big Ten, Big 12, Pac-12, and Southeastern—are guaranteed more than $31 billion up through 2024. The fact that the labor, the athletes themselves, are not receiving any of this revenue while coaches and others are making millions is not lost on too many people, and the athletes themselves have fought back for their fair share. Lawsuits have drawn media interest, and members of Congress smelled headlines so much that Senator Jay Rockefeller (D) of West Virginia held hearings in Washington, DC, on the conduct of the NCAA in July 2014. In May 2014, the House Education and the Workforce Committee conducted a session discussing the potential consequences of unionizing college athletes at Northwestern University. During the July 2014 hearing, the West Virginia senator and others on the Senate Commerce Committee went hard after the NCAA and especially NCAA President Mark Emmert about the conduct of college sports and what they believed to be inherent unfairness in many ways. Rockefeller also indicated that Congress may take a longer look at American college sports governance in the future if issues such as safety, overspending, and unfairness to the athlete continue (Berkowitz 2014).

Even the United Steelworkers got into the act, financially backing the bid to unionize football players at Northwestern and providing legal assistance.[9] The Northwestern unionization effort was one of the more significant athletes' rights movement efforts supported by the NCPA and concerned the attempt to unionize by members of the Northwestern University football team in 2014. While this effort was largely symbolic, since this was just one school and a private one at that, Northwestern athletes were able to secure various decisions by the National Labor Relations Board. Initially, the Chicago office of the NLRB determined that Northwestern football players qualified as employees of the university and could unionize, provided the majority of the players voted for it. Some of the reasons for the finding that the Northwestern athletes were employees included the players' time commitment to their sport, the seeming priority of athletics over academics, and the fact that their scholarships were tied directly to their performance on the field rather than their educational advancement (Bennett 2014).

The Chicago ruling was appealed by the university to the national board in Washington, DC, shortly thereafter. In August 2015, the NLRB announced that it would not take jurisdiction in the matter based on the fact that Northwestern was the only private school in the Big Ten conference. Since the NLRB only has authority over private institutions and not public ones, which are governed by state law, they felt the stability of college sports would be threatened by one school unionizing. It did not address the question of whether or not the athletes were actually employees, as determined by the Chicago office. This issue remains a critical one, and the door is still open for further unionization efforts by college athletes in the future. Certainly this is not the last we have heard on this issue, and the question of whether college athletes are employees will be an ongoing subject of inquiry.

Athletes' Rights at the Primary and Secondary Levels of Education. The struggle for athletes' rights, for their having a stronger voice in the sports they play, and for the improvement of governance is not restricted to intercollegiate athletics. Athletes at all levels are beginning to assert themselves in many different ways. Some of the more notable efforts have included fighting for religious freedom, protesting against the actions of particular coaches and administrators, and demanding better playing conditions and medical care, just to name a few. As many sports at secondary and even primary schools become more and more popular and are televised and commercialized at ever-increasing rates, athletes at these levels will also likely step up and demand greater rights, access to profits, and the ability to market themselves.

One example concerns the performance and skyrocketing popularity of Mo'ne Davis, a female pitcher for the Taney (Pennsylvania) Dragons, which played in the Little League World Series in 2014. While she was not the first girl to participate in the World Series, she was the first to earn a win and to pitch a shutout. Very few females have ever competed in this prestigious tournament, but the performance of Davis will be a likely catalyst to opening it up even more to both sexes in the future.

Davis excelled as a pitcher, regularly outplaying the boys and, predictably, becoming a media phenomenon at the tender age of thirteen. Commercialization naturally followed. She had nothing to do with the fact that baseballs she had signed started showing up on auction websites, but Davis did accept endorsement money for appearing in a Chevrolet advertisement that ran during that year's Major League World Series. Of course, accepting money or any other compensation based on her competitive reputation could have ramifications for her eligibility to play intercollegiate sports. (Davis had often made it known that she dreamt of playing college basketball one day, specifically for the powerhouse University of Connecticut woman's team.) The situation became a major issue, as many asked why a thirteen-year-old should be subject to those types of restrictions, especially when they might be at their commercial and athletic peak. Thankfully, at least in this case, the NCAA showed some ability to adapt and understand reality, and said it would not punish Davis in the future (Wolken 2014).

Davis is likely not the last young athlete who will experience this type of fame and financial opportunity. The landscape is rapidly evolving in this area and the issues arising are important to address, or the athletes themselves will likely force changes. Davis did not have to rely on the courts or government intervention to enact change, but many read the tea leaves and saw that restricting her would have unintended consequences (at least perceived by some) that could lead to more athletes at lower levels asking for expanded rights, involvement in decision making, and access to revenue. The hoopla surrounding Davis and the overall increased media coverage of youth sports make situations like this inevitable in the future.

In a December 15, 2015, ESPN.com column that followed the University of Missouri protests already mentioned above, the outstanding ESPN writer Howard Bryant said it best with regard to the power athletes have to change the current system(s) of sports.

> The players, should it be a mission they choose to accept, are on the verge of revolution. Only to the deniers or the naive is each step an isolated incident, whether the conversation is Ed O'Bannon suing the NCAA, unionization at Northwestern, players forcing an owner's ouster or Missouri football threatening a boycott if student demands are not met. Combined with the resurrection of protest as a weapon on American streets, times are changing. The money in sports is enormous, and the systemic issues of inequity remain heinous: scholarships that ostensibly provide educational compensation in lieu of a paycheck; coaches leaving for more money while most players must sit out a year after transferring. But the generational belief that an unfair system cannot be changed is not shared by students who slept in tents until they received some say. (Bryant 2015)

Reason 3—Legal Challenges

Two notable lawsuits have great potential to force change to the current sports development model in the United States. The first, *Edward O'Bannon, Jr. v. NCAA*, brought by former UCLA basketball star Ed O'Bannon, concerned the right of college athletes to profit off their name, image, and likeness being used in NCAA-affiliated properties after the player's NCAA eligibility has expired.[10] O'Bannon's suit arose from his name and image being used in NCAA-affiliated video games, for which he and other players also depicted received zero compensation. This case, now finished after the United States Supreme Court declined to hear appeals from both sides, did help in changing the legal definition of an amateur athlete, whether in college or at other levels of education. While the O'Bannon case did not specifically allow amateur college athletes to receive a salary, it did prompt the NCAA to fast-track and redefine the value of a scholarship up to the cost of attendance at each particular school. This means that an athlete on a full-ride traditional scholarship of tuition, room, board, books, and fees could receive a stipend up to an amount of the school's actual cost of attendance (COA). COA is set by institution as a total cost to attend a school and includes expenses such as travel, clothing, and other living expenses.[11] This common-sense change was resisted by the NCAA for years as a slippery slope toward professionalism, but the pressure of the O'Bannon lawsuit, the Northwestern unionization effort, and other legal action as catalysts for this change cannot be minimized. As mentioned above in regard to the Mo'ne Davis situation, even very young athletes may have the opportunity to commercially profit off their own name, image, and likeness. Even with the compensation of so-called amateur athletes beyond a scholarship and actual and necessary expenses at all levels, it is inevitable in my view that one day these athletes will be free to negotiate and capitalize on their own marketing utility and share in marketing and sponsorship revenue generated by their institutions, conferences, and governing bodies. This would also give athletes more power and, I believe, the ability to gain greater representation in the governance process.

Well-known antitrust attorney Jeffrey Kessler is also attacking the amateur model via the courts. He is lead attorney in a class action lawsuit, *Martin Jenkins et al. v. National Collegiate Athletic Association et al.*, that many experts believe could have an even bigger impact on educationally based amateur athletics than the O'Bannon case. Kessler has been aggressive in his representation of athletes and has had numerous legal successes against prominent sports governing bodies, including the National Football League and Major League Baseball.[12] In this legal push, Kessler is harnessing the power of athletes and the interest among many of them, such as in the Northwestern unionization effort, in eliminating all market caps on them and allowing them to negotiate the best deal available under a free market system—a system that almost any other person in America enjoys access to, including all other college students. Kessler contends in the class action suit that limiting player compensation to the value of scholarships is price fixing and therefore illegal, and that compensating athletes at their fair market value will have no effect on the product.

I certainly agree with Kessler on this in principle, and certainly don't think the system will implode if college athletes and even precollege athletes like Mo'ne Davis are fairly compensated. We may be heading in this direction regardless, but I do think there are some alternatives beyond straight salaries that can fully compensate what we have called amateur athletes for over a century and preserve educational opportunity for those who desire it. Still, this case and other legal actions will be a major catalyst in changing the system. Where it may end is anyone's guess, but Jeffrey Kessler will certainly not give up. If his past record is any indication, he will likely be successful in some way in changing the definition of what a college/amateur athlete is and how he or she may be compensated in the future.

Reason 4—Legislative Action

As discussed earlier, the federal government of the United States is seriously examining the business of intercollegiate athletics in America. This examination and potential legislative action will not only have ramifications for college sports as we know it in America, but will likely change the way we do sports at all levels of education and through other options currently available outside the professional ranks. Due to the high profile of college sports in America, the cost of them to the taxpayers at public educational institutions, and the immense amount of media coverage they entail, the federal government has many times stepped in to review whether intercollegiate athletics, and most specifically the NCAA enterprise, has its house in order. Over time, the US Congress has reviewed NCAA rules and regulations, athlete health and welfare, recruiting issues, educational aspects such as graduation rates, gambling, and enforcement and infractions procedures, just to name a few. In almost all cases, government intervention or the threat thereof has spurred the college sports enterprise, and by extension even primary and secondary school sports, to make needed changes, including many that would not have been considered but for the involvement of the government.

For instance, the Student Right-to-Know and Campus Security Act of 1990 made it mandatory to publish graduation rates of college athletes, against great resistance from many in the NCAA. The bill that eventually became law was primarily written by three members of Congress at the time, former University of Maryland standout basketball player Representative Tom McMillen (D-MD), Representative Ed Downs (D-NY), and former Princeton and New York Knicks basketball player Senator Bill Bradley (D-NJ). This legislation mandated that graduation rates and financial data for all colleges be publicly available, including the graduation rates of athletes. According to McMillen (1992) and Lederman (1991; 1992), the primary impetus for the Student Right-to-Know Act was the advent in the late 1980s of stricter national eligibility standards for incoming freshman athletes. Research had demonstrated that stricter initial eligibility standards for all students in terms of college preparatory courses and standardized results increased the likelihood of graduation.

Several changes were also made to the archaic NCAA enforcement and infractions process after congressional reviews in 1991 and 2004. Congress established a blue-ribbon panel to review the much-criticized process, led by Rex Lee, president of Brigham Young University and former solicitor general of the United States, resulting in significant and needed changes that many agree made the system much more fair and inclusive for those individuals who might be accused of NCAA violations. The system is far from fixed, but the NCAA adopted most of the reforms suggested by the Lee Commission. Amazingly, before these changes, players accused of NCAA rule infractions were not allowed to have any representation, nor were interviews tape recorded or transcribed to ensure accuracy. None of these things would have happened, but for the involvement of the government.[13]

Government inquiries into the sports industry over the years have had a largely positive effect, certainly with regard to intercollegiate athletics. At the very least due to the impact of rising sports-associated costs on the affordability of higher education for all, it is likely the federal government will continue to look at how college- and university-based sports fit within the overarching goals of advanced education in this country. Many advocates have been pushing to have a presidential commission review intercollegiate athletics and, by extension, school-based sports at all levels. A bill introduced in 2015 and currently in a House subcommittee would do that, at least at the intercollegiate level.[14] Whether by making H.R. 2731 into law or otherwise, it appears the government will get involved again in some way—and this is one issue where it is clear to me that government attention is a good thing. In fact, it is necessary: already, those in charge of college sports have demonstrated little willingness to move without outside intervention. The persuasive power of the federal government in encouraging, if not forcing, reform in sports development in America can be a strong impetus for positive change.

While primary and secondary schools are also due for intervention regarding their sports programs, any action by the government will most likely be handled at the state level because authority over those programs ultimately rests within each individual state. However, high school and primary school sports also need to be part of both a federal review and a national sports policy because of increased interstate and national competitions, commonalities in health and welfare dangers, and the ongoing elimination of participation and development opportunities at these levels nationwide. Potential government intervention in primary and secondary school sports is discussed in greater depth in later chapters.

Reason 5—Educational Priorities

As mentioned previously, America is falling behind other developed countries in educating its citizens. This obviously is not the sole fault of educationally based athletic programs, but the correlation is there. All too often, the educational part of the equation gives way to the pursuit of athletic success at the intercollegiate, secondary, and even primary school levels. It is time for us to make a choice about what we want our schools to be. Do we want them to be about education first, or are we going to focus on limited and commercially based athletic programs?

It is no secret that public education has suffered from massive budget cuts at the state and federal levels over the past years. Stories of overcrowded classrooms, outdated textbooks, and corruption abound in America. While athletics can still be an integral part of American education, the overemphasis on sports and the funds directed to them, essentially for the entertainment of many but participation of few, need to change. Good health practices can and need to start in the schools. We can bring back physical education to our school systems, while still providing a level of competitive sports.

Reason 6—Ensuring a Viable Home for the Other Sports

The competitive and mass-participation opportunities in sports other than football and basketball are dwindling rapidly. At the same time, there are no currently adequate and accessible models for maintaining a safe home for those "other sports"—the ones we might fondly call Olympic sports, or at least which we tend to deem noteworthy at certain times such as during the Olympics or world championships. Sports like men's gymnastics, swimming, wrestling, and track and field are in real danger of no longer having adequate models for developing world-class athletes. The worry that America will suffer in its stature as far as competitiveness in certain sports is real.

In theory, American educationally based sports should provide student-athletes the total package of gaining a valuable education, needed social skills, and health benefits from participation in athletics regardless of ability. I believe that many have succeeded at this effort. My personal and professional life has been enhanced by participation in school-based sports and so have the lives of millions of others. Arguably, that was the goal for everyone when most schools and universities were providing access for students to many more sports than they sponsor now, including sub-varsity teams for less-talented athletes and for those who needed more experience before moving up to the varsity squad. Unfortunately, even at the lowest levels of education in America, those opportunities are becoming less and less available as schools focus more on the entertainment and popularity of certain sports while dropping others, mostly due to financial exigency. College sports are becoming more expensive, and even though substantially increasing revenue is coming in, it is not resulting in more elite development and mass-participation opportunities.

As mentioned previously, now that the NCAA is beginning to understand that it must compensate athletes in some form beyond the current scholarship level, along with providing other benefits such as four-year guaranteed scholarships, the potential increased costs could be astronomical, threatening the existence of sports other than football and men's basketball. Subsequent chapters explore the likelihood of intercollegiate athletic programs continuing to chase the dreams of winning in football and men's basketball while decreasing funding for or outright eliminating other sports that do not generate revenue on the same scale, or perhaps not at all.[15] Currently, even smaller athletic conferences outside the Power 5 say they will provide increased benefits to their athletes, even though most of the athletic departments in those conferences typically run in the red. The money will have to come from somewhere, and the losers will be sports like volleyball, swimming, gymnastics, and wrestling. What will become of these sports if they can no longer sustain themselves on budgets largely provided by revenues generated by the two marquee teams? What about the fact that there are many football and basketball teams that do not break even, financially? Will they be supported adequately at the institutional level via increased student fees and institutional subsidies?[16]

6

Potential Alternative Sports Development and Sports Delivery Models for the United States

AFTER THE review of problems and issues with the current American sports development model in the areas of economics, education, athlete rights, access to sports, and public health, it is time to propose potential solutions to the many existing problems and issues in interscholastic sports, intercollegiate sports, and overall sports development and delivery in the United States. This chapter and the following four chapters propose and discuss four empirically based conceptual models as alternatives to the currently dominant, yet deteriorating, educational model. Potential solutions include the following four proposed models:

1. A realignment and reform of the current education-based sports development model

2. An academic/athletic commercialized solution

3. A "European-type" club sports development model or hybrid model

4. A complete separation of competitive sports from schools

Each of the four proposed models details potential structures and resources in regard to governance, organization, management, potential staffing, and costs versus benefits, but none is intended to be the final word on how these models could be structured and developed. A final workable model could end up including elements of all four, or even something completely different. My main objective here is to contribute to a dynamic, ongoing discussion that will continue to evolve.

INTRODUCTION TO THE PROPOSED MODELS

To me it is not inherently wrong to develop any athlete in the existing American school system, but to take full advantage of all the aforementioned benefits of sports participation and exercise, we need other athletic choices. Changing our longtime and archaic sports system need not have negative connotations. It can and should open up many other opportunities for participation and development regardless of participants' income level, background, or zip code. If changes in any of the proposed models were implemented in whole or even in part, many individuals would likely want alternatives beyond the parameters of the new systems. For instance, leagues like the NFL and NBA would most likely consider a new educational model too restrictive for maximum elite development and their own profit, and thus other alternative systems would likely arise. Currently, Major League Baseball (MLB) has this option via its minor league system, and despite having a minimum age of nineteen, the NBA lowered that age limit in 2006 for its rapidly developing G-League (Gatorade League, or what was once more commonly known as the National Basketball Developmental League) to eighteen years of age.[1] In addition, basketball players can go to Europe to play at virtually any age if they are good enough, and they can leave college to try out for the NBA at the age of nineteen. Still, the bulk of development in this country is happening at primary, secondary, and higher educational institutions. It is time leagues like the NFL and NBA present more alternatives to maximize elite development along with financially supporting and developing methods outside of education to expand and grow their sports, all while providing opportunities that reduce stress on the educational model. To a lesser extent, the USOC and established NGBs can also help fund new developmental systems. In many ways they are already doing this, but they still rely primarily on the various school systems to develop talent. These entities can reallocate funding and revenue-generating efforts to support models outside of the educational system. Given the income that professional leagues receive through ticket sales, sponsorships, and massive television contracts, the money is there to assist with any proposed change and, together with other sources, to provide financial backing for sustained success and operations of new sport development options in America.

INTRODUCTION TO MODEL 1:

A Realignment and Reform of the Current Education-Based Sports Development Model

There has been no shortage of reform efforts at all levels of sport, specifically regarding the relationship of education to sports in America. Despite the involvement of diverse groups such as the NCAA, the American Council on Education, the Knight Commission on Intercollegiate Athletics, the US government, and a host of others, there has not been significant progress in defining and managing the relationship of education and sports in America. One group that has been very active in the intercollegiate athletic and academic reform movement is The Drake Group.[2] The first proposed model (chapter 7), which is essentially a realignment of the education-based model, is primarily derived from the Drake Group's proposals for intercollegiate athletic reform.

The Drake Group was established in 1999 when Dr. Jon Ericson, a former professor and provost at Drake University, invited a distinguished group of college faculty, authors, and activists to a weekend "think tank" on how to end academic corruption in college sports. Participants in the conference included members of faculty senates, athletic directors, journalists, and members of reform-minded groups such as the NCAA and the Knight Commission on Intercollegiate Athletics. The mission that began with that first meeting in Des Moines, Iowa, was later formalized in Chicago in 2003: "to defend academic integrity in higher education from the corrosive aspects of commercialized college sports."[3]

The Drake Group wants faculty to take control of one of their chief roles, which is to safeguard academic integrity at their institutions of higher learning. Simply put, the goals are to create a system in which college students play college sports and to enforce common sense and attainable academic standards. One would think that this would be a popular movement that all could embrace, since the so-called ideals of college and scholastic sports, most notably the perceived educational connection, are something that many hold very dear. In fact, numerous studies have been conducted to gauge the public perception and feeling toward college sports. While there are some well-informed and well-intentioned people who see what college sports and significant parts of scholastic sports have become, much of the American public wants school-based athletes to remain students and not be athletic employees.[4] The romance of the "student-athlete" is no doubt important to many, but the reality is much different, and we need to face what the current priorities in school-based sports are, not what we might hope them to be. Sadly, winning seems to trump everything, and oftentimes the pursuit of success in sports leads to an irrational emphasis on success ahead of educational primacy.[5] One does not have to look too deeply to find academic scandals like the one at the University of North Carolina discussed in previous chapters, covered-up criminal activities, and inconsistent treatment of athletics departments when compared to other entities on most campuses.

A realignment of the educationally based model would be designed to preserve the opportunity for one to pursue development of a sound mind and body—but under very different, strict conditions—and to bring athletics into alignment with the mission of the educational institution. It can be inferred that the rapid quasi-professionalization of intercollegiate sports in America has also given rise to corruption and commercialism at lower levels of educationally based sports. Many high school athletic teams now play football and basketball games on national television in front of large crowds. Traveling across country to compete in a high school sporting event is becoming more commonplace and accepted.[6] Meanwhile, a high school football team in Hoover, Alabama, even had its own reality show on MTV. Academic eligibility standards for both scholastic and intercollegiate athletics have created additional problems concerning academic integrity, thus having the opposite effect on educational primacy than the one supposedly intended.

Why this proposed model is a realistic possibility for effective educationally based athletics reform is simple. It is, allegedly, what we want. Ostensibly, getting access to an education first and foremost while playing sports is the basic tenet that drives educational sports systems in America. These proposals have existed in some form for well over a decade, but they have taken on a greater sense of urgency due to the rapid changes occurring in college sports, particularly in response to ongoing lawsuits and potential legislative action.[7] Such pressures can, and, I believe, likely will forever alter sports development in the United States. As a member of the Drake Group for over a decade and its president for four years, I have been an active participant, writer, and researcher in all of our proposals and efforts since 2001. The work of the Drake Group and other like-minded groups and researchers such as the Coalition on Intercollegiate Athletics (COIA), the National College Players Association (NCPA), and activist professors like Drs. Murray Sperber, John Gerdy, and Richard Lapchick have inspired me and driven the discussion toward reframing how sports fit into our educational lives and maximizing their benefits.

The arguments for retaining some type of educationally based model are many, but they are mostly practical and financial. The current system is already established, with infrastructure, facilities, coaches, governance, and more in place at all levels of the educational spectrum in America. It is a system that is over a century old and not without its tradition and successes, even educational ones, that must be acknowledged. Arguably, that tradition and popularity, as great as they may be, can also present other problems—for sound empirical reasons—in moving some or all sports operations away from the US educational model. There will certainly be powerful resistance to any change from both within and outside the current industry. Highly paid and powerful coaches, lobbyists, government officials, alumni, and students, along with many other constituencies, may find themselves on the defensive and likely will mount a powerful movement against changing the current model. This type of action was recently on display after the University of Alabama at Birmingham dropped its football, rifle, and bowling teams in 2014, ostensibly as a cost-cutting measure. Despite being one of the many athletic departments that does not generate revenue greater than expenses and with a football team that traditionally had tepid fan support in a football-crazy state dominated by such traditional national powerhouses as the University of Alabama and Auburn University, a successful public relations and fund-raising effort led by many of the aforementioned constituencies eventually forced the university administration to bring back all three teams in the spring of 2015. Make no mistake, though: the driving force behind the campaign was their wish to resurrect the football program.[8] Thus, any suggestion of taking away or even merely limiting these opportunities—in what is, after all, popular entertainment for the masses—must be backed by sound reasoning and clear benefits. Students, alumni, fans, television networks, government officials, and many other concerned individuals and groups that have influence over educationally based sports in America must be convinced that change is needed for the greater benefit of all—and that achieving such greater benefit is more important than simply maintaining the commercial viability of entertainment programs. Considering, also, educational institutions' current contractual obligations to coaches, television networks and other media outlets, stadiums, and sponsors, it would be remiss not to look at potential alterations to the current model that would keep the education system as the primary mode for delivery of sports development in the United States, while still honoring those contractual obligations and other agreements.

The first proposed model thus continues with the basis of athletics embedded in the educational system, albeit with some major and potentially unpopular alterations. There are four main reasons to drastically alter the relationship between sports and education in America if we intend to maintain that relationship in some form: governance, financial stability, academic integrity, and the health and safety needs of students and athletes in our colleges and schools. The last reason is arguably paramount, especially since, despite the fact that the NCAA was founded when President Theodore Roosevelt threatened to ban college football because of player injuries and deaths (see chapter 3), the NCAA has claimed in court that it is not its legal responsibility to protect athletes—a stance that must change at all levels of sport in the United States.[9]

The Drake Group is also focusing on Washington, DC, for possible government intervention to reform intercollegiate athletics and shift the paradigm, if there is to be any hope of maintaining an educationally based sports-development model. This is not an endorsement of government intervention per se, considering that there are many issues it has not managed well over the years and that it is too often dysfunctional and overly bureaucratic. However, true reform of how we do sports in America will require changes only the Congress and the president can authorize.

INTRODUCTION TO MODEL 2:
An Academic/Athletic Commercialized Solution

Dr. John Gerdy and former Big 12 Commissioner Dan Beebe are primary inspirations for proposed Model 2 (chapter 8). The model includes the primary underpinning of eliminating the traditional intercollegiate athletic scholarship while also providing more latitude and time to pursue athletic and academic goals. Gerdy, a longtime friend and Drake Group colleague, has a great approach to changing the current athletic development system in America that would preserve many of the things The Drake Group holds dear, more fully detailed in chapter 7, but would also likely lead to creation of more athletic options outside the educational system. As radical as it may sound, Gerdy supports eliminating all college athletic scholarships as they are defined currently and replacing them with need-based athletic and/or academic scholarships that would be available to all students. In his outstanding book, *Air Ball: American Education's Failed Experiment with Elite Athletics*, and in a passionate presentation he delivered at the National Institute for Sports Reform conference in Lake George, New York, in 2003, he stated that the elimination of the athletic scholarship would deemphasize the importance of college sports on campuses across the United States, and, moreover, would "fundamentally [change] the relationship between the athlete, the coach, and the institution" (Gerdy 2006, 152). By extension, it would also logically lead primary and secondary education systems to focus on preparing the student to be competitive for academically based aid options.

Gerdy and many other scholars have long been proponents of the elimination of, or at least a revision of criteria for, the currently existing athletic scholarship arrangement in college sports. This is primarily a response to the control that administrators and coaches exert over the athlete, which essentially makes the college athletic scholarship a pay-for-play contract that can be cancelled or reduced for athletic reasons, and not the academically centered financial aid award it is often touted as being. In reality, the college athlete with an athletic scholarship is too often a professional performer, albeit a poorly paid one.[10] Consequently, the educational aspect of the scholarship turns into a smokescreen for a one-sided relationship that most do not understand fully, and education may or may not fit into the equation. Thus, many parents and coaches during a prospective athlete's formative years focus primarily on gaining a college athletic scholarship through athletic means, rather than concentrating on academic capability and progress, with teachers too often being pressured to "play along." This can and does skew the priorities of primary and secondary school sports in the United States.

Oftentimes, the focus of students, parents, administrators, and coaches is on athletic endeavors instead of education, with access to a college athletic scholarship being the goal as a potential pathway to the professional athletic ranks, however remote that possibility may be.

Gerdy's idea is a bold move that would strengthen the emphasis on academics, give athletes more control over their own academic and social futures, and greatly lessen both the control exerted by coaches over athletes and the time demands currently placed upon them. Recruitment would be based on academic merit, not strictly on athletic ability, even if the money comes from the athletic department. According to Gerdy, "the student will continue to receive his or her financial aid regardless of what transpires on the athletic fields. . . . Under such a contract, the student is less beholden to the athletics department's competitive and business motives and thus freer to explore the wide diversity of experiences college offers" (ibid.). The result would be college students playing college sports, which, again, is theoretically supposed to be the main purpose of educationally based sports.

An unintended consequence of the current system is that many families spend massive amounts of money pursuing the dream of their child's being awarded an athletic scholarship. In the end, they may find out that their child was never good enough to be seriously considered. Maybe worse, they may find out that the scholarship, if awarded, doesn't work the way they thought it was supposed to, with their child receiving in the end neither a quality education nor a degree. The drive to get an athletic scholarship has almost become a blood sport, and a very expensive one at that. Many families are literally gambling on an athletic scholarship for their sons and daughters to help offset the increasing costs of higher education. Opportunists have taken notice. A lucrative cottage industry has developed, as many enterprising individuals and companies such as D1 Sports Training and IMG Sports Academies tout their ability to prepare an athlete to compete for a college athletic scholarship. That promise lures parents and prospects to pay thousands of dollars in the hope of achieving something that they very likely may not get. Meanwhile, the focus on obtaining an athletic scholarship can undermine academic preparation, especially among elite athletes.[11]

Abolishing the athletic scholarship may seem counterintuitive to some. After all, isn't the point of intercollegiate and interscholastic athletics actually to get an education while playing sports? Is it not a worthy pursuit to gain a lucrative financial aid package for that educational opportunity, regardless of what the qualification requirements are? Having an athletic scholarship pay for the ever-increasing expenses associated with attending college sounds like a great deal and a fantastic trade-off for all parties involved. In theory, it is supposed to be just that—but I agree with Gerdy that, even though the athletic scholarship was conceived as a noble ideal, it has been abused by coaches and administrators past the point where it is worth trying to save it. It is hard to argue that the athletic scholarship is primarily an academic award when typical elite college athletes are devoting forty hours or more per week to their sport.[12] Taking into consideration travel time as well as off-season and summer requirements, in addition to the forty-plus hours many athletes already dedicate to their sport during the playing season, it is easy to see how academics are consigned to a lower priority.

This can happen even to student-athletes who are striving mightily to stay focused on getting a complete education, since the stated or implied threat of losing a scholarship is too often used against athletes if a coach or administrator feels they are not devoting enough time to athletics. Many times, coaches and other leaders in athletic departments use the scholarship as leverage to gain the capitulation of the athlete. This can be done by "encouraging" the athlete to take an easier academic major, pushing for academic shortcuts, or simply taking away opportunities for an athlete to be an actual college student by dominating the athlete's time through what has become a system of virtually year-round sports. Athletes justifiably feel extreme pressure if their scholarship is threatened, not only because it provides at least some access to a college education but also because many of them are hoping to advance to the professional ranks. That is certainly the case in football and men's basketball, due to the scarcity of other developmental tracks in those two sports. Thus the scholarship becomes an enforced pay-for-play arrangement controlled by coaches and administrators, and if an athlete's education suffers, then too many institutions are seemingly willing to accept that outcome.

An even more revolting example is flat-out academic manipulation, or what I like to call "eligibility maintenance." This means keeping an athlete academically eligible by virtually any means necessary, including pressuring teachers and faculty, test fraud, grade manipulation, falsified diagnoses of learning disabilities, and, in higher education, academic clustering. Clustering is a term of art for "warehousing" athletes in certain majors and classes to ensure their academic progress and athletic eligibility, and the practice falls far short of providing a real opportunity for education and social mobility. It would take an entire additional book to discuss notable academic clustering and manipulation issues at all levels of education, but make no mistake, this is a not just a problem for college sports.[13] It is happening at all levels of educationally based sports. It is well known that even those athletes who truly want to learn will often find themselves directed into "easy" classes and majors by their coach or other athletic department personnel in higher education. It is less understood how frequently this happens in high schools, where an athlete will many times acquiesce out of fear of losing playing time or a potential athletic scholarship (or one that has already been awarded) and risk forfeiting a chance to potentially compete professionally.

Abolishing the athletic scholarship would reduce the common practice of recruiting academically disinterested athletes solely based on athletic ability. We need to recognize that many college athletes attend American colleges and universities only to compete in their particular sport, without a focused interest in education itself—at least at this time in their lives. It is important to note that I am not saying such students don't have the ability to compete academically, only that college can come at various times in a person's life, whereas there is only a finite window of opportunity to maximize one's athletic utility. In cases like this, college education could be delayed, prepared for, or obtained through various delivery methods that can be made more easily accessible and even more affordable outside the current university-based sports system. Even outside or professional teams could provide educational opportunities for their athletes. This wouldn't have to be for four-year degrees, but could also include community college, trade and professional schools, and other specialized training such as in performing arts. If we would only think outside the box and realize that the educational and sports development options are limitless, we can present more opportunities for everyone.

Beebe in an OpEd piece written for the *Sports Business Journal*, in 2014 suggests that we segment intercollegiate athletics into two distinct categories: spectator sports and participation sports.[14] Within these two groups there would be significantly different sets of rules, and different competition structures would apply. Beebe points out that NCAA FBS football and Division I men's basketball produce net revenue and ticket sales at the highest levels in comparison to other sports. The same observation can generally be applied to interscholastic sports. I agree with Beebe that this does not minimize the effort and importance that these athletes put into other sports. In my view and as a former NCAA Division I wrestling coach I feel that many of those athletes work just as hard as or even harder than elite football and basketball players. However, as Beebe notes, the fan intensity, the revenue from ticket sales and sponsorships, and the pressure brought by the media are simply not comparable between highly revenue-driven sports and almost all other sports.

Certainly, other sports could fit into a more commercialized model. For one thing, because of Title IX regulations it would be likely that some comparable women's sports would also need be designated differently in order to meet the requirements of the law. The devil is in the details, and some women's sports are becoming quite successful commercially, most notably women's basketball. Some Olympic/nonrevenue sports such as baseball are primary sports at some institutions. This could all be sorted out, but initially, I agree with Beebe that we should begin by focusing on football and men's basketball, designating them as spectator sports. Women's and other men's sports programs at participating institutions could then later be similarly designated, based on regional and/or national popularity and commercial viability.

What would be the main difference in college athletics if certain sports were designated as spectator sports? In many ways, of course, we are already seeing some effective differences, as in football and basketball (both men's and women's), which are already treated much differently than most of the other Olympic sports in terms of rules regarding practice and competition. Beebe proposes some other clear delineations. Under this new designation, spectator sports would be defined as "those that are funded at their current or higher level and have national competition" (Beebe 2014). In exchange for their efforts on the field or court, athletes could receive compensation similar to their current benefits (money to pay for tuition, fees, etc.), a cost of attendance/living stipend, or a straight market-based salary. Additional benefits and allowances may end up being required as a result of new rules arising from potential federal or state legislation as well as court decisions expanding athletes' bargaining or commercial rights. This could mean actual pay-for-play salaries or the ability of athletes to profit from their marketing utility. Other benefits that could be considered are lifetime use of a four-year scholarship or guaranteed coverage of medical care for a period of years after expiration of athletic eligibility, with these and others funded by the affiliated commercialized team, not the educational institution. In other words, athletes in these sports can go to school if they want to while playing, as the money will be there for them to finance an education, but they should be allowed to take as few or as many credit hours as they like and remain a student for as long as they need to earn a degree, if that is their wish. It would be the choice of the athlete.

On the other hand, athletes in a spectator sport should be able to devote as much time to their sport as necessary under their playing contract, whatever its form, or more time if desired. If they don't want to take classes during the competitive season, that should be fine. Many will still want to go to school while playing, and I believe that most would take advantage of that opportunity. Those who don't or who want to take longer to finish will still have a lifetime educational grant awaiting them so they can fulfill the educational promise on their own schedule. Meanwhile, whether the athlete is a full-time student, takes a few classes, or none, he or she is still representing the school, and, honestly, I don't think the fans care one way or the other.

In the other sports, what I call Olympic sports, Beebe's proposal generally mirrors Gerdy's. Olympic sports would be grounded in the educational model and governed much like current NCAA Division III participatory sports. All scholarships and other financial aid would be based on need or academic merit, and there would be no athletic scholarships. One variant from Gerdy is that athletes in participation sports would also be allowed to exercise their marketing utility and be remunerated for endorsements and other commercial activities.

Beebe recommends that in the spectator sports there continue to be full-time coaches—and, in fact, in institutionally affiliated commercialized teams, these would almost certainly be full-time positions. He makes an intriguing distinction, though, regarding coaches in the participation sports, who would coach part-time with the potential of taking on other responsibilities at the educational institution, including in academics, or in the community. This would allow a return to the coach-as-educator model. It has been a few decades since it was common, but college coaches frequently used to teach classes instead of being unconnected to the educational mission of the institution. (It is already fairly common to see coaches in high schools and at even lower levels who have minimal or no academic relationship with either the school or the athletes they are training.) Gerdy has also pushed on this point for years, and in fact many agree that making the coach once again an educator would be a major step toward bringing the college back into college sports.

For those in the participatory sports, Beebe also indicates areas of cost containment that could feasibly benefit the institution as a whole, such as severely limiting travel in Olympic/participation sports, which would also have a very positive impact on academics and keep athletes on campus more. While teams in football and other spectator sports would continue to travel extensively, in regard to participation sports institutions could—perhaps by working outside the NCAA with other national governing bodies such as the USOC—form sports federations or alliances that would enable quality competition on a local and regional basis. This would certainly change the existing NCAA divisional structure, but it would not be too difficult to implement, as there are many colleges and universities that could form these local and regional associations and still offer quality athletic competition. In a scenario such as this, it would also be very easy to start a promotion-and-relegation system similar to that found in Europe (see chapter 5).

In addition to reduced travel, there are many other potential savings in participation sports under this model, including eliminating or reducing athletics grants and other current benefits, along with coaching and recruiting costs. With these savings from operating expenses, the current minimum number of sports required for NCAA Division I could be increased, and any financial gains converted to providing athletic opportunities in participation sports. This would in turn have a direct net-positive trickle-down effect on interscholastic sports, as the decline and elimination of participation sports at the intercollegiate level has negatively impacted these same sports in interscholastic athletics over the past thirty years. As participation opportunities increase in intercollegiate sports, more sports would be expanded or started at the lower levels to serve as feeder programs for college sports programs or other external sports development models. As Beebe notes—on a major point of discussion in this book—this would most likely result in saving Olympic sports that are being dropped at all educational levels in the United States without negatively affecting commercially driven spectator sports. Beyond saving already endangered sports like swimming, wrestling, and gymnastics, this model could enable a massive expansion of participation opportunities in many other sports that would benefit even more collegiate, high school, and other athletes. It would also likely lead to opening up more participation opportunities for the greater population, further benefitting public health and wellness.

Dan Beebe's suggested approach is based on recognizing the almost insurmountable odds against fundamentally changing the rampant commercialization of college football and men's basketball in this country. He is essentially calling for us to wave the white flag in surrender to the commercial and monetary pressures those sports present, and, essentially, make certain teams professional franchises attached to their universities. In these sports, teams and players would have much greater freedom to do what they want. If it means paying players' salaries, reducing or eliminating academic standards, and/or allowing players to profit from their marketing utility, then so be it. The toothpaste is definitely out of the tube, and if there is truly no going back, this might be a way to satisfy many constituents. The athletes could go to school if they want to and pay for it themselves. Meanwhile, alumni and other fans, sponsors, and most notably the television networks and other media outlets would still be highly interested in these sports and teams—which would not only survive under less restrictive conditions than the current guise of amateurism, but thrive. Beebe, like Gerdy, also proposes eliminating the athletic scholarship and the negative and often unintended consequences that go with it. Gerdy's approach is to make all athletic aid need-based, while Beebe says all sports except football and men's basketball should be need-based while letting football and basketball be run as essentially professional franchises as auxiliaries of the school with no academic eligibility requirements or archaic amateurism issues.

It's arguable that one of the major obstacles to realistically addressing issues in American educationally based sports is the failure to recognize that there are differences between and even within sports. Applying the same eligibility, competition, and other regulations to all has never made sense, nor has it worked effectively in either intercollegiate or interscholastic athletics. Identifying the differences between sports, specifically between the more revenue-driven spectator sports and ones that are less commercialized or primarily participatory, is a good place to begin offering different options in sports development and competitive opportunity for all.

I have taken these two ideas along with removing the academic and eligibility restrictions currently imposed by the NCAA and other governing bodies and meshed together aspects of Gerdy, Beebe, and my own ideas for a workable possible new approach to sports development.

INTRODUCTION TO MODEL 3:
A "European-Type" Club Sports Development Model or Hybrid Model

The third proposed model is a hybrid approach of using both education and European-style external clubs that can better address the problems facing the United States today (chapter 9). Europe provides an excellent sport development template, as most European countries support an external, non-educationally embedded local sports club system. Overall, these countries have been quite successful at ensuring educational opportunity for the elite athlete, while allowing the athlete to train and compete at an elite level. It is a system that is very successful without having the academic eligibility requirements for educationally based athletic competition found in America.

One of the better articles written about access to both educational and athletic development for European Union (EU) athletes is "Athlete Development, Athlete Rights and Athlete Welfare: A European Union Perspective," by Ian Henry (2013). In this excellent article, Henry explores in depth the ways the European sports club system contributes to prioritizing traditional and vocational education for athletes (particularly, in his study, elite athletes), exactly because their sporting pursuits are typically not taking place within the educational system. His analysis provides an intriguing roadmap for how a hybrid system could possibly work in America.

The primary concern about the relation between elite sports and educational development is clear. Are these athletes receiving a viable education, one that will benefit them and society beyond their sporting pursuits? In America, the potential to receive an athletic scholarship to pay for access to a college degree provides a powerful defense argument against anyone wanting to change the current system. Still, it is important to see whether there are alternatives that would increase choice and access while restoring academic primacy in our school systems. By analyzing the educational opportunities available for European athletes as they compete outside the educational system, it becomes easier to conceive that something similar could also happen in the United States.

According to Henry, European systems were not always what they are today. In fact, there was a time when selecting and pushing the elite athlete to compete at a high level was the main priority. Protection of European elite athletes' access to education or vocational training has been limited in the past, with little focus on dual careers or even a future beyond competitive athletics. Eventually, though, it became an issue of athletes' rights, in a context where access to education and/or vocational training is protected for other citizens of the European Union. As in the United States, there was increasing concern regarding the time demands on athletes and their ability to still receive the sort of education needed for most careers outside of sports. However, European countries effectively addressed the issue and provided the flexibility necessary for the benefit of the individual athlete.

Sports governance was targeted in part because of the convergence of other legal issues in the EU. Several empirical studies were done specifically on the issue of athletes' access to educational opportunities. In 2012 an EU committee submitted its recommended *Guidelines on Dual Careers of Athletes: Recommended Policy Actions in Support of Dual Careers in High-Performance Sport*. From this and other studies, four different models for securing athletes' rights to education and other benefits established themselves.[15] The first, which is found in France, Hungary, Luxembourg, Spain, Poland, and Portugal, Henry calls a "state-centric system of defined legal obligation." While some specifics vary, all of these countries have legal provisions for athletes to have guaranteed access to an education. In Hungary, Olympic medalists are allowed admission to a university without a qualifying entrance examination score. After admission, as in other countries under this model, Hungary provides educational adjustments for elite athletes to accommodate the needs of training and competition. Spain provides financial assistance to elite athletes for living expenses. Similar approaches could work in the United States if we would abandon our long-standing way of thinking with regard to school-based sports. In the meantime, relatively strict academic eligibility and time requirements, coupled with little relief in regard to academic assignments and examinations, make it very difficult for young athletes in America to balance academic and athletic obligations, at all levels of education.

Other countries, such as Belgium, Denmark, Estonia, Finland, Germany, Latvia, Lithuania, and Sweden, have formal processes for addressing the educational and other nonathletic needs of the athlete, but not through legal requirements. Henry calls this a "state-sponsored formal system based on permissive legislation." Essentially, such a system authorizes schools and universities to make provisions for athletes, but it is not a requirement. However, even without the legal requirement, most of these countries are making great efforts to ensure that the athlete's needs, both social and educational, are taken care of to the best of a country's ability. In Belgium, for instance, a cooperative program between the Belgian Olympic Committee, the federal government, and the main sports administration body awards elite athletes up to €20,000 (over $22,000 as of this writing) to pay for costs incurred for both elite sports training and education. Vrije University in Brussels, like "sports schools" in other EU countries (although not a sports school itself), has developed a Study and Talent Education Program specifically tailored for the elite athlete. Enrollees' academic work can be spread out over a significant amount of time, in contrast to the United States, where four years of athletic eligibility must be completed within a five-year window in NCAA Division I while being enrolled as a full-time student—with very few exceptions, such as regarding being enrolled in the final term before graduation.[16] The German government, German Olympic Committee, and higher education institutions have also made provisions for elite athlete development. These include flexible handling of attendance and exams, tutoring assistance, and even providing up to three years of salary to professional athletes who have retired from sports as a bridge to another career—along with the establishment of several sports-themed schools, as discussed in chapter 4. This is definitely outside-the-box thinking for Americans, but these are certainly some ideas that could work in this country.

Other European nations, such as Greece and the United Kingdom, practice a model Henry calls the "representation of athlete's educational interests by sporting bodies." These countries do not have formalized systems of rights for athletes, instead relying on national governing bodies or federations, coaches, athletes themselves, and others essentially to negotiate on behalf of the athletes to broker the best educational deal they can with participating universities, specialty schools, and trade schools. This might include exceptions on certain admissions criteria or increased time allowances for completion of academic work. In Greece, athletes can be students for as long as they wish, taking as much time as needed to complete their studies without its affecting their competitive athletic schedules. Greece also provides financial assistance in the form of scholarships for undergraduate and graduate athletes. In the United Kingdom, elite athletes can have a "performance advisor," employed by the National Institute of Sport, to work with and negotiate on behalf of the athlete. The UK also provides financial and other assistance to promote academic and athletic balance and lessen the effect of life stressors that many elite athletes face, given their high-level training and educational requirements.

The last model type discussed by Henry is the "laissez-faire approach," in which there are no formal structures for educational access. Under such a "system," broader measures to improve access might be encouraged and allowed, but arrangements, if any, still primarily rest on individual agreements. In countries such as Italy, Malta, Austria, the Czech Republic, Ireland, Slovakia, and Slovenia, there are typically no educational concessions made for athletes. For obvious reasons, such as infrastructure, finances, and even sporting culture, many smaller and/ or less-developed countries are typically less likely to directly support sports development. (There is an interesting outlier in the laissez-faire group: while the Netherlands has no specific formal structure or legal framework for supporting the student-athlete, it is still very proactive in working in other ways with the elite athlete to balance academics and athletics, and in limiting restrictions that hurt educational access and athletic excellence.)

A similar approach could also be taken with elite athletes below college age in this model, but I believe that proposed Model 3 works better from a youth and high school perspective, as it suggests that most if not all elite sports development is removed from the school system. From an elite-athlete perspective, an individual has only so much athletic utility to exercise in his or her lifetime. Elite athletes should be allowed to pursue excellence without the shackles of the current unworkable and overregulated educational model—which has little to do with educational primacy anyway—unless they desire to be there and adhere to the revised academic standards while participating in their preferred sport(s). Of course, the revised educationally based model is only one of those presented in the following chapters. Even in the other models, though, education can be part of an elite athlete's career, either during competition or after his or her playing days are finished. One must understand that education is so diverse in the twenty-first century that putting anyone in a box and saying they must go to college between the ages of eighteen and twenty-two is misguided, and, candidly, not keeping up with the times and the choices people should have with regard to education. There are numerous examples of students who wait to pursue higher education for various reasons, whether for service in the military, church missions, or other choices—including, as some athletes have done, attending college when their professional career is over, or even during a professional career.[17] Arguably, at least in football and men's basketball, saying that one must get an education at ages eighteen to twenty-two is more about ensuring we have elite athletes at their peak for entertainment in commercialized college sports than it is about providing them real access to a valid college education.

In Major League Baseball (MLB), there is an extensive developmental system via Minor League Baseball (MiLB) and the opportunity for athletes to go directly into the professional draft after graduation from high school. If a baseball player decides to go to college, he must then wait three years to reenter the professional draft. While I still think athletes need the freedom to go the professional route at any time if their ability allows it, this system is certainly much better than the alternatives presented in football and men's basketball. In American baseball, at least there is no requirement to go to college, but the option is there, and MLB actually offers educational financing options for those who desire to pursue or finish their college education once they turn professional. I have seen several former Ohio University baseball players return to school in the offseason largely funded by their professional clubs. The educational option for them does not go away, thus providing more choices for the athlete.

The resistance to men's basketball and football athletes being allowed to do the same as baseball players often rests on the argument that the football or men's basketball athlete will miss out on an education if allowed to go professional, even in a minor league. Rhetoric like this just masks the real reason why athletes in these sports are restricted, and that is the revenue, other indirect commercial utility, and prestige those sports bring to colleges—or at least are perceived to bring. A somewhat egregious example of this is the massive yearly turnover of University of Kentucky men's basketball players, many of whom only compete as freshmen and then turn professional, using higher education as a mere stopping point to get to the big leagues. Elite athletic development is the priority, not education, and I question the wisdom of allowing this to be a primary option within a supposedly education-based model. Some understandably see this as a waste of scholarship money on students who only complete one to two years of their degree program (if that), when there are other students (and athletes) who could use that money to obtain a legitimate education.[18] While "one and done" can be part of a broader sports development structure, and while elite athletes certainly have the right to make it part of their individual strategy, it should not turn into a default and it should not necessarily be subsidized. While there are some options for basketball players in the United States to develop through European or other international clubs, along with the NBA G-League, the marquee and current best pathway to a career in the NBA or NFL is through American college sports.

The NBA and NFL are not off the hook here, in that the NCAA has provided a free developmental system for those leagues, enabling them to save millions by not having to support their own developmental systems as in professional baseball. It is a mutually beneficial arrangement, and it is hard not to catch at least a whiff of collusion here due to the monetary benefits to all. Not the least of these are valuable television and multimedia contracts such as the NCAA's current fourteen-year men's basketball tournament contract with CBS and Turner Broadcasting System, valued at $10.8 billion, which provides 96 percent of the NCAA's overall revenue.[19] There is an obvious advantage to colleges in having the best players, if only for a short time, and the NBA gets a better, more developed player.

In contrast, the NBA and NFL could develop and maintain a system similar to baseball's, while providing educational benefits to those who desire them—or they should pay the colleges and universities a fair value (that is, handsomely) for the privilege of using them as their primary farm system. I have no problems in principle with college and university sports being part of the process of developing athletes for professional leagues, but intercollegiate football and men's basketball should no longer be the primary source of talent for massively profitable leagues at the expense of educational institutions. Any of the proposed models could force these leagues to take on a greater role in player development themselves, using colleges and universities as one part of a larger development system to build their franchises. Most importantly, educational primacy—not winning and revenue generation—could once again be the fundamental goal and purpose of institutions of higher education, without the distortions that have been introduced under the present system.

INTRODUCTION TO MODEL 4:
A Complete Separation of Competitive Sports from Schools

While the first three models propose retaining some aspects of the educational system's governance of sports, the final proposed model, Model 4 (chapter 10) is the nuclear option of completely separating sports development from the educational system in the United States. Educationally based sports are part of the fabric of American society, with over a century's worth of popular history, but this country is not managing the fragile marriage between education and sports very well. Frankly, I am not sure it's managing that relationship at all, to the extent that the only certainty is that the model will be forced to change at some point in the future. There is a big difference between what Americans believe educationally based sports should be and what they actually are, and we need to recognize that reality and do something about it. America is in a sports development and public health crisis. A cost-benefit analysis would very likely show that a complete separation of sports and education could have greater, farther-reaching benefits for more Americans than existing systems currently provide.

In this model, the complete separation of competitive and, to a lesser extent, mass-participation sports from the American public education system would occur at all levels, from K–12 through higher education. Obviously, private educational institutions could continue to run athletic programs. However, many private educational institutions still receive some federal and state government funding, so there could be restrictions placed on what a private school could or could not do, assuming such funding continues and the government supports and partially funds these changes. Meanwhile, many private institutions are part of state high school associations or the NCAA. Because of this membership, even private schools must follow the rules and regulations of the governing body. If state high school associations and the NCAA as we know them ceased to exist as academically related sports governing bodies, it would be interesting to see what private institutions would decide to do with their sports when confronted with a new, segregated model such as this. If they decide to maintain an educationally based model, that would not be inherently wrong. However, if a club system flourishes, most athletes will want to participate at that level, whether in elite or participatory sports, even if they attend a private school. I believe it's likely that private schools would follow the majority and allow their students to gravitate toward the club system.

CHAPTERS 7 through 10 explore each of the four proposed models in greater detail.

7

Model 1—A Realignment and Reform of the Current Education-Based Sports Development Model

AS MENTIONED in chapter 6, it is critical to examine how the current educationally based model can be improved and enhanced, given the infrastructure of sports that currently exists throughout the United States. While proposing different sporting and recreation options beyond the educational space, reforming educationally based sports in America should be the first action we take if we accept that sports will likely always exist in US schools in some form. This model proposes largely keeping sports in our school systems, albeit with a much different academic-centered paradigm. Essentially, athletes who choose an educational development model must be students first, under stricter academic guidelines This model also presents solutions to major problems of current governance in school sports and addresses the aforementioned current problems in American sports development of economics, athletes' rights, lack of access to a wide range of sports, potential government intervention, and mostly educational priorities. This model presents several processes that likely will need to happen to return educationally based sports to what they were once intended to actually be in the United States.

In spite of all the issues covered in previous chapters, it is still important to consider whether there are ways to keep sports participation as an integral part of the educational process in America. As stated before, I do believe the current model is irretrievably broken, but the option of still having educationally based sports integrated in public and private schools at all levels should still be considered, albeit with a drastically different structure in the future. The focus needs to be on how we can change this and make educationally based sports programs what they are designed to be, which is an effective augmentation to a better educational experience. To ensure that athletes who compete in this proposed model are actual students first and athletes second, some core principles must be adhered to in this model.

This model is attractive because it satisfies those purists who believe that educationally based sports development is not only uniquely American but works well as both an educational endeavor and a means of developing life skills—which I believe is still somewhat valid reasoning despite all the negative issues mentioned thus far. The model's primary goal is to strengthen academic primacy and make athletics a secondary, but still very important, activity within higher education. By extension, the same goals would apply at the primary and secondary education levels, as intended when sports became part of education in America over a century ago. It is believed by many scholars, including those in the Drake Group, that changes at the highest level of educationally based sports development would have a dramatic trickle-down effect on the primary and secondary levels of American education. In other words, we must start at the top in order to fix the problem throughout the system.

It is in fact critical to remember that these issues are not only confined to college sports. Corruption is rampant in high school sports, as many athletes struggle academically to meet initial NCAA eligibility standards. The trickle-down effects of sports being seen as the only way to get a college education for those who might not go to college otherwise, or of the drive for an athletic scholarship to help pay the bills in a very expensive higher-education marketplace, have put a very unhealthy emphasis on sports, from high schools down to our middle and even elementary schools. As one example, many young elite athletes have been drawn into a cottage industry of advisors and programs promising access to college scholarships and even a "free" education. The fees for these services are often substantial, with families spending thousands of dollars to chase scholarships that may well never materialize.

ESTABLISHING A PRESIDENTIAL COMMISSION TO EXAMINE INTERCOLLEGIATE ATHLETICS AND SCHOOL-BASED SPORTS PROGRAMS

The Drake Group and other reform groups believe that a need exists for a president's commission on intercollegiate athletics reform to undertake a comprehensive examination of mechanisms for returning intercollegiate athletics to levels of academic integrity, athlete welfare, and financial sanity appropriate for nonprofit institutions of higher education. I believe such a commission should also be charged with examining scholastic and other youth sports, to consider how the current setup of college sports affects those systems in ways that have pulled high schools, and even middle and elementary schools, away from their own educational missions. In these lower-level schools and beyond, the effects of the current system in higher education include loss of participation opportunities and health benefits to students and their communities. The Drake Group's primary call is to specifically examine college sports, but I do think that follow-up or concurrent examinations of scholastic and other youth sports by the same or similar commissions are vitally important, and there is no reason that these inquiries should be mutually exclusive.

There is precedent for both a presidential commission and positive impetus for change in long-practiced traditional sports models. This in itself justifies optimism regarding the potential of still having school-based sports, but with a drastic paradigm shift. In 1975, the President's Commission on Olympic Sports addressed athlete protection, championship exclusivity, and integrity and governance issues in Olympic sports. The reason for establishing the commission to review Olympic-level amateur sports, as set forth in President Gerald Ford's executive order, applies just as well to our current need for a similar commission to examine school-based sports: "Because there are conflicting views on the best methods of addressing the problems facing international amateur athletics, it is desirable and appropriate that a Commission of outstanding, knowledgeable Americans undertake an immediate study of our Nation's problems in the Olympic sports."[1] The efforts of this commission eventually led to the passage of the Amateur Sports Act in 1978 (later revised as the Ted Stevens Olympic and Amateur Sports Act of 1998, named in honor of the Alaska senator who sponsored the latter bill).[2] These two laws were designed to organize, streamline, and

more effectively govern US Olympic sports programs. Steps taken toward these goals included chartering the already-existing United States
Olympic Committee (USOC) as the official US governance authority
in regard to Olympic sports, establishing several National Governing
Bodies (NGBs) to administer individual Olympic sports, granting exclusive use of the Olympic rings and other related intellectual property,
and charging the USOC and related organizations with promoting and
supporting Olympic sports in America. They provide an effective template for discussing and addressing the serious issues now facing educationally based sports.

The challenges are so complex and controversial that most experts
agree that only congressional intervention, with an endorsement from
the president, has the potential of resulting in meaningful reform, by
considering a range of solutions that only Congress may enact. For
instance, only Congress has the power to place conditions on Higher
Education Act funding and other federal funding of public primary and
secondary schools. State governments could also be part of a new oversight process, helping to ensure that education is paramount and athletics are only a proper educational augmentation, not something that
overwhelms an institution's academic mission and fiscal responsibility,
or damages the health and welfare of the student-athlete.

Funding of the most commercialized higher education athletic
programs could be predicated on continued membership in a national
governance association that requires such programs to demonstrate
educationally sound practices and fiscal restraint. If the government is
as focused on education and educational costs as it claims to be, then
this would be a great way to prove it. Steps in this direction could
include establishing federally chartered nonprofit organizations to replace and/or restructure the NCAA (and even set a potential template
for governance of youth sporting programs). A president's commission would provide the opportunity to assemble national experts to address these complex issues in a comprehensive way, protected from the
power of coaches, administrators, and television networks and without
the "conflict of interest" barriers that prevent the NCAA from enacting
any real, education-friendly reform. A reformed NCAA or replacement
organization could be granted exclusivity in the conduct of national
championships, while mandating that proceeds be used to enable all
member institutions (not only those at the top of the heap) to provide

health programs and protections, including athletic injury insurance, and tangible educational benefits for all of the current half-million collegiate athletes, not only elite athletes. For elite athletes, this model could allow for equal and fair revenue sharing in some form, and might also include lifetime access to education, the ability to profit from outside income, post-graduation trust funds, and insurance against injury and other related health issues, such as is seen and mandated in professional sports leagues.

Another needed change that only Congress can enact is to grant governing bodies in intercollegiate athletics and potentially even high school sports a limited antitrust exemption. The only real way to permit the NCAA or any other national governing body to impose cost controls on member institutions without facing antitrust lawsuits is through an antitrust exemption. Currently there are college athletic coaches, mostly in football and men's basketball, making millions of dollars per year, and although many stakeholders generally agree that most coaches are overpaid, this is the market that exists. The only legal way to cap coaches' salaries and control athletic costs is through an antitrust exemption granted by Congress. The intent in this model is to not grant school-based sports or intercollegiate athletics free rein with an unlimited exemption. This narrow exemption would allow the NCAA or other national governance association(s) to impose cost controls on member institutions without facing lawsuits under the Sherman Antitrust Act. Such an exemption would be conditioned on the governing body meeting its own education, health, and due process mandates, as well as on it being governed by an independent board of expert directors, none of them currently employed by any member institution and otherwise devoid of conflict of interest.

This is a vital part of the proposed model and not a granting of complete antitrust protection to educationally based sports. Controlling costs in a nonprofit educational system is crucial. Without such limited antitrust protections, institutions of higher learning and even high schools are spending outrageous and unneeded amounts on athletics and sports in order to maintain and attempt to strengthen their athletic programs, without any regard to the impact on education spending and sustainability. This idea of a limited antitrust exemption is controversial, and many see it as a way an organization like the NCAA could procure even more power and control over both the enterprise of sports and athletes. I profoundly disagree and believe it is likely the only way to reign in runaway spending and refocus the model on educational primacy. It has already been proven with bright clarity that athletic costs are not being managed effectively. Very few intercollegiate athletic programs cover their own costs and are instead largely dependent on student fees and other institutional monies to fund their operations.[3]

In college sports there are coaches and administrators making millions of dollars while spending on other university infrastructure and education is plummeting. One glaring example is found in Louisiana, where the state had already cut higher education funding by millions midway through the 2015–16 fiscal year, while at the same time many boosters and some administrators at Louisiana State University were actually talking about paying a potential $15 million buyout to its current football coach in hopes of finding a better one.[4] Thankfully, LSU changed its stance when the coach, Les Miles, won his last regular season game, so the buyout question at least at that point was dead, but Miles was eventually fired the next year and the university still owes him $10 million. Still, it is virtually nondebatable that college sports have become caught in an arms race, with many schools maintaining that they are only paying "market rate" for coaches or that they need to build facilities that will enable them to recruit better athletes. Meanwhile, in what is after all a nonprofit higher education market, most of these programs cannot even support themselves without massive and unbalanced financial assistance from the institution and general student body.

In order to ensure that reforms take hold, Congress would have to require that current major Division I public institutions, such as Football Bowl Subdivision (FBS) schools, remain as part of the NCAA or any replacement organization. The challenges of reform are so complex that it is reasonable to believe that only the threat of loss of federal funding will move the needle toward meaningful change by forcing colleges and universities (and even primary and secondary school systems) to comply.

ESTABLISHING FINANCIAL STABILITY AND ECONOMIC IMPACT ON EDUCATIONAL INSTITUTIONS

Recent events pose grave threats to the financial stability of college athletic programs and demonstrate that change will happen whether we like it or not. The most notable include

- the recent court decision in the antitrust suit *O'Bannon v. NCAA*, which mandates raising the allowable limits for athletic scholarships, as well as the provision of trust fund accounts, drawing from group licensing revenues, for Division I Football Bowl Subdivision (FBS) football and Division I basketball players;

- the NCAA's granting of further decision-making power to sixty-five of its most commercialized athletic programs, which will allow more expensive practices in those programs and reinforce competitive imbalances among Division I institutions;

- the Region 13 Office of the National Labor Relations Board's classification of Northwestern University football players as employees;

- an alarming escalation of coaches' salaries in a manner inappropriate for nonprofit educational institutions that are provided with significant tax preferences; and

- additional pending multimillion-dollar antitrust and concussion lawsuits.[5]

All of these developments put pressure on institutions of higher education, particularly those with Division I athletic programs, to increase spending on athletics in the hope of generating needed revenue—ironically, revenue that is largely being chased in order to cover the increased spending. This means that all of these institutions will consider one or more of the following means to raise new funds or to shift existing funds:

- increasing the subsidization of athletic programs through general funds and/or mandatory student fees, at a time when rapidly growing student loan burdens and high tuition rates and student fees are causing great national concern;[6]

- appealing to donors to increase their gifts to athletics at a time when such gifts are needed to support the institutions' educational missions;

- ceasing already insufficient efforts to achieve Title IX compliance for women's athletics;

- pressuring state legislatures to utilize already stressed education funds to supplement athletics budgets; and

- eliminating or further reducing funding for nonelite ("Olympic") sports.

The last point to me is one of the most worrisome. Without a change to the current educationally based model, it is virtually certain that opportunities to participate and compete in Olympic sports will be lost at higher education institutions across America. This will eventually affect the growth and development of these sports at all levels, including in scholastic and other youth programs and even internationally. If the college sports industry and primary and secondary schools decide to focus exclusively on commercialized, high-revenue sports, there will need to be a home for these other sports if the United States wants to continue its international athletic success—and, of course, if it wants to preserve not just elite but mass participation opportunities. This proposed educational realignment plan preserves those programs and offers a platform for expansion of sports participation at all levels of education.

ENSURING ACADEMIC INTEGRITY

The most essential goals of any truly academically based sports-development model should be obvious: ensuring academic integrity while improving the athlete's opportunities for educational access and social mobility. This has to be emphasized because it is so difficult to challenge the widespread current belief that educationally based sports are in fact primarily about augmenting education, with athletics themselves being secondary. At least that is what people want to believe, because it is cleaner and more acceptable to believe it. The fact that a disproportionate number of athletes in football and men's basketball are African American makes this belief even more compelling, as a supposed path to educational opportunity. After all, these young men (and a smaller number of women receiving athletic scholarships) may be getting something they would never otherwise have had a chance at, right?

To me, this is an unfortunate assumption and close to being racist as well as classist. Education is the true path to social mobility and success. Communicating to those who are members of a racial or other minority and/or lower socioeconomic classes, who may have received substandard educations, that athletics is their most likely and perhaps only way to advance in society contributes to the "dumbing down" of America and disproportionately affects the black athlete. As long as popular opinion continues to hold that for many students athletics is the "only" path out of a bad situation, thousands and thousands of kids will be tempted to limit their pursuit of excellence to the field or court.

Already at the middle-school level the trickling down of what is going on in higher education has pushed parents, schools, and school systems to emphasize athletics to the detriment of education. The situation gets worse as young athletes advance through high school, where the problem has been growing for decades. Through no real fault of their own, many of these outstanding athletes come to colleges and universities woefully underprepared, but are kept academically eligible as "student-athletes" so we can all be entertained and continue to cheer for our alma mater. It is a vicious cycle and one that must be broken. During my time working and coaching in college athletics I do not remember meeting a "dumb" athlete. I did, however, meet many overworked and academically underprepared athletes who—if they were to be given proper educational opportunity and remediation before participating in team practice or play, along with dramatically reduced demands on their time when they did participate—could then have a real opportunity at social mobility in a very competitive world, instead of being tossed away or forgotten about when their athletic eligibility and commercial usefulness ends.

American education itself is threatened by increased incidences of academic fraud involving college athletes, as well as by the exploitation of academically unprepared athletes who are admitted to institutions without meeting regular admission standards. This creates academic eligibility challenges and leads to pressures on administration and faculty to keep an athlete playing by any means necessary. It is an incessant cycle, and not surprising, as academic shortcuts and exploitation at all levels of athletic participation have been part of American college sports for well over a century.[7]

Current initial eligibility standards for incoming freshmen, as determined by the NCAA through its Eligibility Center, are set on a sliding scale that measures performance according to predetermined core course standards in combination with an entrance exam score (SAT or ACT). This puts extreme pressure on high schools to assist athletes in meeting these standards so they can compete in college sports.[8] Thus, the same pressures experienced by colleges and universities to keep athletes academically eligible are found at the high school level, when it means the difference for a favored athlete between getting an athletic scholarship or not getting one. Academic corners are being cut at all levels. As the college admissions dance continues, many athletes are admitted to selective institutions where they have almost no chance of succeeding academically without being provided proper educational remediation. This occurs irrespective of any usual admission standards that a particular school may have. In other words, an institution may have higher admission standards than NCAA initial eligibility requires, but will admit an athlete who at least meets NCAA minimums. Some schools, such as public universities in Mississippi, have simply relented and made their common admission standards the same as NCAA initial eligibility standards, as it was when I was a faculty member at Mississippi State University in the early 2000s.

This affects an academically underprepared athlete in many ways. First, it encourages a "teaching to the test" mentality among teachers and professors—from a focus on getting the athlete initially eligible while in high school to maintaining eligibility after admission, often to a college or university with a significantly higher academic profile than NCAA standards represent. This should be understood in light of what my Drake Group colleague Dr. Gerry Gurney of the University of Oklahoma calls the "original sin" of college sports: asking underprepared athletes to essentially work (and it is work) in their sport for forty-plus hours a week while attempting to be a college student. With that kind of time demand, the academic workload can be challenging for the most prepared athletes, much less the ones who are not ready. This scenario has led to distortions of academic advisement for elite athletes at the university level that too often turn it into nothing more than eligibility maintenance, rather than giving the athlete true access to an education and a better chance at social mobility outside of sports (Gurney and Willingham 2014). Again, this has a massive trickle-down effect in high schools and at even lower levels. Athletes are many times pursuing the lowest common denominator of just getting eligible, often at the behest of parents, teachers, and advisors who may not have the athlete's best academic and future interests at heart.

The solution, as long as we are in a (revised) educationally based model, is to not have athletes who are competing for an educational institution be either considered or effectively treated as employees. It is within the authority of higher education institutions and national sports governance organizations to define a "professional athlete" and to prohibit professional athletes from participating in college athletic programs. In short, admission of students into any university is the prerogative of that institution. If an institution wants to lower its standards and can live with the effects of that, including repercussions in regard to accreditation and research rankings, then so be it. I tend to think that the faculty and even some of the most jaded sports fans would not allow it, because the damage to the academic status of an institution could be irreparable.

However, this does not mean that schools should not incorporate special considerations in admissions decisions, including for athletes. To the contrary, everyone should have access to an education, but keeping educational primacy the priority is still the key. For members of the NCAA or any other voluntary athletic association, there should still be some baseline academic standards for athletic eligibility. However, the Drake Group believes it is time to end the practice of having a national-level eligibility clearinghouse run by the NCAA.[9] In this proposed model, and also as proposed by the Drake Group, any incoming athlete who is more than one standard deviation below the mean academic profile of the incoming class at a given institution would be ineligible for competition and only allowed limited practice opportunities, while still receiving athletically related financial aid (athletic scholarship). This preserves the ability of the school to admit anyone they want to, but also ensures that an athlete will not be put in a situation where his or her education does not effectively matter.

With regard to athletically related financial aid, the Drake Group wants it mandated that "athletes are treated as students, rather than employees, by mandating scholarship awards that extend through graduation and prohibiting cancellation for reasons of athletic performance or injury. A committee of each member's faculty senate should also review rules created by coaches and athletic directors to ensure they are consistent with academic best practices."[10] In essence, the athletic scholarship would be explicitly redefined as an academic award that is guaranteed throughout the enrollment of the athlete. Any reduction or cancellation of the scholarship would have to be for reasons common to all students (academic underperformance, violations of codes of conduct or law, etc.), so that scholarships cannot be unilaterally adjusted or withdrawn by a coach or athletic administrator. The days when a coach could choose whether to cancel or reduce an athletic scholarship should end immediately and athletes should be treated like all other students in financial aid matters. The present-day influence or control over athletic aid by a coach or athletic department is a major reason why many believe that athletes are essentially employees. Having the same standards as for all students would help ensure that student-athletes are not employees, but college students playing college sports.[11]

This part of the proposal contributes to achieving many of the goals involved in creating a true educationally based sports development model. It puts admission decisions back in control of the school, with the only condition being that academic remediation must be provided for students who are likely to have difficulty meeting the academic standards of the institution. We owe the student a chance to be raised to a level where he or she can compete academically as well as athletically. This can also influence high school and secondary school achievement. The athlete would no longer be striving to meet an arbitrary national standard, but institutional standards. If a student wants to be eligible to play as a college freshman, they must either meet the profile of that institution or be effectively academically immersed prior to being allowed to play. The best way to do this for those below the standard deviation threshold would be to mandate a year of academic remediation with limited athletic activity. While I strongly believe that athletic ineligibility for all college freshmen is a promising idea that should be considered, there certainly are new students who can handle both athletic and academic demands effectively. Using the standard deviation threshold is a way to treat all athletes fairly—and, in the long run, especially the ones who need remediation to be academically successful. I also believe that this action alone would at least push the NFL and NBA to think about adjusting their age requirements or enhancing and/or creating their own developmental programs.

Another requirement that has been a cornerstone of the Drake Group plan is to mandate academic disclosure of athletic team academic benchmarks in comparison to the general student body. This is not about controlling the academic practices of institutions nor embarrassing the athlete. It is about holding institutions publicly accountable for how they are educating athletes they promised would get a college education. If an institution wants to have a "paper class" system, as the University of North Carolina did to keep athletes eligible, as discussed previously, that is up to them, but it will be public knowledge. For public institutions, federal funding could be made contingent on transparency, while private institutions could be mandated to comply with transparency rules as voluntary members of any athletic association such as the NCAA. Once institutions are exposed as allowing substandard programs and shamed publicly, as with North Carolina and Auburn University, they tend to make quick, positive, long-needed changes. Disclosure is about institutional, not athlete, behavior. It can be mandated by faculty senates or as a condition of voluntary membership in a governing body, and can be done within the confines of the Family Educational Rights and Privacy Act (FERPA), also known as the Buckley Amendment, since the individual athlete would not be identified.[12]

For those who do not want to meet these new academic requirements, there should and likely will eventually be other sports-development choices they can pursue outside of the educational system—hopefully, more than they have now. Currently, there is no reason for the intercollegiate athletic system to change, nor is there a reason for professional teams to spend time, effort, and money on sports development, as it is being provided cost-free via the established educational model. This academics-first model will not only encourage more systems to manifest themselves, but will likely determine whether this country continues to maintain itself as a worldwide athletic powerhouse.

ENSURING ATHLETE HEALTH AND SAFETY

As covered in chapter 4, one issue that has become much more prevalent over the past few years is the health and welfare of athletes, most notably at the youth level. Growing knowledge about continued exposure to the physical and mental dangers of playing certain sports has led many to believe that such sports have to be fundamentally changed, or even simply banned altogether. As unlikely as that may sound, there has been a great deal of damaging recent news of the harmful effects of playing American full-contact football and, to a lesser extent, other sports, especially concerning potential long-term effects of head trauma and concussions. We are in a situation where protection of the athlete has become of paramount importance. Football and likely other sports may be changed significantly in the future. This is more acute at the educational and youth sports level, where athletic-induced trauma and injury can significantly affect the ability of an athlete to be an effective student and could cause lifelong negative health issues. In addition, there may be potential legal liability that educational institutions may be exposed to if these sports continue to be sponsored within the educational system. If contact sports are to remain part of the educational system in America, they will likely be altered to better ensure safety and wellness for the athlete. Considering that many schools have banned certain types of playground equipment and other activities that could cause injury to students and increase legal exposure, it is not too big a leap to predict that there will be changes to how contact and even traditional noncontact sports are conducted for school-based and youth athletes in the future.

In fact, it is already happening. While traditionalists may blanch at some of the changes, many are being made and more improvements are likely forthcoming. Some recent common-sense changes that are already happening include eliminating two-a-day football practices at NCAA institutions and within most state high school athletic associations, along with restricting the number of full-contact practices. These recent changes are not perfect measures but do go a long way to bolstering a revised academic model such as the one this chapter proposes. Any significant change like Model 1 will generate discussion and controversy if ever enacted in whole or in part. That is a good thing, in my view, as I strongly believe if we do reform our academic-based sports system, other systems outside education will manifest themselves and that will be beneficial for all stakeholders. Other systems that can potentially be created in addition to a new academic model or that can operate independently as the primary model in the United States are discussed in the next three chapters.

8

Model 2—An Academic/ Athletic Commercialized Solution

THIS PROPOSAL is modeled after suggestions by prominent scholars in the field and expanded further based on what would be logical extensions of such suggestions. The main drive for this model comes from distinguished thinkers with immense knowledge of educationally based athletics in America, notably including Dr. John Gerdy.[1] It also draws on the significant experience of athletic leaders who recognize the urgent need for change, including former Big 12 Conference commissioner Dan Beebe.[2] This model, the "Academic/Athletic Commercialized Solution," draws on proposals Gerdy, Beebe, and others have discussed over the years, particularly in regard to the elimination of the athletic scholarship. My proposal includes an important additional desired outcome: spurring an increase in other sports development options, outside the educationally based context.

A unique feature of this model is a proposed restructuring of intercollegiate athletics in the United States with a focus on the NCAA as the largest governing body. It involves revamping the current divisional structure, potential promotion and relegation of teams as in European club sports, and reframing how sports are defined and financed at the university and scholastic levels. It recognizes the commercial entrenchment of college football and men's basketball at the NCAA Division I level and essentially surrenders to those financial and commercial pressures for those sports, while keeping these two sports loosely associated

with the university. In this proposal, these two sports—and potentially others—would exist as for-profit auxiliaries of the institution,
structured as outsourced entities. The teams would be financially self-
sustaining and pay a franchise fee to the universities they represent.
Most important, the athletes would not have to be full-time students,
or even officially enrolled students at all. They would be paid a salary
to play and be defined as employees who could essentially go to school
on their own time, having an opportunity to pursue educational opportunities at the university of their own choosing. However, there would
be no academic eligibility requirements for these sports at schools that
wish to compete at this level.

All other sports under this model would be considered actual educationally based participatory sports. No athletic scholarships would be
given: any financial aid the athlete receives would have to be need-based
or otherwise merit-based, as determined by the same analysis used for
the general student body. The money saved by doing this would enable
more participation opportunities (thus enhancing public health), the
return of many sub-varsity teams, and the resurrection of many Olympic sports that have been dropped due to the arms race of funding football and men's basketball. This would augment the commercial viability
of these sports while enhancing the country's national and international
competitiveness. The lack of athletic scholarships also levels the playing
field between NCAA divisions. In this model, a European-style system of promotion and relegation between divisions could also be instituted to increase competitiveness and excitement. For the athlete in
non-marquee sports, competition and practice time would be strictly
regulated, including with regard to out-of-season activities. Most competition would be regional in order to limit missed class time and offer
athletes the ability to pursue an academic path of their choice that is not
overly influenced or dictated by their athletic endeavors. There could
still be national competitions, but they would be structured around the
academic calendar and not commercial interests.

This would involve forcing or at least persuading some significant
stakeholders, notably the NBA and NFL, to consider establishing other
sports development and development league options, simply because
an intercollegiate model that no longer offers athletic scholarships
would likely not be as attractive to many athletes and coaches, most certainly the ones at the elite level who are looking for the best potential

path to the professional ranks. This is not a bad scenario and should be encouraged, as more options can be developed, ultimately benefitting everyone.

This model adopts Beebe and Gerdy's basic premises and proposals. Step 1 would be eliminating the athletic scholarship for all sports, allowing for only the need-based athletic aid or academically merit-based scholarships generally available to all students. Step 2 would be to designate certain sports as spectator sports. Certainly, football and men's basketball are the two obvious candidates. As Beebe mentions, due to Title IX and gender equity issues it would be important and likely mandated to designate two or three women's teams as spectator sports to give a certain number of women the same opportunities as male athletes to earn the salaries, educational options, and marketing opportunities available in men's spectator sports. Based on their potential marketability and popularity, I propose that women's basketball, volleyball, and softball be considered spectator sports. All of these women's sports have professional playing opportunities around the world, and I would argue that they are three of the most popular women's sports in intercollegiate and interscholastic athletics.

Step 3 would be to designate all other sports as being within the nonrevenue or participatory category. There would be no athletic scholarships, no off-campus recruiting, and competition would be organized more regionally and locally. Coaches would not be full-time and would have educational and/or administrative responsibilities with the school and be more vested in the institutional mission. Finding the right mechanism to structure a model like this should not be extremely difficult, but it would involve a paradigm and philosophy shift that particular institutions would undertake with varying difficulty. However, since the commercially driven sports are being saved with fewer restrictions, this model would be very palatable and popular with the public, and likely tolerable among colleges and universities, thanks to the budgetary and academic benefits outlined above.

There would likely be a legitimate concern that a model such as this, or any of the other proposed models for that matter, could have a disparate effect on minority athletes and their potential social mobility via obtaining a college education. I strongly believe this would not be the case. This model can actually make education more accessible for all by changing requirements and offering lifetime educational opportunities.

In this and other models, admissions decisions should be solely controlled by the colleges and universities. All institutions would still have the ability to admit whom they like, with the same proviso as in Model 1: freshman eligibility for competitive athletics should be limited to those who meet the incoming mean academic profile of the institution. Individuals more than one standard deviation below the institutional mean, as in Model 1, should be academically remediated with limited competitive athletic activity until they are brought up to the academic standards of that institution and are in a position where they can academically compete while maintaining involvement in athletics. Competitive and travel restrictions would also help athletes focus more on academic rather than athletic success. Eligibility standards can be set by individual schools or groups of schools. If there are to be national or regional standards, I would recommend only a 2.0 GPA, but it certainly does not have to be a requirement. All other rules regarding progress toward degree requirements and part-time versus full-time enrollment should be governed by each individual institution.

The checks and balances put in place to ensure academic integrity would require that each school be fully transparent by publicly disclosing academic information in the aggregate through their faculty senates. This can be done without identifying individual students and therefore violating individual student privacy rights under the Buckley Amendment (FERPA). It has been proven that public disclosure is one of the best ways to ensure that all educational institutions are actually giving their athletes an opportunity to receive a legitimate education (Salzwedel and Ericson 2003). While institutions can have different academic requirements, being transparent makes it highly unlikely that an institution will stray away from common institutional standards because of the embarrassment and scandal it would cause. Academic disclosure is about institutional behavior and academic integrity, not about athlete behavior. Since no individual would be identified, the focus would be on what the institution did or did not allow with regard to academic integrity and athletics.[3]

A model like this would actually have a positive educational impact on lower socioeconomic classes and minorities. Need-based aid would be available, so that the lack of an athletic scholarship should not be a barrier to higher education access for anyone. The ability to participate in sports would still be available. Meanwhile, the focus would be on education first and not athletics. The priorities would be changed and codified. Athletes participating in the spectator sports would still have access to an education. Although they would not be required to be full-time students or even enrolled students, for that matter, when they are competing, they would still have the opportunity to receive an education should they desire it. Forcing education on an athlete who may be academically underprepared or simply not at a viable time in his or her life to pursue an education is a recipe for academic integrity issues. Oftentimes, people mature and realize the benefits of education and college later in life, as many have, including myself.

As stressed, individuals can have access to educational opportunities throughout their lives, certainly more so in the twentieth-first century, with accessible online and affordable educational programs. Even the professional leagues that almost solely rely on educationally based athletes for their talent pools can provide educational options for their athletes, as Major and Minor League Baseball currently do. Elite clubs and sports schools in Europe still provide educational options for their athletes, and we can do the same in the United States. The bottom line is that we do not have to pigeonhole all American athletes as we do in the current system: all athletes should have other competitive options. This model recognizes the cultural importance of commercialized elite sports, but also focuses on reviving mass-participation options and physical fitness for all, making them of primary importance.

There might be great fear that school-based sports would not be as marketable or popular if many would-be elite college athletes begin to try other sports development systems that are or could become available to them. Nothing could be further from the truth. I contend that we will watch the games in an educationally based sports system regardless of the level of play. We want to be entertained by athletes who can perform at a high level, but I cannot emphasize this point enough: we will still watch. A prime example of this was when prospective NBA athletes could enter the draft right out of high school. Many elite and commercially impactful players skipped college and went directly to the NBA. Names like Kobe Bryant, LeBron James, Kevin Garnett, Darryl Dawkins—and even, digging into the past, Moses Malone going right to the American Basketball Association (ABA)—proved without a doubt that many elite players could make an immediate impact in the professional leagues after being drafted out of high school. At the same time, though, we still watched college basketball in ever-increasing numbers. The predictions of doom for college basketball did not come true. Similarly, college baseball is popular even though many elite players go straight to the minor leagues, bypassing college.

We want to watch the athletes who represent our alma maters, our local colleges and universities, or simply our favorite teams. As middle school, high school, and even college sports fans, we ultimately cheer for the name on the front of the jersey, not the back. Candidly, the skill level should not even matter; we simply want to watch the product. Two prominent television executives—Loren Matthews, a former senior vice president at ESPN and ABC, and Mike Aresco, then a senior vice president at CBS Sports—stated as much at separate Knight Commission on Intercollegiate Athletics meetings in 2001 and 2003.[4]

Considering that these were two individuals whose job it was to generate viewer interest, sponsorship and advertising dollars, and other revenue for their networks, their opinions on the effect the then proposed NCAA academic standards could potentially have on the quality of the games and fan interest in them were illuminating. In 2001, Matthews stated, "If you still had either scholarship athletes in total, at all participating universities, or non-scholarship athletes participating in all universities, there would still be a level of play that would be consistent across the board. I would think from a fan's end it would be at an acceptable level."[5] Aresco was even more direct in a November 2013 Knight Commission meeting, stating that there would not even be a product if the athletes were not students, and that there would not be a significant dilution of talent among educationally based athletic programs. Speaking to the fear of losing talent to the NBA when elite basketball prospects could go straight from high school to the pros, Aresco noted that "we have already seen most of our top players leave for the NBA and it has not affected, in the end, the quality of what we put on the air. We still have a vibrant, terrific tournament."[6]

Ultimately, only so many athletes will go to the professional ranks in any sport, and there still would be fantastic athletes to play in college sports under Models 1 and 2. Take a powerful college football program like those at the University of Alabama or Ohio State University, along with basketball powerhouses like Duke and UCLA. These are some of the best college teams in the land. In any given year, how many of the athletes on those teams get drafted into the pros? The answer is, very few, if any. When Ohio State won the inaugural College Football Play-off championship over the University of Oregon in January 2015, they were, without a doubt, the best team in college football that year. Of twenty-two seniors graduating from the best college football team in the country, most of whom were at least being considered as prospects, only five players were drafted. None of them were picked in the coveted first round, where rookie athletes typically get guaranteed contract money from the NFL.[7] Currently, only three of those five Ohio State draft picks are on active NFL rosters. So, even playing with high-level skills for an elite team, the chances of going pro are infinitesimal.

This may sound like all the more reason to keep scholastic and intercollegiate athletics unchanged, so that a so-called "student-athlete" can have an education to fall back on when his or her competitive days are over. However, as has been made clear, we have lost our way at all levels of educationally based sports—whether it's a question of commercial powerhouses like football and men's basketball or of less commercially popular sports—because of the overwhelming desire to win and the emphasis we put on early specialization and overtraining of young athletes. These factors are squeezing out their educational options, while turning institutions of higher learning and many secondary schools into nothing more than farm clubs for certain professional leagues and elite sports-training operations.

OTHER SYSTEMS OF DEVELOPMENT

Where would changes like those proposed in Models 1 and 2 potentially leave us? I believe that other development systems would begin to manifest themselves both inside and outside the educational context. Even if the bulk of sports development remains grounded in educational institutions, it will be imperative to have other options for many sports, particularly sports open to international competition, including the Olympics. While primary and secondary schools and colleges would still compete in such sports under this model, I believe we'd very likely see a comprehensively developed sports-club system begin to manifest itself in response to a new structure and format of educationally based sports.

These clubs could focus on elite sports development and more opportunities for Olympic sports, along with enhanced health and wellness opportunities for all ages of America's population. Financing would likely be similar to what is found in Europe, in that increased government and private support would be needed to encourage the establishment and growth of this new system. Although there would be a cost to the taxpayer, the individual and societal savings on future costs (e.g., in the form of health care and insurance) would be significant. While many health-care delivery systems in Europe are often lauded in themselves for their efficiency, low costs, and accessibility, in the best cases they also benefit from a model of prevention through physical fitness and access to sports for all via local club sports.

Obviously, there would be great resistance to this model and, frankly, other proposed models—especially from those athletes who would not want their athletic endeavors limited as proposed. Many would likely want other practice and competitive options, including ones entirely detached from education. In other words, a model such as this would virtually force, or at least encourage, other systems to manifest themselves to preserve options, mostly for the elite athlete. Why would this happen? The answer is very simple and has been demonstrated repeatedly. When athletes are restricted in competition and practice time, most notably elite athletes, they will find other outlets.

An example of this is when the NCAA instituted a limit of twenty hours per week for practice and competition in the late 1980s.[8] Many athletes, such as Stanford's Janet Evans, an elite collegiate and international swimmer at the time, did not want their training time to be reduced and thus hinder their Olympic and other international aspirations. Many either temporarily dropped out of school or simply gave up competing for their college teams so they could maximize training and competitive opportunities. The point being, athletes who want to train and compete at the highest level will find ways to do so—and I believe that coaches, national governing bodies, and the country itself would almost certainly build alternative systems to sustain and support just that. We do not have to have 90 percent of our sports development grounded in education, where opportunities in Olympic sports are being limited or even eliminated. This does not mean that an elite athlete cannot remain in school or get an education. The opportunity for an education will be always be there. The chance to compete at an elite or sub-elite level will not. Athletes in other, new sports-development systems would be able to go to school at their own pace and receive the education they desire for their future, as opposed to an incomplete education often manufactured to keep athletes eligible.

Adopting at least some of the ideas that Gerdy and Beebe are proposing, and modifying them into a codified athletic and academic model, would go a long way toward keeping sports embedded in education, but now prioritizing education and using sports participation as a broad-based educational tool rather than a commercial one. Paradoxically, a model and measures that might appear to some to be moving us away from the ideal of balance between education and sports participation could instead be key to restoring and preserving it.

9

Model 3—A "European-Type" Club Sports Development Model or Hybrid Model

THIS BRINGS us to proposed Model 3, the Hybrid Model, for short, which is essentially a combination of the previous two models with some modifications. Overall, the European approaches detailed by Ian Henry (see chapter 6) relate closely to Model 2 with regard to athletes having more freedom in their athletic and academic pursuits. In Model 2, elite athletes would still be affiliated with a certain school in the spectator-driven sports, while others can still potentially engage in participatory athletics via the school. Model 3 focuses on outside sports development that would manifest itself primarily through clubs more or less based on the European model, including elite training and competition for athletes who do not want to have any educational restrictions on their pursuit of athletic excellence. Participation opportunities for the nonelite athlete can also be provided by external clubs, even while such opportunities can still exist in the schools. Having these two options by combining components of both systems under the hybrid approach would open many more sporting opportunities for both the elite athlete and the more casual participant. The hybrid model builds on what likely would happen if Model 1 and/ or Model 2, or parts thereof, were ever implemented. While Model 3 combines parts of the previous two proposals, it could conceivably be implemented on its own. However, it is unlikely that this hybrid approach would ever be considered without the wholesale changes to educationally embedded sports outlined in previous models instigating further substantial action.

Underlying this model is the belief that it is vital to present as many elite, mass-participation, and recreational sports as possible—in various venues and systems—in order to create opportunities for everyone. It is a virtual certainty under this model (as well as the previous two) that other sports development systems will emerge to satisfy those who want either high-level activity or mass-participation opportunities outside the educational system. Meanwhile, although allowing for increased access to a broader range of sports, such developments inside and outside the educational system do not have to inhibit one's access to an education. Generally speaking, the model aims to offer a wider selection of sports in schools and colleges, in a less competitive format for all students, while better preparing both elite and subelite competitive athletes for higher levels of competition in a distinct external club system. However, this does not mean there would not be opportunities for mass participation in a club system, in addition to sports experiences available in school. As in Europe, those recreational options would be available, as would elite development programs taking place in the same facilities.

In this hybrid model, education and sports are both prioritized and one does not have to be subservient to the other. The educational mission benefits by reducing the distorting impact of athletic competition on schools, teachers, and students. On the other hand, by lessening this impact and achieving a better balance of elite and nonelite programs in both academically based and external sports-club systems, we can actually improve our ability to emphasize the educative, social, and character-building aspects of sports and athletic recreation. Many skills and character traits can be developed through sports participation at all levels. While education is the true path to social mobility, sports promote personal development, social skills, and even awareness of and positive engagement with social justice issues (Foster, O'Reilly, and Dávila 2016).

Of course, in this sense, it should not matter when or where the athletic opportunity is delivered for the participant, whether in the school, in outside competition, or through a combination of both. However, the struggle in America to combine mass participation and elite sports development within the education system is seriously undermining these timeless and all-important aspects of athletic endeavor. When elite participation is predicated on an arbitrary standard of academic eligibility, coaches, administrators, and even teachers, parents, and athletes are under pressure to find ways of gaming the system. Nonelite athletes tend more and more to be underserved and to be seen (or to see themselves) as somehow less important than the elite. This is where the bulk of the problems with the current system in the United States begin and end: in allowing the effects—and the meaning—of competition to spin out of control. To find a solution, it is vital to look across the Atlantic Ocean for viable alternative approaches that, with adjustment, could be successful in America through a hybrid approach.

USING BOTH SCHOOLS AND CLUBS FOR YOUTH AND ELITE SPORTS DEVELOPMENT

An overarching goal under any model of sports development in the United States, but especially acute to proposed Model 3, should be to encourage all students, including elite athletes, to sample more sports and not specialize in any specific sport at an early age.[1] Playing one sport virtually year-round and limiting or even completely eliminating exposure to other sports and physical activity is detrimental to total athlete development (whether in competitive sports or other participation and exercise options) because the athlete loses the skill development that can come from participating in multiple sports. This growing phenomenon also leads to early burnout and injuries for many athletes. According to the 2016 NCAA GOALS study, a high percentage of the athletes surveyed questioned the wisdom of sport specialization at an early age (defined as twelve years old and up). Most wished they had had greater exposure to a variety of sports development options during their formative years (NCAA 2016).

Thus, one key goal of this hybrid model is to expand options for participatory sports in the primary and secondary school systems, first and foremost, as well as through internal and external sports clubs. This closely follows how sports are introduced and experienced in Europe. Most European students at the primary and secondary levels of education have the opportunity to sample several sports through their schools and being introduced to sports via sampling, they may eventually want to concentrate on at a more competitive and/or participatory level within a sports-club system. In the United States, there still could be limited competition between schools, but with far less emphasis on winning as a value that crowds out all others. Placing participation and competition in something more like a festival weekend format would help students maintain their focus on academic obligations, without letting athletic competition, extensive travel, and even academic manipulation interfere. The primary competitive sports, such as football and men's and women's basketball, could be housed completely outside the school system in external clubs or athletic clubs sponsored by the school—but with no academic eligibility requirements, so as to prevent the all too often corrosive effects on the education system. This provides, as in the previous models, more choices for the athlete inside and outside the educational system, and increases mass participation opportunities for all.

Students who are enrolled in elementary, middle, and high schools would be required to participate in either school-based sports or competitive club sports as part of their educational program, with several different competitive and participation levels offered in both the clubs and the schools. Again, this is very similar to what most European countries are currently doing. Having several teams at many different levels along with a broad menu of sports can make this method much more attractive to the community and to students, while promoting physical activity that will benefit individuals and society in the long term. This sort of mandatory but varied and fluid system can make sports participation and physical fitness more enjoyable for our youth. It would also bring our schools back to pursuing, on behalf of all students, the "sound mind in a sound body" aspect of a complete education.

I have had direct experience with similar hybrid models when I was on research sabbatical in Germany in 2014–15. My son and daughter were typically out of school no later than 12:30 p.m. each day in Bayreuth, Germany, and then the afternoon was dedicated to sports and/or the arts. There were also in-school and post-school-day physical fitness classes and other exercise options. Twice a week my son had a basketball class as part of his curriculum; on two other days he had swimming and chess. He also played soccer regularly for a local sports club, as part of one team among others that were segregated by age and ability. He practiced no more than twice a week with his soccer club and never had more than two games per week, although it was typically only one game per week. My daughter joined a local swim club and had various physical fitness options during a typical school day. She would also spend many afternoons attending piano lessons and dramatic arts practice.

Although this goes beyond the proposed model per se, we should explore shortening the school day and revamping the traditional school calendar in order to more easily allow increased time for and ease of participation in not just sports but other activities. Easing into a different competitive sports schedule is an intriguing step to help prevent the burnout and early injuries now prevalent in American youth sports (Farrey 2009). The European school calendar is much different from that in the United States. Typically, there is only a six-week summer break, but there are several breaks during the school year that most American schools do not provide. America's school-based sports—and, for that matter, even external sports clubs—could benefit from a revised and more consistent school calendar. In my opinion, and that of others, the US school calendar is outdated, being mostly based on agricultural needs (Ballinger 1988; Ballinger 1995). Although it's not yet widespread, there is a steadily growing belief that the United States needs to look seriously at revamping the school calendar in order to allow needed changes not only to sports and other activities, but to the curriculum itself. In terms of sports, changing the school calendar could help school systems better regulate practice and competition schedules so as to interfere less with the educational process. There would also be less tendency to force certain athletes to practice during breaks, including the summer break. The revised summer break, while shorter, would allow families to spend time and vacation together without this pressure.

There can be many different formations, in either school-affiliated or completely external club systems, with regard to competitive viability, size, and formal structure. As mentioned in the discussion of Model 2, these newly formed clubs can have a system of relegation and promotion that could enable even a small, local club to grow and become more commercially sustainable—if that is desired. School systems would have the option to govern their own approach to sports competition, but, with a fully functional, broad-based club sports system in place, the likelihood of the state of competition in scholastic sports remaining anything like it looks today seems minimal. Given that strictly school-based sports options would be somewhat limited, while offerings through clubs are intended to be broader, the external sports-club system would become the primary mode of development for elite athletes and for mass participation. Schools can still provide physical education, unstructured and structured play options, and limited intramural and extramural sports, but the main focus in the educational context would be exposing kids to multiple sports and physical fitness options that, hopefully, will become a normal part of their future lifestyle.

This model can draw on several components of Models 1 and 2. For instance, football, men's basketball, and other commercialized spectator sports can be handled as proposed in Model 2: teams can be affiliated with the educational institution, but players can be paid and/or otherwise profit from their marketing utility while not being required to be full-time students (or students at all, for that matter). As in Europe, athletes would have the flexibility to tailor their education to fit with the demands of a competitive athletic schedule, pursuing any of several different educational options as they wish. Education can be encouraged, but it does not have to be a requirement. The participatory sports could be pursued within the schools (as in Model 1), or athletes could have the choice of participating in an external sports club (as in Model 2) without participation being tied to specific academic requirements.

Another option is that all sports, including both spectator and participatory sports, could be embedded in the education system—therefore involving the academic standards of Model 1—but that an external system for all sports, including noncommercial as well as revenue-driven ones, would be developed. In this vein, everyone associated with any sport would have a clear choice, including both athletes and fans. There would still be educationally based sports, albeit with fewer games, less stringent time requirements, fewer off-season responsibilities—and, crucially, a real, encompassing focus on education. As discussed earlier, there would still likely be a strong fan base and commercial market for educationally based sports played in this scenario. Meanwhile, the external sports club could serve in part as something like a minor league/developmental system for elite athletes in a myriad of sports, including football and men's basketball. There would also be fan interest (and a spectator market) in these teams, but athletes can be developed for future professional opportunities in both systems. For the most part, elite athletes would likely gravitate more to the club system with its flexible approach to academics, but that does not mean that they would not also be able to develop and thrive within a strictly educational context, if they wish to go that route. As noted, another alternative would be to have external clubs attached to the schools themselves, in part because of the availability (or provision) of facilities and other infrastructure, but still as separate entities without the imposition of academic eligibility requirements on their players.

Although not directly applicable, this is closely similar to what is currently happening in baseball and hockey at the high school and college levels in the United States. When a baseball player graduates from high school, he can either enter the major league draft or enroll in college. If the athlete chooses to enroll in college, then he must wait three years to reenter the MLB draft. In baseball there are thus essentially two main paths for the elite athlete. The same options exist in hockey. On the one hand, there is an established minor league system and junior-level competition. On the other, many great ice hockey players come up through the college ranks before going professional. In both sports, NCAA competition provides great development opportunities for elite or aspiring elite athletes. While some players do reenter the draft before actually finishing college, Major League Baseball has provisions to financially assist these athletes toward degree completion if they do leave school early. While this is not an exact match to the proposed model, it is certainly a hybrid example that is working quite well for baseball and ice hockey.

This model can be a win-win for all involved and interested in American sports development and delivery. It can satisfy the purist who still believes in the redeeming value of school-based sports in America along with the fragile amateur ideal while also satisfying the reformers who believe the current educationally based model has survived far beyond its usefulness and is overdue for a change. Regardless of what one thinks of amateurism and sports embedded in the educational system, Model 3 is a way to give athletes a clear choice of how to possibly pursue their sporting endeavors outside education along with clear parameters and boundaries should the choice be to participate in sports within the educational system. It is not as though these approaches have not been done before or are currently without success. Despite its flaws, the American educationally based sports development model has shown extreme resilience for the past hundred-plus years, as has the external European sports club system. The Hybrid Model brings together the best of both systems in a workable model that can change American sports forever for the better.

GENERAL EXPENSES IN EUROPEAN SPORTS CLUBS

Besides discussing potential models for change under a European-type club sports model, it is necessary to review revenue streams in European clubs and potential sources of revenue for a proposed American sports club system. It is also important to review typical expenses that a local sports club may incur, specifically with regard to proposed Models 2 and 3. Funding for current forms of American sports development is a combination of many different sources, so the broad-based aspect of revenue sourcing is not the same in Europe, but many of the expenses are similar. As mentioned, the three primary ways a European sport club is funded are through government and state subsidies, membership fees, and ancillary revenue such as lottery proceeds, businesses, ticket sales, and sponsorships. In 2012, the DOSB conducted a survey asking German sport clubs about their expenses. Most of the money was spent on coaches, maintenance of facilities, equipment, sports events, and membership and affiliation fees paid to sport organizations (Breuer and Feiler 2013, 33). Since German sport clubs are volunteer-based, most of the coaches are paid minimum wages, if they get paid at all. In contrast, for-profit sport clubs, such as those in the Bundesliga first league, pay their coaches, and even many administrators, huge sums of money. Since soccer is the most popular sport in Germany and throughout Europe, soccer coaches are the best-paid coaches in European countries. This would likely be a similar phenomenon in America, where the free market would govern compensation for workers, staff, and coaches based upon the size and revenue-generating potential of the club. How any sports club–affiliated system in America would work and be financially feasible is covered in chapter 11.

CHALLENGES AND ISSUES WITHIN
THE EUROPEAN CLUB SPORTS SYSTEM

While there are many advocating other approaches to sports development in America, including the creation of a local sports club system, some challenges and issues within parts of the European club sports system need to be addressed, as many of the same challenges would likely exist in America if a similar system is ever enacted. Some of the current issues in European clubs, aside from some smaller clubs needing additional financial resources, are the recruitment and commitment of volunteers, younger athletes, coaches, and referees, and generating more members overall. Among the challenges are the same ones that exist today in America, including time poverty, especially for students and young people. Time demands are increasing for the younger population (eighteen to twenty-five years old) through growing expectations in school, college, and universities, as well as job entry requirements (Bundesministerium für Familie 2010, 104–6). Despite having a shorter school day that enables greater access to physical and sport activity, a recent major change in the German public school system was a reduction from nine required years of high school study to only eight years. This led to overcrowded schedules and less space for leisure time as the hours per school day were increased. Even with these changes the German school day is still shorter than most American school days (Breuer and Feiler 2013, 23). Another important reason why members are staying away is that sport clubs seem to be not as trendy for the younger population as they used to be. Young adults keep leaving clubs in search of fun and individual disciplines without obligations, such as attending individual training sessions or helping out as a referee at other games. New trends and exciting sports like CrossFit or stand-up paddling are becoming more and more popular, putting original club sport disciplines in danger (Opaschowski 1996, 2–3). This can be looked at as a negative or as an opportunity. Like anything, local sports clubs need to evolve to adapt to the membership. Sports activities like CrossFit and integrating technology can be popular additions to any club to attract and keep members.

Increasing stress and demand in today's jobs might be a reason people do not want to volunteer. Since most coaches are volunteers who usually have another "real" job that can conflict with sport club responsibilities, it can be difficult to spend a whole weekend coaching the local swimming team at a tournament without compensation. Many training sessions can only be conducted during the night hours, and an inflexible timetable might be another negative aspect for athletes, particularly college and high school students. Another challenge for "old-fashioned" club sports—and certainly something America would face—is the advancement of technology. One does not need to be on a team to compete or stay in shape: self-measurement via cellphone apps, video game–based exercise programs, and other technologies are getting more popular these days. All of these challenges currently exist even with the educationally based model. Any move to a comprehensive sports club system would also need to incorporate the new aspects of sports development to attract members and sustain interest. The issues are many, but funding options for reimagining sports development in the United States do exist. With some effort and creativity, a sustainable funding model can be established that insures the long-term success of a local sports club system in America.

10

Model 4—A Complete Separation of Competitive Sports from Schools

MODEL 4 is based on a complete severing of ties between sports and education in America and a pivot to a more inclusive external sports-club system. While actually removing competitive sports from their educational base in the United States might seem far-fetched and impossible to accomplish, it is at least worth discussing as an option. Although it could be thought of as a "nuclear option," there is reason to believe that this model could change the relationship between sports and education in a constructive way.

This proposed model would build on many of the principles discussed in regard to the previous models. It would not be a hybrid model, as in Model 3, but would instead be essentially very similar to the current sports development system in Europe. A European-style, community-based club system would become the primary mode of sports development and delivery. Primary and secondary schools would focus on physical education, intramural sports, and exposing the country's youth to the benefits and habits of lifetime physical exercise and to several different sports. Note that in this model there would be intramural sports, and even some limited extramural competition between schools—but, as in Europe, extramural sports would be rarer and more recreational, with a deliberate de-emphasis of the competitive aspect we see so strongly at work in the United States today. This would enable primary and secondary schools to establish a structurally and financially sound basis for returning to daily physical education classes and providing more choices in intramural sports. They could have great latitude in exposing boys and girls to stick and ball sports, racket sports, running, swimming, and a host of other opportunities, and even to things like ballroom dancing and other activities out of the mainstream that can be part of a vibrant, daily physical education program. Meanwhile, not having competitive sports programs in our schools would release a large amount of government, institutional, and community capital to fund mandatory and inclusive physical education programs—not to mention a return of many arts and other enrichment programs that are a necessary part of a well-rounded education.

A new sports club system—especially one that becomes the truly primary basis for sports access for all—could flourish throughout communities large and small in the United States. Even smaller clubs, properly dispersed and managed, can provide many options for members. If certain sports can't be made available in a certain club, there are ways to balance access across a defined geographic area. As most sports club systems are organized in Europe, there is virtually always a nearby club that will offer a sport not available to an interested athlete via his or her local club. In case this sounds burdensome, we should remember that in many parts of the United States we currently have young athletes regularly traveling hundreds of miles with their school or college teams, and even thousands of miles with the teams that are most successful. Many believe that this approach, along with pushing athletes to focus on one particular sport year-round, is greatly contributing to athlete burnout and injuries at a very young age (Farrey 2009; Aspen Institute 2015). Robust competition, including elite competition, can instead happen locally and regionally, limiting the extensive travel and time commitments that our youth, especially the athletically gifted ones, must often undertake to advance in their sport. The commitment to a more local approach is overt in many European countries—not just in major metropolitan areas but in small cities like Bayreuth, Germany, where there are five separate sports clubs in a community of less than seventy-five thousand people, and that does not include clubs in the surrounding communities within ten to thirty kilometers (roughly six to eighteen miles).[1] While most citizens will go to the closest sports club, the option of joining another club, usually because of its different offerings, is readily available.

On the macro level, a fully developed sports club system in the United States could serve the population through a "Sports for All" focus similar to the one found in Europe—that is, a focus on sports as a primary driver for social development, social integration, and public health. At the same time, the club system can provide elite sports options as a driver for national pride and international prestige. On the micro level, for communities the sports club can become a positive social anchor as a focal point for all kinds of activity, sports-related or not. It can be a central location for neighbors to exercise and participate in sports, but also to socialize and engage in many other activities—in Europe, these commonly include informal and league play of chess or card games, and entirely noncompetitive pursuits such as book clubs— along with taking part in the governance and management of the club.

As in Model 3, this model could certainly include the option of having school- or college-affiliated clubs, somewhat integrated into existing educational systems although still structured as separate entities. This would allow communities to use and leverage existing and planned infrastructure in the form of facilities and fields, along with other resources such as equipment and personnel. As with other clubs, those affiliated with schools or colleges would be open to the larger community. Students attending the affiliated school could be required to participate in club sports as part of their educational program. More realistically, though, the model would only require participation by all students in an expanded school-based physical education curriculum.

Creating a sports club system in America will take more than just removing competitive sports from schools; it also requires justification and examples of a functional sports club system that serves all levels of competition, age, and desire that could conceivably work in the United States. A good workable template is provided by the current youth-development model of the notable Amsterdamsche Football Club (AFC) Ajax in Amsterdam, the Netherlands.[2] While a typical local sports club will offer recreational opportunities as well as several sports and teams, a main function of most will be elite athlete development for the parent team(s) and for national and international competitions. Which sports and leagues are represented differs from club to club. For instance, most European clubs have a parent soccer team that competes in one of the various competitive professional divisions throughout the country. Ajax is a first-division team in the Netherlands. My son's sports club in Germany had a seventh-division soccer team, while a nearby club had a fourth-division team. My wife's hometown had a first-division handball squad. Other sports are also represented at most clubs, any of which teams might be highly competitive in its division. An example of this is Bayern München, which has one of the most recognizable sports brands in the world as a Bundesliga first-division soccer powerhouse, while also having a first-division team in the Basketball Bundesliga (formerly Beko BBL, now referred to as easyCredit BBL under sponsorship agreements), along with other sports offerings at various levels. Other clubs also commonly have such "parent" teams at different competitive levels, whether in the sports already named or in ice hockey, volleyball, wrestling, or a host of others.

In all cases, the youth development programs at these clubs are partly intended to develop athletes for the top competitive teams in their particular club. If the skill level of a player exceeds what the local sports club can accommodate, the athlete can easily transfer to another club that more appropriately fits his or her skill level and athletic goals, such as Philipp Lahm did when he transferred to Bayern München. The goal at Ajax is to have at least three players advance to the first squad every two seasons. This is not set in stone as a goal at any club, including Ajax, but most European clubs do want their players to advance. Obviously, top-division teams like Ajax or Bayern München will draw players from all over the world, so while their player-development systems are strong, the need to have any more than three or four players advance from within every couple of seasons is not as critical as it might be for a lower-division team, which will likely draw the bulk of its players locally and through their youth teams.

The main vision of Ajax, however, as championed by Dutch soccer legend and former Ajax player Johan Cruyff, who managed the team from 1985 to 1988, is to have a developmental program that serves as a consistent feeder program for the first-division team. The Ajax Youth Academy includes around 250 players in total. On average, there are 45 players leaving and 45 joining the Youth Academy every other year. These players have security for two years to acclimate to the academy without fear of being kicked out, but if their ability does not meet the standard for eventually moving up to the first or second teams, those players will be separated from the Youth Academy. However, those athletes can certainly go to another club and play at a level that suits their skills and desires.

THE STRUCTURE OF THE AJAX YOUTH ACADEMY

In order to counter the injury and burnout issues prevalent in American youth sports, we should seriously consider adopting the structure of the Ajax Youth Academy and similar European sports club and their approach to the time commitments required of boys and girls and young men and women. The Ajax approach is similar to that found in almost all other European clubs, with a focus on bringing athletes along slowly and deliberately while allowing them significant time to do other things— above all, to primarily focus on academics. Athletic commitments increase with age and skill, but even at the top levels you find most youth teams spending less time than is common in the United States on practice and other athletically related activities—yet these teams achieve a high level of regional, national, and international success in many sports. At the Ajax Youth Academy, players participate at one of three levels, each called a "wheel" (*Bouw*). The first wheel (*Onderbouw*) contains players 7–12 years old, the second (*Middenbouw*) players 13–16 years old, and the third (*Bovenbouw*) players 17–20 years old.

THE FIRST WHEEL (AGES 7–12)

While this example illustrates youth development in soccer, the principles are largely the same for all sports throughout Europe and differ dramatically from how we manage youth sports in America. At Ajax, the players in the first wheel practice only three times per week and play just one match on the weekend. Most European clubs believe that children have to live their own lives and experience as much quality time as possible with families and in their social environment. When boys and girls in the first wheel are not training they are encouraged to participate in unstructured play within or outside the club. It is strongly believed by many European sports-club managers that this engagement in other physical activity can actually enhance the creativity and technical skills of the players, while allowing them a normal life. Part of the vision of local sports-club systems in Europe is allowing kids to take risks, express their creativity, and, from the youngest age, not get punished for their mistakes but learn from them.

This first wheel is segregated by both age and skill. The U8/U9 teams play eight-on-eight on half a soccer field, the U10 team plays nine-on-nine on a slightly larger field, and the U11 team is the first that plays eleven-on-eleven on a full-size regulation soccer pitch. They start with the smaller fields in order to increase the number of ball touches in a game and from a belief that, when soccer is played in a smaller area, a player will automatically improve his or her technical skills. Age-appropriate differences in physical and mental development are taken into account to enhance self-confidence. At this level, the academy spends a great amount of time, often in mixed-gender training sessions, helping children develop various motor skills that enhance general physical coordination rather than promoting sports specialization. This is accomplished by conducting spatial, rhythm, reaction, and balance exercises within normal practice sessions and incorporating elements of gymnastics, judo, and running and agility exercises. Key knowledge goals for this age group focus on gaining fundamental understanding of the sport. This is achieved by offering instruction in three basic areas—possession, receiving, and specific game situations—in order to enhance players' technique, motor skills, and tactical awareness.

The education of athletes is not forgotten at any competitive level. Simply allowing for more time away from competitive sports is in itself a great advance in prioritizing education. At Ajax, the club maintains contact with its athletes' primary schools and even provides significant study and tutor time at the club. Ultimately, though, remaining focused on success in school is seen as the responsibility of the students and their parents. The club acts as an educational facilitator and offers encouragement and resources, but does not take a primary role in educational delivery.

THE MIDDLE WHEEL (AGES 13–16)

In the middle wheel, players are at a difficult age and often need special attention. They are reaching puberty, which brings with it "growing pains" both emotionally and physically. Toward the end of the wheel they will be entering high school, an exciting but often problematic transition. Meanwhile, they will of course have different types of home situations. While coaches and other staff in sports clubs like Ajax are focused on young people's sports development, they are certainly aware of these significant life changes and their impact.

As with many other European clubs, once a player enrolls in high school, Ajax, the school, and the player will enter into an agreement regarding his or her involvement and progress both in the Youth Academy and at the school. The seriousness regarding competition increases at this age, but it is still managed closely. This wheel involves practice up to four times per week with one match on the weekends. From a training and development perspective, players enhance their skills and knowledge through a focus on refining technique, developing decision-making skills, understanding in-game situations, and a progression from simpler drills up to more complex ones that capitalize on their increasing strength and speed at this age.

At Ajax, while the families of first-wheel participants are responsible for the child's transportation to and from training sessions, in the second wheel the player is transported from school to the academy in buses provided by the club. Upon arrival there is mandatory study time, with homework support provided, before the athletes start their training sessions. As in all age groups, students who don't finish their homework can't participate in training sessions that day. Thus, even without an academic eligibility requirement, there is educational oversight and measures are taken (including punitive measures) that are more proactive than the largely reactive approach often seen in American educationally based sports. School comes first and athletics second, with no exceptions. The view that most European clubs share is that education is a need, while playing sports is an additional opportunity. This philosophy is, arguably, exactly the opposite of what we too often find in America, and our entire country could benefit from cultivating a similar approach.

THE UPPER WHEEL (AGES 17–20)

The age of 16 is when most elite athletes are identified and given options to pursue a professional career at some level. For those who are not considered athletically ready for that jump, there are other options, including with other nearby clubs. While the upper wheel consists of players ages 17–20, it also overlaps with the club's second-level professional soccer team, which may have some older players. Players in the upper wheel who make it onto the team are considered fully professional athletes. In Europe, it is pretty standard that players can earn a contract in a professional sport from the age of 16, if they are good enough. At Ajax, youth soccer players who advance to this level can earn €30,000–50,000 a year ($34,000–$57,000 as of this writing).

However, in this grouping, most of the players are still attending school, and Ajax has the same commitment to academics as it has with the two younger groups. Even these players will only practice four times per week for no more than two hours at a time, and there are only two matches per week. Practices for this advanced group are focused on mental discipline, developing self-confidence, and performing under pressure. Training in tactics and decision making is centered on choosing proper position, understanding individual game-image patterns, and the ability to analyze and recognize when to get the ball. One main difference from the other wheels is that, after these athletes are brought from their respective schools by Ajax buses, they immediately go to training, with study hall reserved for afterward. Since these players are older, the bulk of educational responsibility is put on their shoulders, but the club is there to support them as with the other groups. The club feels that even though they are now professionals, the priorities do not change. School comes first, and the club supports that notion until they leave school, but many of their top players on the first and second teams are attending university while also making significant money. However, earning that money does not undermine individual or club prioritization of education, a value explicitly promoted by European clubs. They encourage education and provide an impetus for younger players who have graduated high school to pursue a college degree. As a club, Ajax also provides connections for athletes to take university sports management courses and opportunities to complete their internship requirements within the club, should that be a career interest for a player.

European sports clubs, exemplified here by Ajax, show a way that sports development in America can be made completely separate from the existing educational system without sacrificing quality of competition, educational opportunity, social mobility, or fan appeal and commercialism. Clubs like Ajax are proving that a robust and competitive sports club can be maintained with education still being of paramount importance, with little or no incentive to corrupt academic primacy in order to maintain athletic eligibility behind an educational façade. When one views a philosophy and management approach such as this, it is possible to imagine how American sports could one day be held completely separate from the educational system. This is a model that should not be dismissed quickly, as other developed countries demonstrate on a daily basis that it can be done, all while benefitting more citizens and even enhancing national and international competitiveness.

PARTICIPATION IN the club system would still be voluntary, although students could receive physical education credit for participating on a club team. Model 4 would not have any academic eligibility component, but the club itself can be an integral part of educational growth for any of its members. Physically fit children learn better, and exercise and sports participation can improve self-confidence, self-esteem, and work ethic (American Heart Association News 2015). Having several teams at any given club at many different skill levels, along with a broad menu of sports available for different ages, can make this model attractive, inclusive, and beneficial to more citizens, very much including our youth. Shortening the school day and revamping the traditional school calendar, as suggested in the discussion of Model 3, could additionally provide many educational, competitive, and health-related benefits by allowing more access to club activities.

This model could certainly work in the United States, but likely would not be adopted unless portions of the previous models are attempted and fail—or if the current educationally based model simply implodes. That could happen because of ubiquitous lawsuits, athletes' rights movements, academic issues, shaky television and marketing revenues, outpricing the fans, or people simply pursuing other forms of recreation, just to name a few things that could force a scorched-earth reaction and radical move to separate competitive sports from systems of education in America. In other words, many of the problems affecting American sports development today could very well be the tipping point to severing the long-standing relationship of education and sports in the United States.

If we as a country were ever in a position to make such a change, it is now, and the obstacles are not insurmountable. We have an already existing model that works similar to Model 4: the European system. Realizing that there will be immense resistance, debate, and certainly inertia working against moving to any new model, arguments for such change as Model 4 proposes should start with addressing the problems mentioned in previous chapters and focus on improvements to public health, lower health-care costs, and the financial and wellness benefits, short- and long-term, to be gained by Americans of all ages. In almost any election these days, federal, state, and even local, there is fierce debate over health care, health insurance, and health access. While many in this country point to European and other "socialized" models as at least partly showing a better way, many others are deeply concerned about losing freedom of choice and paying higher taxes. It is true that taxes in Europe can run to levels most Americans would frown upon—but it's also arguable that in many cases we are talking about political and economic systems where taxes are higher than ours in great part to pay for a frequently broader range of social services for all citizens. However, I am not here to argue the merits of a fully funded socialized health system.

It needs to be noted, though, that many European countries base much of their health care model on individuals and families taking primary responsibility for their own wellness through diet, exercise, and balanced living. The scourge of obesity is much less pronounced in most European countries because people eat better, ride bicycles and walk more, and have more opportunities for exercise and sports participation through the local sports-club system. European health-care and wellness programs strongly emphasize prevention through a healthy lifestyle in order to reduce the impact of preventable diseases and conditions—and they appear to do it better than we do.[3] Having a healthier and more active population can obviously reduce health-care and insurance costs for everyone. Even if America continues to eschew a taxpayer-funded social medicine system for all, improving sports access and wellness would be an unquestionably positive change. Whether we're talking about the radical scenario proposed in Model 4, or any other model, this should be something we can all agree on as an explicit goal.

11

Funding and Sustainability of Alternative Models of Sports Development and Delivery in America

WHEN PROPOSING to overhaul a nationwide sports development system—especially one that is widely accepted, popular, and financially lucrative to some—questions of course arise as to how much the proposed system will cost to implement and whether it offers a long-term sustainable business model. Without satisfactory answers to such critical questions, it will be impossible to justify any changes to the current system. I believe that the answer to these questions can be an absolute yes because of the short- and long-term benefits that positive changes can bring to all citizens. This chapter focuses on potential funding sources and structures for the models discussed in the previous chapters, in part by looking to European nations, most specifically Germany, as providing potential templates and roadmaps for a newly configured American sports development system.

POTENTIAL FUNDING SOURCES FOR AMERICAN SPORTS CLUBS

Using many of the same financial anchors that Europe does to fund its sports club systems for both mass participation and elite development, even a tax-adverse and capitalistically oriented country like the United States can fund alternative sports development models successfully in the short and long term. A robust funding system would draw on most or all of the following sources:

- Targeted federal, state, and local tax appropriations
- Membership fees

- Lottery proceeds
- Private philanthropy and partnerships
- Professional franchise and national governing body support
- Ancillary business operations
- Volunteerism
- Shared use of facilities and other resources

FUNDING OPTIONS THAT CAN BE APPLIED IN AMERICA

Targeted Federal, State, and Local Tax Appropriations

Public funding must be considered to be a major financial lynchpin for any of the proposed plans, and a review of how it works in Europe is needed when studying potential changes to the American way of funding sports. Among the European countries there are huge differences in public tax and levy funding regarding sports in general and sports clubs specifically. This is demonstrated by the fact that in Sweden roughly 0.5 percent of the gross domestic product is devoted to sports and recreation development, while the figure dips to 0.3 percent in Portugal. On average, European Union countries spend about 0.7 percent GDP for sports and recreation development.[1]

Meanwhile, in most European countries, overall community funding to support local sports facilities and clubs is typically higher than overall state funding. European tax-supported funding for sports clubs and activities is thus basically divided into two models. The first is defined as having a lower level of state funding and higher community financial support, such as in the Scandinavian countries, Austria, and Germany, where a decentralization of sports is dominant. In Germany, for example, local community funding is on average about ten times higher than state support. The other model is found in countries where state and community funding complement each other relatively equally, including Belgium, France, Italy, Portugal, and Spain (Miège 2011, 47–48). In the United States, we are already providing public funds for school-based athletic programs while at the same time requiring families and students to pay more and more out of their own pockets to participate in school sports. A redirecting of some or all of those public funds could assist in financially supporting any of the proposed models.[2]

The German federal government has declared that sports clubs are a place where people can meet and learn from each other, since physical exercise and sports participation connect people and overcome cultural, social, and language barriers. In fact, it infers that sports have vast potential to positively influence social change (Bundesregierung Deutschland 2010, 12). This demonstrates that health, wellness, and sports are valued by the government and explains why a large part of the funding of clubs and the sports sector comes from the government. These governmental goals are supported in the scholarly literature, which has repeatedly found that sports and sports development programs are important to countries because of their positive effects on values, health, entertainment, and social identity (Foster, O'Reilly, and Dávila 2016, 169).

Even with these worthy objectives, the basic law of Germany does not mention sports explicitly, and public authorities actually do not have a financial duty to promote sport. However, there is an accepted although unwritten responsibility of the German state to encourage sports participation, represent the country through promotion of its participation in the Olympic Games or world championships, and support the Deutscher Olympischer Sportbund and its member associations and clubs. Besides such efforts by the federal government, however, it is primarily the individual states' task to take measures that directly affect the clubs. This might be done, for instance, by financially supporting the construction or enhancement of facilities, the purchase of sports and other equipment, or the compensation of coaches and sports leaders, as well as through promoting sports-injury insurance programs (Foster, O'Reilly, and Dávila 2016, 12; Wegener 1992, 79).

Regarding public sports administration, German sports policy covers three basic areas: the autonomy of sport, subsidiarity of governmental sports promotion, and partnership and cooperation.[3] The autonomy of sport means that clubs and associations are guaranteed freedom of action under the basic law of the Federal Republic of Germany, assuring that any action taken by the state has to preserve the self-government and independence of the clubs. This is something that would resonate in America, where even with government funding there is widespread concern about unneeded government influence and regulation.

The subsidiarity of governmental sports promotion means that financial support is only provided by the state if sports organizations cannot afford to achieve particular goals on their own. Very large and commercially successful clubs like Bayern München can generate significant revenue streams, whereas the smaller clubs generally must count on public funding to maintain operations. Of course, smaller clubs in the United States could pursue similar revenue streams of the types discussed below, even if on a limited scale. Currently, some college athletic departments and, to a lesser extent, high school athletic programs in this country do generate significant revenue—through ticket and merchandise sales, donations, sponsorships, and partnerships—yet most rely greatly on public funding, and it should be expected that under a new club system the situation would be similar. Obviously, to the extent a club can generate independent revenue, it would receive less public funding.

Good partnership with the community and cooperation among sports clubs themselves are necessary for efficient sports promotion (Bundesregierung Deutschland 2010, 17). Cooperative measures among clubs will be addressed below. It should be noted here, though, that federal, state, and local government in the United States can do much to contribute to the financial viability of clubs and encourage partnership with the community. Assuming that clubs are set up as nonprofit organizations, there would be both direct tax relief for the clubs and indirect government support of community donations and partnerships through tax and other policies.

Of course, flaws can be found in Europe's various systems for government subsidy and other support for sports clubs. One that should be kept in mind is the difficulty of establishing solid measures of accountability. This is in part based on the fact that, even though most sports clubs in Europe have similar goals, as stated above, club charters are often very unclear about those goals and the organization's larger purpose, which can make it difficult to quantify management functions and monitor efficiency and effectiveness. The number of members in a club might be seen as one indication of success—but, on the other hand, smaller clubs don't serve their purpose any differently than bigger ones. A club's overall performance in athletic competitions might be seen as another—but that sort of athletic success doesn't necessarily mean that a club is meeting its other goals and fulfilling its other purposes, especially in regard to mass participation. A club's financial situation is another obvious indicator—but, again, it doesn't reliably tell us whether the club is achieving its other goals and purposes. There continue to be attempts in Europe to monitor clubs along these lines, but these criteria ultimately do not establish whether or not a club is successful in fulfilling some of its most important purposes (Thiel and Mayer 2009, 86–87). If America moves in this direction, it would be important—both in itself and as a way to ensure continued public support for government funding—to establish standard quantitative and qualitative measurements of success that can be evaluated against clear goals and statements of purpose.

Membership Fees

In one of its periodic "Eurobarometer" surveys, conducted in 2013, the European Commission examined sports and exercise participation across the European Union to determine what percentage of the population was engaging in athletic activity and where and how it was accessed (European Commission 2014). It found a high degree of variance in membership in sports clubs from country to country, ranging from low single-digit percentages to as much as one-quarter of those surveyed. There were also differences in participation across sociocultural and demographic groups, including by age and gender. Alternatives to sports clubs included membership in for-profit health clubs, exercising on one's own, or engaging in privately organized sports.

It should be expected that we would see similar variation in sports-club membership in such a large and diverse country as the United States. Of course, membership fees represent an important source of revenue for many nonprofit organizations, and it would be no different for sports clubs. However, the current cost of participation in American public and private sports and athletic clubs, teams, and developmental programs can be quite prohibitive, both for mass participation and for elite athlete development. If a broad-based club system were to be introduced, membership costs should be kept nominal (and should arguably be needs-based) in order to encourage and enable access across the economic spectrum. The losses to clubs from reduced participation fees can be offset by government and private funding. Membership fees are kept extremely low in Germany and elsewhere in Europe. In a recent report, the Deutscher Olympischer Sportbund found that roughly half of the sports clubs in Germany charged a monthly fee of no more than €2.50 for children (or approximately $3.10 in 2012, when the data was gathered), €3.10 ($3.85) for adolescents, and €6.20 ($7.70) for adults. Family memberships at an average cost of €12 ($15) per month were available at 62 percent of clubs (Breuer and Feiler 2013, 7). Of course, there can be other expenses involved beyond basic membership fees, but extremely low-cost barriers like this can guarantee that local sports clubs are able to offer sports and/or fitness programs that are affordable to almost everyone. Still, membership fees do have to be regarded as a critical source of funding, even with other subsidies available.

Lottery Proceeds

Lotteries and other gaming activities have been used across the globe as a way to fund many public projects and ongoing expenses. Most European countries with a robust sports club system turn to these options to provide financial support for operating expenses, equipment, facilities, and fields (Petry and Hallmann 2013, 79). In America, lottery proceeds in several states support such various government programs as public education, community development, crime control, environmental remediation, and public works projects. There are already examples of fitness and sports being funded by lottery proceeds in the form of parks, trails, school-based sports, and community recreational programs.

Setting aside the moral and ethical dilemmas involved in government-sponsored gambling, this certainly is a funding pool that can be tapped into to support new sports delivery models, especially given the public health benefits. There has been controversy in several states, as it has been claimed that some legislatures and government agencies have used lottery proceeds in ways that were never intended. Political controversy notwithstanding, there are of course good and bad points to using funds from lotteries and similar measures, and there have been varying degrees of success in their application—but, if managed properly, funds from state or national lotteries can go a long way toward assisting new sports-development programs to get off the ground and go on to achieve long-term success.

Private Philanthropy and Partnerships

As mentioned above, European countries provide tax deductions to private and corporate donors to sports clubs. Meanwhile, there is a long history in the United States of philanthropic efforts to support athletic programs at all levels, greatly encouraged by similar tax breaks. That type of support can easily transfer to a new sports-club system. Considering the elite-development aspect, one strong incentive for donors would be the prospect of enhanced national and international competitiveness for American athletes, as individuals and corporations want to be affiliated with winners. Even without that consideration, many donors would simply want to support good health and athletic achievement at all levels. Since companies and individuals are already funding health programs and athletics, we can expect that under a new model these funding flows will continue and potentially even increase.

One interesting source of direct funding, public-private partnership, and other forms of cooperation and collaboration can be found in the health and medical sector, including among health-care organizations, hospitals, and insurance companies. Currently, athletic organizations at all levels in the United States have cooperative and financial agreements with health-oriented organizations and companies. Many of these outside organizations and companies also pay sponsorship and affiliation fees to athletic organizations, colleges, and professional franchises. Further assistance is found in the form of directly providing or underwriting the cost of athletic training, health education, medical or paramedical personnel, and safety programs. There is often a mutual benefit, since providing personnel offers great experience for athletic trainers, emergency medical technicians, doctors, nurses, nutritionists, and dieticians. Many for-profit health-care and insurance companies are also in a position to contribute significant financial support to a local sports club or to offer free or low-cost health-care services.

Professional Franchise and National Governing Body Support

This may be one of the more controversial funding ideas, but it is time for the professional leagues in America to pay their fair share for sports development, from the lowest to the highest levels of development and competition. Many clubs in Europe do fund elite developmental programs and academies that produce professional players, but they also provide support for mass participation. Granted, there are professional leagues in the United States that already have developmental programs, academies, and minor leagues for elite development—notably, in baseball, soccer, and ice hockey—and these leagues often do, although to a much lesser extent, help fund mass-participation opportunities. Still, a large part of even elite development, and most especially health and sports development for the rest of our youth, goes on without such support.

Interestingly, the NFL—a league that might actually make a profit without selling a single ticket for three-plus years, due to the massive size of its television deals—provides no such support for its main source of talent: intercollegiate and interscholastic sports.[4] It is similar for the NBA, which, while it probably would not be able to sustain itself for three years based on television deals alone, could certainly do more for grassroots and developmental basketball. The money is there, but these leagues simply do not have the motivation to support developmental leagues and clubs because they already enjoy, for all intents and purposes, a free farm system provided at the expense of high schools and colleges. Yet, given that most professional sports leagues around the world provide significant financial support for developmental leagues and clubs, there is no reason the same can't be done here.

To a lesser extent, the United States Olympic Committee and other national sports governing bodies could also help fund new developmental systems, and not necessarily just for elite athletes. In many ways, they are already doing this, but we still rely primarily on school systems and colleges to pay for developing talent. These entities can reallocate funding and revenue-generating efforts to support either alternative models within the educational system, or models that move elite development and mass participation outside of it.

Ancillary Business Operations

Sports clubs in Europe have evolved from their origins as private initiatives driven by a community of like-minded people to become suppliers of sports and exercise opportunities that have to survive in a competitive market of commercial providers such as fitness clubs or yoga studios. Any American sports club system would face the same challenges. Many of the big sports clubs in Europe (with two thousand members or more) have already turned into multiservice providers. Their commercial enterprises are still under the umbrella of the actual club, but are often either outsourced or spun off as limited liability companies or stock corporations (Zimmer 2013). Of course, there are potential problems under any of these arrangements, in that sports clubs and companies pursue different goals. Sports clubs are focused on their community and make decisions cooperatively, whereas companies are hierarchically structured and designed to maximize efficiency and profit. It can be a difficult dance to have the people and missions involved coexist happily, as has often already been evidenced by the establishment of for-profit entities within American higher education.

However, having ancillary business operations within a club can be a great source of sustainable revenue. While the sports side might be operating in a nonprofit mode, club-based businesses would be operating for profit, with proceeds going to support the nonprofit mission. There is already a trend toward this kind of structure among US nonprofit organizations in many spheres, under the banner of "social enterprise." In European sports clubs, one often finds restaurants, pubs, or facilities that can be rented for various events such as festivals, weddings, and even town meetings. Some have theaters, studios that can be rented for yoga or dance classes, or even host academic and trade courses. These are not only a source of revenue, but can also contribute to the community cohesiveness that is such a prevalent aspect of European sports clubs. The club essentially becomes a community center that enables participation by everyone, in sports and many other activities. Certainly, the enormous difference between nonprofit and for-profit enterprises can possibly lead to an undermining of club and community values and goals, but it does not have to. In fact, it can actually support them, both philosophically and practically (Zimmer 2013).

Volunteerism

Since European sports clubs need volunteers to survive within their existing governance structures and as a business model, volunteer participation rates were also part of the survey referred to above. Again, there was great variety in rates of participation (European Commission 2014; Petry and Hallmann 2013, 79). Still, it is clear that most clubs in Europe can only operate thanks to volunteers, and it is not unusual and even common for a European citizen to have a paid job and also provide significant volunteer help to support the community, whether in a sports club, in social services, or elsewhere. Many volunteers in local sports clubs serve as officials, administrators, and coaches.[5] On average, 25 percent of German sports clubs engage paid workers, while the other 75 percent operate without any paid employees or with minimal paid staff. In total, 1.7 million volunteers (or 8.6 million, counting both "full-time volunteers" and "casual volunteers") put in a total of 24.1 million hours a year to support the mission of the German club system.[6] These numbers are similar to those found in other European countries, adjusted for total population. This type of active volunteerism creates a certain relationship between volunteers and clubs that leads to a more passionate and detailed level of involvement.

Even so, as in America, it is getting more difficult to recruit volunteers for sports operations. The German government set a goal in 2007 to improve conditions for volunteer work in all spheres, and new laws were eventually passed to stimulate volunteerism. Most important—and indicating areas where the United States can continue to look for ways to increase volunteerism—are laws that reduce the liability risk of volunteer managers and workers and that provide for tax and other financial incentives and benefits (Bundesregierung Deutschland 2010, 15).

As a result of commercialization and professionalization, the management of sports clubs in Europe has gotten more complex. Therefore, paid staff are hired in some cases because they have the knowledge and experience to cope with those complexities. The concern would be that this might increase conflicts due to differing motives, values, or expectations between volunteers and paid staff, which could diminish the commitment of volunteers. This is particularly problematic if volunteers become peripheral when it comes to decision-making power, since European sports clubs have traditionally been governed through democratic structures as autonomous entities (Jütting 1999, 54–55). However, strong leadership and standards should be able to mitigate this, and the need for dedicated volunteers will likely never fade. It will be important in Germany and elsewhere in Europe to continue to incentivize volunteers to serve, or more cost and effort will have to be expended to employ paid workers in their place (Thiel and Mayer 2009, 92–93).

Of course, America has its own long, proud history of volunteerism, including in youth sports. In fact, the Bureau of Labor Statistics consistently finds that about a quarter of the US population age sixteen and above volunteers at least once over the course of a year, and a large portion of those tens of millions of people volunteer on a regular basis. Although I am certain that all of the challenges and opportunities faced by sports clubs in Europe with regard to attracting and retaining volunteers would also be found here under a new sports club system, I am just as certain that we are up to the challenges and ready to seize the opportunities.

Shared Use of Facilities and Other Resources

Offices, sports facilities, fields, related equipment and supplies, and athletic equipment represent major cost areas. This is true whether we are talking about construction, expansion, improvement, or simple upkeep, and it may not be cost-effective to build additional facilities in the United States to support any new model. On the other hand, it may not be needed, at least on the scale that one might imagine. Just as in Europe, there is the possibility here of using existing public facilities, such as school and community gyms and fields. This is how many sports clubs in Europe manage such costs. In Germany, it was recently found that only 46.9 percent of sports clubs own sports facilities outright, and not all of them rely entirely on the ones they own. In fact, 61.6 percent of German sports clubs use municipal facilities, including school facilities (Breuer and Feiler 2013, 32).

Examples from Germany show great variety. The Nürnberg Rams do not own training grounds and are allowed to use city-owned fields either rent-free or at a nominal cost. TSV Ochenbruck uses a gymnasium that belongs to the local government, but also has its own outdoor training facilities, with two soccer fields and six tennis courts. SV Wiesenbronn and TSV Winkelhaid, on the other hand, use only club-owned facilities and do not need access to external facilities and fields. At the far end of the spectrum, FC Schalke 04, long known as one of Germany's best first-division soccer clubs, owns several facilities. The main club contains two fields, one gym, and the stadium for the professional Bundesliga team. The youth development program uses another two fields, one inside with artificial turf and one outside. In the United States, many such facilities and fields already exist, so that many sports clubs would be able to use what their communities already possess. Agreements for any use of external facilities can be negotiated and managed by local governments and organizations, with the possibility of subsidies by government and/or the private sector.

The cost of maintenance and upkeep is certainly a concern for European sports clubs, and it also will be a concern for American clubs. The pressing need to renovate sports facilities in Germany is reflected in an estimated €42 billion ($47.7 billion) of deferred and preferred maintenance projects, creating a significant bottleneck in the development and sustainability of German clubs (Deutscher Olympischer Sportbund 2014, 2). The condition of some facilities is so bad and so unfriendly to spectators that many stay away, a contributing factor to decreases in revenue. This is a problem that is being addressed more aggressively in Germany and many other European countries, and it is one that we should address more aggressively here. I believe that establishing a broad-based club system would actually serve as the needed catalyst to do so.

Since most of the external facilities that sports clubs use in Europe belong to schools, other public institutions, and municipalities, there can be issues in terms of overlapping demand. As a result, around 17 percent of German clubs claim that there are problems with the availability of gyms, swimming pools, playing fields, and the like. To some extent, this arises from the fact that German clubs offer so many sports, but the problem remains. In the United States, this will be another test of facilities management skills and of the relationships between organizations at the local level, but I am confident that such problems can and will be overcome.

Obviously, any major changes to sports development systems in America will come at a massive cost, and that funding has to come from somewhere. While this chapter has identified numerous potential sources of funding to make potential changes financially feasible, in my view the source of the money is not even the most difficult challenge to overcome if any of the potential models are in enacted in some form. The biggest challenge is the justification to change the current processes of sports delivery in America. The proposed cures can certainly justify the costs if the new system or systems are managed and implemented correctly. If areas like economics, public health, greater access to sports, academic integrity, and the fundamental rights of athletes at all levels are changed for the better in a more inclusive system, then potential savings later certainly justify the costs for needed change.

12

The Potential Future of Sports Development in America

> There is nothing more difficult and dangerous, or more doubtful of success, than an attempt to introduce a new order of things.
>
> —Niccolò Machiavelli, *The Prince*

NICCOLÒ MACHIAVELLI'S words from 1513 still ring true today as an apt description of the obstacles that must be surmounted in changing, re-imagining, and reframing sports development in the United States to positively influence current and future generations. This final chapter is an overview of the problems and solutions presented in previous chapters but also poses the "so what?" question and argues why you the reader should care. While the way sports are done in the United States is working very well for many, every day one can witness the negative effects of problems continually plaguing sports and sports development in the United States via scandal, injury, overtraining and even corruption. The primary issues that the proposed models can potentially solve, or at least certainly ameliorate, include economics, education, health and safety, access to sports, and athletes' rights. The problems in American sports will only get worse if the system does not change. Cracks in the educational façade are getting larger and more apparent to the American public, and the stated purpose of educationally based athletics is becoming simply an oxymoron.

It is clear to me, as well as to other scholars and to many stakeholders, that the system of sports in America needs to be changed. Our current approaches are simply not working as intended, and extreme external pressures will force changes sooner rather than later. The main barrier to change likely is widespread resistance to change itself, even among those who have the ability and power to effect positive changes in sports development and delivery. People are often afraid of change and terrified that a new way of doing things will not work as intended. Comfortable with the status quo, they end up in a mindset of believing what they want to be true, instead of facing the reality of what is actually happening. Despite any perceived flaws in our day-to-day lives, we tend to accept the familiar ways of doing things or adjust only incrementally to mimic change without any real substance. However, as Einstein stated, the very definition of insanity is to repeat the same thing over and over again and expect a different result. We seem to be doing just that in American sports development. Change is not comfortable, and implementing any of the proposals discussed in this book would not be a smooth and easy process, but we do have functional templates and models around the world that we can emulate.

What is the future of sports development and delivery in America? In my view, if we stay on the current path, the future is not promising. Maintaining the focus on certain sports because of their commercial viability will continue to harm multisport opportunities and widespread access to sport and exercise. Out-of-control spending on more commercially viable sports at all educational levels will produce many of the same effects. Moreover, the educational system will continue to erode as the broken union of education, elite sports development, and even mass-participation and recreational sports in America becomes even more of a potential economic burden through higher medical costs and a less active populace. Many changes are needed and the time to act is now. The myth that educationally based sports development meshes perfectly with academics will not survive much longer, and all stakeholders need to accept that change is critical. To me it's an easy sell. We have to care because the very foundation of American education is being threatened. We have to change how we fund and use education— and not sports—for primary social mobility in this country. True social mobility in society is primarily through education. While sport can certainly be a complement to a well-rounded education, it is not a panacea that replaces it. Sadly, with the increased emphasis on single sport specialization and elite sport development in our educational systems, sport has overwhelmed education as a supposed way to get ahead for underserved populations in America. This is largely a myth of access to educational opportunities that may not have been there without the chance to play sports simultaneously. While that is a larger and needed conversation to have concerning the overall educational system and access to a quality education regardless of zip code, it is a fallacy to assume that one can get access to a quality education based on athletic ability alone, especially when that athletic ability is valued more and is very valuable to others. Education can often be an afterthought.

Educational primacy in the United States, or what was once thought of as the best educational system in the world, has been falling behind countries that aren't nearly as developed. Our higher education system is crumbling under funding challenges and rudderless leadership. The lack of opportunities for participation in sports is having a dramatic negative effect on the health and welfare of Americans. We can and we must improve our educational and sports participation infrastructure in the country before we shut out more and more people based on our thirst for elite athlete performance at the expense of greater benefits and access for all.

We want to believe that the way we are conducting and managing educationally based sports development in America is actually working the way it was intended, because in theory it sounds perfect. Getting an education while playing sports—that sounds great. Receiving a full athletic scholarship to cover massive college tuition costs—well, sign me up! It is easier to believe in what are essentially myths of school-based athletics than to face the facts of the transformation that is needed. The ideal of school-based sports as initially conceived more than a century ago is no longer the current model, and many of the tenets that may have applied then—if they ever really did apply—certainly do not apply now. Times have changed, and if amateurism and the purity of school-based sports did not work as intended a century ago, they won't work now. America must forget its assumptions about the uneasy marriage of education and sports and develop a system—or better yet, systems—that will benefit more citizens today both educationally and athletically.

We need to deal with what our sports development system actually is, and not what we hope it is or wish it could be, and take concrete action to fix it.

Why is this important to the future of our society? And should it be a political and legal priority, considering everything else going on in the country, not to mention the world? I often say that although on the surface the current way of doing sports in America looks great, the infrastructure and purpose are flawed. My favorite analogy with regard to sports development and sports governance compares them to the experience of dining in a favorite restaurant. Patrons are often advised to stay in the dining room and not to go into the kitchen to see what is really going on there. With regard to sports development, many observers, myself included, have nevertheless gone "into the kitchen" of American educationally based sports and have viewed firsthand the corruption, economic imbalance, lack of access, overzealous pursuit of victory, and degeneration of the educational purpose of American athletics. The current system has failed, to the extent that I believe it cannot be tweaked, adjusted, or saved in its current form. It is time for a radical departure and paradigm shift from what we are currently doing. The proposed models present templates to accomplish just that.

Think for a minute about what Tom Farrey said in his foreword—"Do not marinate in nostalgia." We as a society need to accept that there can be a better way of doing things, especially in sports, to benefit a large segment of the populace. If any politician said to this country that there is a way to improve education and educational access for all income levels, enhance the health and welfare of American children and adults, and accomplish all that by reinvesting and recalibrating public tax dollars via massive medical costs savings, and also using and capitalizing on private investment, I believe many would jump on board and support the effort. However, if one proposes changing educationally based sports forevermore by creating a federated National Sports Policy with a local sports club system supported primarily by tax dollars, while improving health and wellness and lowering medical costs for everyone, I would wager most people would be very skeptical and against it. Adding to that a proposal to relocate competitive sports development primarily outside the educational borders while moving schools toward a greater emphasis on physical education, exercise, and mass participation than on elite development would cause an uproar from many who remain comfortable in the current educationally based system and benefit financially from it.

The proposed models or portions thereof are a foundation for discussion to improve the unworkable system we have now. If education is the most important issue, then there is a pathway to achieving that in all of the models. If access for all alongside elite development is a primary driver, there are models for that also—or at the very least, alternatives can be created to relieve stress on America's educational system at all levels. In other words, there are better ways to accomplish sports development and delivery in the United States; we just simply need to have the will to act. Make no mistake, the resistance to any change will be formidable. The uproar would largely be from those who crave the exciting entertainment, passion, and emotional connection that educationally based sports provide, but I hope this book demonstrates that at least a discussion of potential changes needs to be considered, if not fast-tracked. America is under immense economic pressure caused by subsidizing ever-growing and expensive athletic operations that support fewer athletes and fewer sport opportunities while often depreciating education. A considerable amount of angst and powerful resistance to any change would also come from the minority that benefits financially from the current system, such as shoe companies, individual agents, the schools themselves, and of course the media, just to name a few. Paradoxically, the resistance would likely not be from the people who actually deserve the change the most—the athletes and others who are being left behind. Just as the world's wealth is controlled by a few people, educationally based athletics in the United States, most notably in the sports that generate revenue, are also controlled by a few, but we cannot lose sight of how a reframing of athletics in America can advantage all levels of athletic and healthy activity. The athletes and participants at all skill levels will find not merely a marginal benefit with any of the new models proposed, but also a lifestyle change that could benefit society overall. I strongly believe a movement like this should not be resisted and extinguished by the powerful few and their greed, though resist they will. However, this is a battle worth fighting.

CAN AMERICA BE CONVINCED?

During my time in Europe conducting research for this book, many sports professionals and students I interviewed expressed the feeling that America's system was near perfect. Some even believed that Europe should move to an American-style educationally based sports system, convinced by the façade it presents. Who could really blame them, considering the public relations and commercial success of US education-based sports programs? Many in America feel the same way and passionately believe in the current system. It was not until after several discussions with my European colleagues and students and the opportunity to present empirical evidence and films such as *Schooled: The Price of College Sports* that most opinions were swayed. Almost all of the people I spoke to in Europe had a clean slate with regard to opinions on college sports and not, as in the United States, a historically embedded fervent and positive belief in the hundred-year-old system. By "clean slate" I mean that even though many in Europe had some idea of educationally based sports in America, specifically college sports, they did not have the culturally embedded and significant feelings (positive and negative) that many Americans have because of over a century of existence in the United States. It is a much tougher sell in America because many have long-standing biases toward the current model and many benefit from the current system. I was encouraged by my interactions in Europe with regard to getting the message out and believe that as more Americans are educated about the problems in the sports development system in this country, we can finally begin to have a rational discussion on how to repair it.

This project was not intended to sugar-coat where we are with our current model of sports development. I firmly believe that we must change and that there is no single best change. The models presented earlier are intended to encourage conversation about alternatives. Interscholastic and intercollegiate sports purists maintain that the connection to academics and educational institutions is what makes these sports competitive and attractive to the masses. In essence, the claim is that there would be no market for these sports without their being tethered to and embedded in education, and they would cease to exist. I profoundly disagree, but also ponder whether that would be the worst thing that could happen—or do we even really care? Personally, I don't think so. If we did truly care, we would already be clamoring for the changes called for in Model 1 or even Model 4 to bring school-based athletic programs back to being an actual part of education and not something that exists in spite of it.

Ideally, the United States will move toward other development models and leagues rather than completely blowing up the educationally based system. That system can surely survive, if not thrive, as Aresco and Matthews noted many years ago in front of the Knight Commission, without elite athletes who would and should have other sport development options outside of the educational space. It is tempting to believe that any problems with educationally based sports are on the periphery and not endemic to the entire system. Unfortunately, the exact opposite is true. Study after study and book after book, many of which are cited here, detail many problems and solutions for American sports development. This book presents options and solutions to consider for change and to begin again. Most important, my research and these ideas demonstrate that there is not a single best approach to change, but potential combinations of many ideas and models that can replace the archaic and outdated educational model that we have currently in the United States. These proposals, or parts thereof, can and will bring the United States more in line with other countries and provide greater benefits to citizens.

DO WE NEED SUCH RADICAL CHANGE?

The answer is yes, and I hope readers understand that better at this point, given the empirical research and external pressures that will eventually mandate adjustments. America's current educationally based model will not survive, and the pressure points for change are becoming overwhelming. Funding, sport elimination, and the continuing erosion of educational primacy in America, often due to an overemphasis on elite athletics, will only continue to get worse. We cannot continue to express concern, claim financial problems, and look away from a disaster just so we can keep the entertainment and money flowing. At the end of the day, we really just want to watch the games. America needs to be honest about what we are doing, or change it for the better. Holding on to the tenet of amateurism and tethering most sport activity to education is not helping America in sports development, education, or public health, and it is damaging overall because the focus is currently on winning and revenue generation rather than on participation.

Education in America is suffering, and as a nation we need to refocus on how we deliver education, how much it will cost, and how it can best prepare college students for the workforce and leadership roles of the future. Focusing only on their success as high school or college athletes while making education secondary is essentially criminal. While educationally based sports can be an important part of education in presenting opportunities for exercise, creating better and healthier students and workers, the current model does not have the far-reaching and systemic benefits for more citizens that the proposed models could have. Numerous empirical studies have confirmed the educational value of sports participation. Learning the valuable tenets of sports participation can be an important part of one's educational advancement, but it is important to acknowledge that it does not have to be in the current educational and/or overpriced external sports development model. Changing the way sport is managed in the United States will have significant beneficial effects for many more people.

The Drake Group founder and my TDG colleague Dr. Jon Ericson, the former provost at Drake University, has one of the best responses to sports reform. Simply put—*no tinkering!* We cannot make adjustments along the edges to attempt to modify a thoroughly broken system. Components of our educationally based model may have existed for well over a hundred years, but it really has never worked in the way it was intended. It is time to try something else, but it must be something different and tangible that will benefit athletes and participants at all levels. New proposed models, like the ones discussed in previous chapters, can enhance elite development and performance of American athletes who find that competitive and high-level training opportunities are vanishing at the scholastic and intercollegiate levels. New models can address where education fits and can encourage participation in sports and physical exercise. Prompting the citizenry of America and the government to create new opportunities for competition and physical exercise can deliver a cultural change to American society for the next generations and make society healthier overall, but it cannot be done incrementally or partially. It must involve wholesale changes, and the time to start is now.

DO NOT FEAR BLOWING UP THE SYSTEM!

The sky will not fall and we as a country will not cease to exist if we examine, consider, and adopt new models of sports development inside and outside the current educational model. We must acknowledge the truth of our current educationally based sports system and then take steps toward meaningful change. Predictions of gloom and doom did not cause professional sports to disintegrate when free agency and greater player rights became legislated and commonplace in the 1970s. Sports fans in America are resilient. We have learned to live with and accept the huge salaries, free player movement between teams, salary caps, and contract holdouts as part of professional sports. We survived the three-point shot, player strikes, owner lockouts, dunking in college basketball, and even interleague play in Major League Baseball when many sports fans, administrators, and scholars said those innovations and interruptions would be detrimental to those games and sports. The Olympics did not become immaterial when professional athletes were allowed to compete in the 1980s and former "amateur" athletes were allowed to profit commercially. As fans, we may have preferred the way things were in pro sports and the Olympic Games many years ago, but we adapted to the changes, and we continue to love these sports entities today. American sports have evolved in many ways, and sports fans have continued to stay with them for better or worse. I contend the same will happen if we make the wholesale changes this book proposes.

The easiest course is to do nothing and just hope and pray that the system doesn't derail on its own. Oftentimes that is what many stakeholders such as coaches, administrators, athletes, and fans are doing in college sports, and to a lesser extent in high school sports. The bottom line is winning, and everything else has become secondary. Revenue generation and the belief that a successful athletic program can drive the nonathletic success of an institution are to blame. To me it is clear that if we want to maintain some semblance of educationally based sports in America and if that system is as important as claimed, then we should not be concerned about potentially paying athletes or letting them capitalize on their marketing utility. How would that affect the value of the sports experience? It certainly would not keep us from watching competitive sports. We should already be outraged at the state of educationally based sports in our country. We should be outraged because of the educational façade, the time that we are requiring athletes to spend on their sports, sports specialization, and the public health crisis we have now in our country. As historian Barbara Tuchman once wrote, "*Telling the truth about a given condition is absolutely requisite to any possibility of reforming it.*" We need to acknowledge where we are going and begin to make the needed changes. Even some of the most jaded supporters of the status quo of the system, such as current NCAA president Mark Emmert, add their voices to groups working for change, such as youth sports advocates like the Aspen Institute's Project Play and the Drake Group, in acknowledging that the system is on its last legs and that some type of reform is imminent.

This is precisely why we need wholesale changes that will provide the greatest good for the greatest number and not just keep billions of dollars in the pockets of a few. The long-standing principle of Utilitarianism can serve as a moral and ethical compass for any future changes to American sports development. Utilitarianism, the philosophy of Jeremy Bentham and John Stuart Mill, holds that morality is determined by its usefulness for as many as possible. Arguably, the current system is one of selfishness and greed that is moving further away from the educational model, while benefitting only a few. This type of greed and power that guides many other industries, institutions, and the government has also been a powerful force in American sports at all levels. Even with this struggle, we can frame it and get in front of the changes to advantage as many citizens as possible. The challenges for modification in the way we do sports in America can be equated to how few people actually control the wealth and political systems in America along with making the most of the decisions, good or bad, that affect so many. It can be inferred that these political decisions are often made with an eye toward donors, companies and political expediency that benefit individuals rather than the larger citizenry. Politicians often state a piece of legislation is good because it can do the greatest good for the greatest number of citizens. As individuals we justify our own actions because they are perceived to be for the greater good. This is the moral and ethical approach we must take as this country is moving toward certain alterations and evolution in sports governance and sports development.

Changing the mindset and recognizing the flaws in the system and its governance are absolute prerequisites and a baseline to start reform. New models of sports development and governance need to be part of a larger revolution—a revolution that can empower people to have choices about how and where to participate in sports and exercise, make people healthier and more productive, and preserve educational importance. Mass-participation opportunities and multisport options continue to be eliminated for our youth and throughout our educational institutions, but as a country we have not asked the hard questions nor made the hard decisions to enable change. The aforementioned proposed models, or even parts of them, can bring positive change. It is a long-term generational effort, but it is an effort worth undertaking. It is not mere tinkering, as the models are proposals for real change that will benefit many more than our current sports system does. We must act as a country now.

Notes

PREFACE

1. Frank (2015), presentation, Ohio State University Sports and Society Initiative, u.osu.edu/sportsandsociety/files/2015/10/SportsandSociety-1pkzj8s .pptx. See also Scott Frank, University of Findlay (Ohio), pending dissertation on sports fees for interscholastic sports.

2. Taylor Branch's (2011) epic takedown of sports in higher education can be found in "The Shame of College Sports." See also Morgan 2012.

3. Christian Papay, chair of business administration, University of Wurzburg (Germany), in discussion with the author, April 2015. Papay was also the venue media manager for the Gdansk site in the 2012 UEFA European Championship (Euro 2012).

4. The number of students from US universities representing other countries in international competitions is growing. During the 2008 Beijing Summer Olympic Games, out of the approximately 10,500 athletes competing, 317 of the non-US athletes had competed at just ten US universities (Farrell 2008).

5. *Sport Development in the United States* is the most comprehensive book to date not only in addressing the potential crisis in American sports development but in providing a workable theory for positive change. The authors propose an "ideal-type model for an integrated elite and mass sport system" (Smolianov, Zakus, and Gallo 2015, 14–19). Their proposal, the "Smolianov and Zakus model," was first put forth in 2008. It includes three levels of support. The first, the "macro-level," includes balanced and integrated funding of structures for both elite and mass participation in sport, along with public and private partnerships with supporting agencies. The second, "meso-level," includes educational, scientific, medical, philosophical, and promotional support, along with a system of competitions and training centers. The last is the "micro-level," which addresses the elite athlete and consists of operations, processes, and methodologies for talent development and support. Other notable

works on sports-development models are Dittmore, Mahony, and Andrew 2008; and Sparvero, Chalip, and Green 2008.

6. My Ohio University and Drake Group colleague, Dr. John R. Gerdy, has been a leader in the sports reform movement for several years. A former star basketball player at Davidson College, legislative assistant for the NCAA, and associate commissioner of the Southeastern Conference, he has also been pushing for increased funding for music and the arts in schools. His *Ball or Bands* (2014) is an excellent overview of how sports funding has displaced arts and educational funding, and the massive problems that have come with that.

CHAPTER 1: WHY AMERICA NEEDS ALTERNATIVE MODELS OF SPORTS DEVELOPMENT AND DELIVERY

1. Canada recently released its 2016 ParticipACTION report on physical activity and sports development in the country and its 2015 Report Card on Physical Activity in Youth. These excellent reports detail means of getting an entire country involved and the impact that physical activity can have on the health and well-being of its citizens. https://www.participaction.com/sites/default/files/downloads/PA-ImpactReport-2016_final_no_crops.pdf; https://www.participaction.com/sites/default/files/downloads/Participaction-2015ReportCard-FullReport_4.pdf.

2. There are several works that discuss national lotteries and the taxation of other forms of gambling as a sustainable funding source for sports clubs. Among the best is one mandated by the European Union, "Strengthening Financial Solidarity Mechanisms within Sport" (Expert Group on Sustainable Financing of Sport 2012).

3. The sportswriter Frank Deford speaks to this in the outstanding documentary *Schooled: The Price of College Sports* (Finkel, Martin, and Paley 2013), shown on EPIX television and produced by Andrew Muscato, Taylor Branch, and Domonique Foxworth. Branch, one of the world's foremost civil rights historians, wrote an article for the *Atlantic* titled "The Shame of College Sports" (Branch 2011) that became the basis for *Schooled*. Branch, who did not consider himself a sports fan, was asked by former University of North Carolina president William Friday to essentially provide an unbiased review of the state of college sports. His article, while not surprising to many observers, was groundbreaking, and brought many problems of educationally based sports to the surface. Not surprisingly, members of the NCAA's national office refused to be interviewed for either the article or the documentary. See also Coakley 2014; Lumpkin 2015; Sack and Zimbalist 2013.

4. National Collegiate Athletic Association 2014, 59. See also Huma and Staurowsky 2012.

5. The International Olympic Committee (IOC) began to accept professional tennis, ice hockey, and soccer players for the 1988 summer and winter games. After 1988, the IOC decided to open up all events to professional athletes, subject to the approval of international sports federations—which, predictably, complied. Although the IOC allowed for athlete compensation

outside of sports activities starting in 1971, all US Olympic athletes still had to be amateurs until 1978, creating a definite unequal playing field. This was a major reason for the United States to move to allowing its athletes to receive compensation and still join the US Olympic delegation, as they otherwise found it difficult to compete against those from other nations who were sponsored by their governments and able to train full-time. In 1978, the United States adopted the Ted Stevens Olympic and Amateur Sports Act, allowing athletes on the US Olympic team to receive financial awards, sponsorship, and payments for the first time (Thomas 1985).

6. The long-standing argument is that many college (and, for that matter, high school) athletes already meet the definition of professional athletes because they are receiving measurable compensation in the form of merchandise, meals, travel, and, of course, college scholarships. Others would argue that, because of the money generated through sports at these levels, the athletes are professionals even if they are not directly paid.

7. It is very easy to see that an emphasis on eligibility rather than education is prominent in higher-profile sports like football and men's basketball. In a study published in the *Journal of Legal Aspects of Sport*, Dr. Gerry Gurney, Dr. Eric Snyder, and I found that almost half of the major academic violations since the NCAA started tracking this information involved football and men's basketball (Ridpath, Gurney, and Snyder 2015).

8. Most of the information here on Parker and Schröder was gleaned from the master's thesis of Carolin Frei, one of my graduate students and research assistants at the University of Bayreuth (Frei 2015).

9. Simeon Career Academy has consistently been one of the top high school basketball teams in the nation. Anderson played thirteen years in the NBA with three teams. Rose recently moved to the New York Knicks after eight seasons with the Chicago Bulls. Wilson, who was considered by many to be the top high school player in the nation as he entered his senior year, lost his life to gun violence in November 1984 at the age of seventeen.

10. Revenue from the NCAA Division I men's basketball tournament, estimated to have been $700 million in 2014, is largely derived from a fourteen-year, $10.8 billion television, internet, and wireless rights agreement with CBS Sports and Turner Broadcasting System that started in 2011. The $700 million funds the operations of the NCAA national office in Indianapolis, Indiana, which can run the gamut from salaries, travel, and external meetings to legal defense. While it is often said that 96 percent of the revenue goes back to the athlete, it is really a sleight of hand. While some money is returned to the member institutions in the form of scholarships, academic assistance, and other student-centered funding, the $700 million also funds championships in all three divisions, enforcement operations, membership services, and other business operations.

11. According to the NCAA's own statistics, only a very small percentage of college athletes make the professional ranks, with football and men's basketball showing among the lowest rates: only 1.2 percent of college basketball players are

drafted by the NBA, and 1.6 percent of football players are drafted by the NFL. The average professional careers are five years or less. See http://www.ncaa .org/about/resources/research/probability-competing-beyond-high-school.

12. A great collection of Kane's work and an overview of the entire UNC academic athletic scandal can be found at http://www.newsobserver.com/news /local/education/unc-scandal/article72207687.html.

13. Hesburgh is referring to the Knight Commission on Intercollegiate Athletics, established in 1988. Although the commission is not a policy-making body, the NCAA has adopted, in whole or in part, many of the recommendations presented during its various iterations over the past decades. More information can be found at www.knightcommission.org.

CHAPTER 2: INTERSCHOLASTIC AND INTERCOLLEGIATE ATHLETICS DEVELOPMENT IN THE UNITED STATES

1. In 2014, the NCAA membership passed permissive rules allowing, but not mandating, institutions to pay a stipend up to the level of the cost of attendance (COA) at NCAA institutions. The traditional athletic scholarship covers, wholly or in part, the cost of tuition, room and board, books, and course-related fees. COA is a federal formula determined by each institution that includes items beyond the traditional scholarship elements, like travel, clothing, additional bills, and spending money. In the 2015–16 academic year, COA figures varied widely, from around $1,600 at Boston College to a high of almost $7,000 at the University of Cincinnati. Many coaches feel a higher COA is a recruiting advantage, but it is hard to justify that when actual cost of living levels are different across the country, and COAs, at least in theory, track those levels. At this point, any real advantages or disadvantages in recruiting have not been systematically studied.

2. Even though the one-year scholarship system lasted more than forty years, it was continually debated as a problem due to fact that the athletes could lose their scholarship for any reason (including athletic ability) at the end of the period of the award. Subsequent legislative pressure and legal and advocacy challenges, specifically by athletes' rights groups, led the NCAA in 2014 to allow schools to offer four-year scholarships that ostensibly cannot be taken away for an athletics-related reason, but only according to the same university-determined standards used for all students.

3. NCAA v. Board of Regents of the University of Oklahoma, 468 U.S. 85 (1984).

4. While there were legitimate worries that some schools would become more powerful than others if allowed to negotiate their own TV contracts (ultimately proven true), the main concern was that unrestricted televised games would damage the live gate and atmosphere. Arguably, this has not happened—but there appear to be more recent signals that both overall ticket sales and student attendance are dropping, likely due to the ability now to access hundreds of games on many platforms.

5. Drake University currently plays in the non-scholarship Pioneer League, a Football Championship Series (FCS) (formerly 1-AA) conference. Many 1-AA

teams used to play in Division I with the major schools until 1978, when NCAA Division I football was further subdivided so that lower-resource institutions could compete against each other. Currently, NCAA Division I football, or Football Bowl Championship Series (BCS), teams are permitted 85 head-count scholarships, while 1-AA (FCS) teams can offer 63 equivalency scholarships. The equivalency designation means that FCS awards can be segmented and spread across more athletes, while in FBS/BCS schools it is one scholarship per player.

6. Like a return to the four-year scholarship, restoring freshman ineligibility (or "year of readiness") has been getting serious consideration among scholars, critics, and supporters alike. Recently, the Big 10 (Division I) conference has been considering freshman ineligibility for football and men's basketball. See the white paper *Education First, Athletics Second* (Delany 2015), distributed by Big Ten commissioner Jim Delany. Others, like The Drake Group, recommend a year of readiness for all who do not meet the profile of the incoming class by falling more than one standard deviation lower than the mean incoming class average, measured by performance in high school and standardized test scores. This would also include restrictions on practice time and competition (Gurney et al. 2015).

7. Amateurism and extra benefits are covered primarily in NCAA Bylaws 12 and 16.

8. The judge in the case seemed to agree with Bloom that his compensation was not a violation, but decided not to rule in Bloom's favor because of the NCAA restitution rule under Bylaw 19. This bylaw states, "If a student-athlete who is ineligible under the terms of the Constitution, bylaws or other legislation of the Association is permitted to participate in intercollegiate competition contrary to such NCAA legislation but in accordance with the terms of a court restraining order or injunction operative against the institution attended by such student-athlete or against the Association, or both, and said injunction is voluntarily vacated, stayed or reversed or it is finally determined by the courts that injunctive relief is not or was not justified, the Board of Directors may take [action] against such institution in the interest of restitution and fairness to competing institutions." The judge did not want to put the University of Colorado in further jeopardy, effectively killing Bloom's hope of recourse through the legal system.

9. Hearing transcript can be found at http://commdocs.house.gov /committees/judiciary/hju95802.000/hju95802_0.HTM. Also YouTube video (Ridpath Congressional Testimony Part 3) at https://www.youtube.com /watch?v=Dhc-hN5fqd0.

10. The NCAA has asserted "procompetitive justification" in the O'Bannon case, which in simple terms would allow it to prohibit college athletes from receiving any form of compensation. The NCAA cites four reasons for procompetitive justification, including the preservation of amateurism, competitive balance, integration of academics and athletics, and increased outputs. Underlying all of this, though, is their claim that intercollegiate athletics would

become less popular and the market in college sports would therefore suffer. Details on the judge's ruling in the O'Bannon case regarding procompetitive justification can be found at http://www.bgsfirm.com/college-sports-law-blog /obannon-v-ncaa-summarizing-the-courts-opinion.

11. LeBron James had several issues regarding his amateur status and eligibility at Akron's St. Vincent–St. Mary High School. These included his allegedly receiving a sports utility vehicle and, in a separate incident, two sports jerseys. James was cleared regarding the vehicle but ruled ineligible because of the jerseys (Wise 2003). He appealed and, after missing two games, was reinstated.

12. Broh (2002, 72) suggests that "sports participation offers student-athletes higher peer status that facilitates membership in 'the leading crowd'" among the student body as a whole, as well as status in the separate social sphere developed among high school athletic participants.

13. In American high schools, athletic eligibility is typically determined by a grade point average and being a full-time enrolled student. Standards vary by state, but for public schools the minimum grade point average (GPA) generally falls between 1.6 (around a D+ average) and 2.0 (C average). Private schools also have their own rules on athletic eligibility.

14. The *Raleigh News and Observer* led the media exposé of this scandal, pressuring the university for answers and uncovering major facts to which UNC eventually admitted. Dozens of articles are available that document the scandal, primarily written by investigative reporter Dan Kane over a period of four years. See http://www.newsobserver.com/news/local/education/unc -scandal/article72207687.html.

CHAPTER 3: THE EUROPEAN SPORTS CLUB AND SPORTS DELIVERY SYSTEMS

1. In most of the world's professional sports leagues, most notably in Europe, "relegation and promotion" means that team performance is rewarded and punished, with the worst teams in a particular league being demoted to a lower league, while the best teams are promoted to a higher league. As one who experienced this as a fan and a researcher, I felt it made the entire season much more worthwhile, competitive, and exciting, compared with the set system of teams in American sports leagues. Noll (2002) provides a valuable discussion of the economics and benefits of a promotion and relegation system.

2. Muscular Christianity is discussed in Miracle and Rees's *Lessons of the Locker Room* (1994). This is a movement originating in Victorian England based on the belief that physical activity, especially team sports, makes a great contribution to society and develops morality and patriotism along with transferable skills used later in life. These are many of the same arguments currently used in favor of school-based sports in the United States. *Lessons of the Locker Room* is primarily an attempt to debunk popular, long-held "myths" about the positive connection between school sports and social values.

3. Although it is somewhat different today, students in the German education system have long been separated on the basis of academic achievement

and early testing to determine aptitude. The three levels of primary and secondary schools (Hauptschule, Realschule, and Gymnasium) still exist, but admission requirements are looser than before. However, the same issues still arise regarding school location, the separation of youth in particular neighborhoods, having classmates from a variety of neighborhoods, and interaction with sports-club teammates who are typically neighbors.

4. The Philadelphia 76ers, once a proud National Basketball Association franchise, have become a prime example of accepting losing in hope of gaining early-round draft picks to aid a long-term program. Even with this strategy, and gaining high-profile picks like Nerlens Noel, the 76ers have consistently been the worst team in the NBA for the past three years, as of this writing, and ended a 28-game losing streak on December 1, 2015.

5. Much of the information on Lahm was gathered by University of Bayreuth undergraduate student Simon Von Schwedler during my sabbatical there.

6. In Europe, the age of sixteen is the typical point when athletes are identified in the local sports clubs as candidates for elite preparation. Many options are then available for the athlete who chooses to go on to elite training. Those can include sports academies such as the one Philipp Lahm attended, a Sports School, an Olympic Base camp, or some combination thereof.

CHAPTER 4: THE POSITIVE GAIN FOR PUBLIC HEALTH AND THE CITIZENRY OF THE UNITED STATES

1. Institute of Medicine (2013), *Educating the Student Body: Taking Physical Activity and Physical Education to School.* Report can be found at http://iom .nationalacademies.org/Reports/2013/Educating-the-Student-Body-Taking -Physical-Activity-and-Physical-Education-to-School.aspx.

2. Centers for Disease Control and Prevention, "Deaths and Mortality," last updated October 7, 2016, https://www.cdc.gov/nchs/fastats/deaths.htm.

3. The figures following are from Bundesministerium für Gesundheit 2014.

4. Body Mass Index (BMI) is a formula that demonstrates a weight-to-height ratio. It is calculated by dividing one's weight by the square of one's height and is expressed in units of kg/m^2. A BMI of 25 is considered borderline overweight, while 30 is the threshold for obesity.

5. Deutsche Gesellschaft für Kardiologie 2014; Centers for Disease Control and Prevention, "Heart Disease," last updated October 7, 2016, https://www .cdc.gov/nchs/fastats/heart-disease.htm.

6. Information on the study can be found in the Forbes article linked below by Bruce Y. Lee of Johns Hopkins University. Lee holds several positions at Johns Hopkins, including Associate Professor of International Health at the Johns Hopkins Bloomberg School of Public Health, Executive Director of the Global Obesity Prevention Center (GOPC: www.globalobesity.org), and Associate Professor at the Johns Hopkins Carey Business School. https://www .forbes.com/sites/brucelee/2016/05/17/getting-children-more-physical -active-could-save-well-over-50-billion/#291c58761133.

CHAPTER 5: THE EDUCATIONAL CONUNDRUM AND THE NEED
FOR A COMPREHENSIVE NATIONAL SPORTS POLICY IN THE UNITED STATES

1. A good overview of the 1998 The Ted Stevens Olympic and Amateur Sports Act (36 U.S. Code § 220501) can be found at the Legal Information Institute of Cornell Law School website at https://www.law.cornell.edu /uscode/text/36/220501.

2. Littlefield (2015) provides information on Reed and Nader's plan. Reed (2014) also discusses the need for a national sports policy or ministry to open access and increase participation in sporting activities rather than continue to morph into a nation of sedentary sports spectators. Seehttp://www .huffingtonpost.com/ken-reed/is-it-time-for-a-national_b_5600613.html.

3. For an excellent discussion of the need for a national sports policy and several ideas on how to create and scale one, see the panel presentation "Call for Leadership: From Treetops to Grass Roots: How to Scale a Culture of Health in Sports?" held on May 17, 2016, at the Project Play Summit in Washington, DC (accessible via https://aspenprojectplay.org/events/2016-project -play-summit). Many of those ideas are presented in this chapter. Panel members included moderator Tom Farrey, ESPN reporter and executive director of the Aspen Institute's Sports & Society Program; Mary Davis, CEO of Special Olympics International; Benita Fitzgerald Mosely, CEO of the Laureus Sport for Good Foundation USA; Dr. Risa Lavizzo-Mourey, president and CEO of the Robert Wood Johnson Foundation and member of the President's Council on Fitness, Sports and Nutrition; Jorge Perez, senior vice president of YMCA of the USA; and Jim Whitehead, CEO of the American College of Sports Medicine.

4. Personal email exchanges with Tom Farrey of the Aspen Institute and Sally Ann Reiss, CEO and founder of PlayyOn.com.

5. Since leaving Ohio, Hocutt has been the athletic director at the University of Miami (Florida) and is currently the athletic director at Texas Tech University.

6. Section 901(a) of Title IX of the Education Amendments of 1972 provides: "No person in the United States shall, on the basis of sex, be excluded from participation in, be denied the benefits of, or be subjected to discrimination under any education program or activity receiving Federal financial assistance." While initially the statute didn't specifically deal with athletics, the growth of women's sports dictated the need to address continuing inequities between women's and men's sports. In 1979, the Department of Health, Education, and Welfare's Office for Civil Rights issued a policy interpretation that did so (Office for Civil Rights 1979). In brief, it stated that female athletes and teams must be provided equity in financial assistance (mainly scholarships) proportionate with overall female enrollment, in treatment (e.g., equipment, travel, per diems), and in meeting the interests and abilities of female athletes. Title IX remained virtually unenforced until Congress passed the Civil Rights Restoration Act of 1987, which clarified that Congress had intended Title IX to

apply to an entire school if any of its programs or activities receive federal funding (20 U.S.C. § 1687 [1987]). The law finally went into effect in 1988—sixteen years after Title IX's enactment.

7. There have been numerous strikes and lockouts in professional sports. It is clear that public, legal, and government pressure will often bring an end to any work stoppage, with the players many times gaining some of the concessions they seek. When the NFL Players Association went on strike in 1987, the league chose to continue operations with replacement players. While some teams had success at the box office, most suffered, with abysmal attendance, fan protests against replacement players crossing the picket lines, and low television ratings, forcing a settlement between the league and the NFLPA—likely sooner than it would have come without the use of replacement players.

8. Sack and Zimbalist (2013) wrote an excellent white paper on college sports and the shifting definition of amateurism, the best line of which, in my opinion, is that "amateurism is whatever the NCAA says it is" (5). This is an accurate reflection of how we see—or are expected to see—the amateur athlete in the United States.

9. This support was provided by way of the National College Players Association, which has longed received backing and funding from the United Steelworkers (USW), one of the most powerful labor unions in the world. On the USW website, the NCPA is listed as an ally and partner and described as follows: "The National College Players Association (NCPA) is a group started by UCLA football players that serves as a powerful advocacy group for college athletes across the nation. Since its first press conference on Jan. 18, 2001, the NCPA has established itself as the voice for college athletes. The NCPA mission is to provide the means for college athletes to voice their concerns and change NCAA rules." Information on the USW and its partners can be found at http://www.usw.org/union/allies-partners.

10. Updated information on this case can be found at https://www.ca9.uscourts.gov/content/view.php?pk_id=0000000757.

11. A full explanation of the details of the NCAA's cost of attendance stipends rules and restrictions can be found at http://www.ncaa.com/news/ncaa/article/2015-09-03/cost-attendance-qa.

12. The complete text of the complaint in *Jenkins et al. v. National Collegiate Athletic Association et al.* can be found at http://a.espncdn.com/pdf/2014/0317/NCAA_lawsuit.pdf. Farrey (2014) offers more on Kessler.

13. The Special Committee to Review the NCAA Enforcement and Infractions Process, or "Lee Commission," made its recommendations in November 1991. Lee stated that the group had three primary objectives: that the system for dealing with infractions should be based on cooperation between academic institutions and the NCAA; that the system should be fundamentally fair; and that the process for addressing infractions should be uniform and applicable in all states. Several recommendations were made and adopted, including the tape recording of interviews held during investigation of infractions and access to those recordings and transcripts; access to adequate representation; creating

an appellate process; and establishing a clear separation between investigators on the enforcement staff and individuals in the decision-making body, the NCAA Committee on Infractions. The NCAA was under no obligation to accept the findings of the Lee Commission, and two of its recommendations were not adopted: having an independent trier of the facts in cases of infractions, and holding open hearings. A 2004 congressional hearing addressed those issues, but, as of this writing, the NCAA still has not adopted these two recommendations. See http://commdocs.house.gov/committees/judiciary/hju95802.000/hju95802_0.HTM.

14. Among other provisions, the National Collegiate Athletics Accountability Act proposed under H.R. 2731 would "establish a commission to identify and examine issues of national concern related to the conduct of intercollegiate athletics." This bill draws from the model "College Athlete Protection Act" drafted by members of and supported by the Drake Group. The bill's main sponsor is Congressman Charles Dent (R-PA). Details and updates can be found at https://www.congress.gov/bill/114th-congress/house-bill/2731/text.

15. The NCAA made it permissible, but not mandated, that institutions can award four-year guaranteed scholarships and cost-of-attendance stipends above and beyond the institutionally fixed amount of a full scholarship, which typically covers tuition, room, board, books, and course-related fees. The stipends, determined by the cost of attendance for all students, are typically going to all athletes due to Title IX equity reasons, and can cost an athletic department one to two million dollars in extra expenses.

16. Dure (2015) poses these and other questions.

CHAPTER 6: POTENTIAL ALTERNATIVE SPORTS DEVELOPMENT AND SPORTS DELIVERY MODELS FOR THE UNITED STATES

1. The NBA does have the Gatorade League, the former National Basketball Development League (NBDL), and this league does provide options outside of college, but most would agree that college basketball is a better developmental and commercially successful system very attractive to potential players. Thus virtually no athletes who are recruited to play basketball at colleges and universities in the United States will choose the NBDL over a college scholarship, especially given that they will only have to play a year of college basketball before being eligible for the NBA draft. Most players in the G-League have already played college basketball and are using the league to get up to NBA ability. The G-League signs about 180 players each year, including college players, international prospects, and players who were recently waived by NBA teams following training camp. Players must be 18 years old to be eligible for the NBA G-League Draft, as opposed to the NBA's age minimum of 19. http://dleague.nba.com/faq/.

2. The Drake Group is a national organization of faculty and others whose mission is to defend academic integrity in higher education from the corrosive aspects of commercialized college sports. The Drake Group goals are to: (1) ensure that universities provide accountability of trustees, administrators,

and faculty by publicly disclosing information about the quality of educations college athletes receive; (2) be a major lobby for proposals that ensure quality education for students who participate in intercollegiate athletics, (3) support faculty and staff whose job security and professional standing are threatened when they defend academic standards in intercollegiate sports; (4) influence public discourse on current issues and controversies in sports and higher education; and (5) coordinate local and national reform efforts with other groups that share its mission, goals, and/or proposals (see "Vision, Mission, and Goals" at http://thedrakegroup.org). The Drake Group is currently "in residence" at the University of New Haven.

3. See "Vision, Mission, and Goals" at http://thedrakegroup.org.

4. A survey conducted during the O'Bannon "names, images and likenesses" (NIL) case showed that 69 percent of those surveyed opposed paying college athletes. While the survey's methodology can be debated, along with the findings, it does show how complicated and how misunderstood these issues are. See Wagaman 2014.

5. The statement regarding sports making rational people irrational is actually drawn from my Drake Group colleague Murray Sperber, who stated it during the National Institute for Sports Reform conference at Lake George, New York, in November 2003. Sperber is a noted reformer and famously called for Bobby Knight to be fired at Indiana University when Sperber was an English professor there.

6. When I was growing up it was almost unheard of for high schools to compete on a national level, unless with a border state. However, high school sports teams (and even some in Little League baseball and Pop Warner football) have become nationally "branded" commercial properties. Although not confined to them, this is especially true at schools like Oak Hill Academy, which plays a national schedule in basketball and counts Carmelo Anthony and other noted college and professional players as alumni. LeBron James played several games around the country while he was a student at Akron's St. Vincent–St. Mary High School, including against Oak Hill. There are also many national high school football games and tournaments. It makes one wonder how long it will be before certain sports in high schools and even at lower levels are fully national rather than local endeavors. See Windhorst 2012 and Collings 2014.

7. For discussion of this model primarily derived from proposals by the Drake Group, see Lopiano, Gurney, et al. 2015.

8. The elimination and eventual resurrection of the three sports at UAB has been widely covered in the media. Some of the best sources and explanations come from local media outlets such as the *Birmingham News* and the Alabama Media Group (www.al.com). See especially Talty 2015 and Scarbinsky 2014.

9. See Fenno 2013 and Lopiano, Porto, et al. 2015.

10. Byers (1995) provides a useful history and discussion of the athletic scholarship, which came into being in 1956. It remained essentially unchanged for over fifty years, during which it was restricted to covering tuition, course-related

fees, books, and room and board. It could be cancelled or reduced for any reason at the end of each one-year period of the award (or at other times in the event of serious transgressions by the student, such as academic misconduct or failing out of school). In practice, then and now, such cancellations or reductions often occur at the behest of a coaching staff that is seeking or has already procured better athletic talent. Only recently was the year-to-year scholarship allowed—although, crucially, not required—to be changed to a four-year guarantee, with a spending stipend that varies among schools and is determined by their offices of financial aid.

11. Two notable companies offering to enhance one's chances of getting an athletic scholarship are Athnet (www.athleticscholarships.net) and D1 Sports Training (www.d1sportstraining.com). While it is good to seek advice on the scholarship process, and while these services are sometimes beneficial, it is my view, after years of experience, that a young athlete is either good enough to obtain a scholarship or not with or without these often expensive services.

12. According to a recent NCAA study (NCAA 2016), athletes reported spending much more than the NCAA's officially allowable twenty hours per week on athletic pursuits. Division I athletes reported spending an average of thirty-two hours per week on their sport in season, with Division I football players reporting spending an average of thirty-nine hours per week in season.

13. Some of the more notable academic manipulation and fraud cases in American educationally based sports have occurred at the University of North Carolina (still ongoing), Marshall University (2001), the University of Miami (2013), Florida State University (2009), and the University of South Carolina (2013), to name a few. See Ridpath, Gurney, and Snyder 2015.

14. The information that follows concerning what I am calling the Beebe model draws on Beebe (2014) as well as several email conversations and a Skype interview with Dan Beebe in 2014.

15. Among the reports cited by Henry (2013) are Amara et al., *Education of Elite Young Sportspersons*; European Parliament, *Combining Sport and Education*; INEUM Consulting and TAJ, *Study on the Training of Young Sportsmen.*; and the paper mentioned, European Commission, *Guidelines on Dual Careers of Athletes: Recommended Policy Actions in Support of Dual Careers in High-Performance Sport.*

16. The rules on four years of eligibility within five years of enrollment are found in NCAA Bylaw 14.2. During this period, the athlete must be a full-time student in virtually every academic term to be able to compete. This usually means being enrolled for twelve academic credits during a semester or trimester (NCAA Bylaw 14.01.2). There are some exceptions, such as for students with learning disabilities, or to allow less than full-time enrollment in one's last term. Typically, though, in order to meet all other NCAA academic requirements for satisfactory progress, an athlete needs to be continually enrolled full-time. Consequently, academic advisement for athletics has been more about tweaking the system to keep athletes eligible than about providing a real educational opportunity. I experienced this myself when I worked in intercollegiate athletics.

17. Probably the best examples are baseball players who have gone immediately into the minor leagues, only to decide to give college or another sport a shot. Chris Weinke became a starting quarterback for Florida State after a number of years spent playing minor league baseball, including a stint playing with Michael Jordan and the Birmingham Barons. Drew Henson became a University of Michigan quarterback, splitting time with Tom Brady, after playing a few years in the New York Yankees system. Many others have attended advanced courses of study while playing professionally, such as Oliver Luck of the Houston Oilers and Steve Young of the San Francisco 49ers. Both quarterbacks attended and/or graduated from law school during their professional careers.

18. Under the current NBA Players Association collective bargaining agreement, athletes must be at least nineteen to play in the NBA. The NCAA benefits from this because players who are good enough to try out for a spot in the NBA right out of high school (e.g., Kobe Bryant, LeBron James) are essentially forced into at least one year of college ball, during which educational requirements are low or frankly non-existent. As of now, the athlete only has to pass six credit hours in the initial term in order to continue to be eligible for the more competitive spring term, when the NCAA March Madness tournament takes place. Many premier athletes will cease attending classes during this final term and leave school after the NCAA tournament to prepare for the NBA draft. The institution may be penalized on their Academic Progress Rate (APR), but it is a negligible risk many are willing to take. North Carolina coach Roy Williams once famously said he didn't worry about the APR "at all." Coach John Calipari of the University of Kentucky, who has been both reviled and praised for recruiting and promoting these players, is all for bringing them in and for letting them move on: "What I do is recruit the best players I can and if they're prepared after a year to go, I influence them to go. Then you just keep reloading." http://www.tampabay.com/sports/basketball/college/one-and-done-early-exits-hurt-college-basketball/1080201. See Folsom 2010.

19. See the NCAA press release dated April 22, 2010, available at http://www.ncaa.com/news/basketball-men/2010-04-21/cbs-sports-turner-broadcasting-ncaa-reach-14-year-agreement.

CHAPTER 7: MODEL 1—A REALIGNMENT AND REFORM OF THE CURRENT EDUCATION-BASED SPORTS DEVELOPMENT MODEL

1. Exec. Order No. 11,868, 3A C.F.R. 174 (June 19, 1975), "President's Commission on Olympic Sports," available at http://www.presidency.ucsb.edu/ws/?pid=23939.

2. See Amateur Sports Act of 1978, 36 U.S.C. § 380, and Ted Stevens Olympic and Amateur Sports Act, 36 U.S.C. § 220501 et seq.

3. The number of NCAA Division I athletic programs that actually make a profit usually hovers around twenty. The rest are supported by massive subsidies and student fees. See Berkowitz, Upton, and Brady 2013.

4. Amazingly, after the school winning a national championship and being a consistent top 20 football team, many associated with LSU wanted to fire Les

Miles and replace him with Florida State head coach Jimbo Fisher. This was at a time when, in February 2016, the governor of Louisiana actually said that football programs at public colleges and universities were in danger of being dropped because of plummeting state funding (Fornelli 2015). See also Kalland (2016) on governor John Bel Edwards alluding to the dropping of football.

5. See Lopiano, Gurney, et al. 2015.

6. Some great studies on the financing and subsidizing of intercollegiate athletic programs can be found at the website of the Center for College Affordability and Productivity (www.centerforcollegeaffordability.org); see especially Denhart and Vedder 2010. See also Chapman, Ridpath, and Denhart 2014; and Ridpath, Porto, et al. 2015.

7. Numerous empirical research articles and books establish this. Ridpath (2002) provides a bibliography of sources that cover the subject.

8. Information on the NCAA Eligibility Center can be found at http://www.ncaa.org/student-athletes/future/eligibility-center.

9. The NCAA has maintained initial eligibility certification since 1986 with the enactment of "Prop 48," which mandated a year of ineligibility and no scholarship aid, ostensibly to bolster academic primacy and allow for the academic preparation of incoming freshman athletes. The rule was widely assailed, but, despite many adjustments after lawsuits and political intervention, similar rules do still exist today. The NCAA Clearinghouse, now called the Eligibility Center, was put in place in 1993, taking the initial eligibility decision out of the hands of the schools. See Pound 2009.

10. Details on these proposals can be found in The Drake Group white paper entitled The Drake Group Calls Upon NCAA, Its Member Institutions and Higher EducationRegional Accreditation Agencies to Fulfill Athlete Academic Protection Responsibilities athttps://drakegroupblog.files.wordpress.com/2015/04/tdg-position-protecting-athletes-from-acad-exploitation-final.pdf.

11. In the National Labor Relations Board decision that deemed Northwestern University athletes to be employees, one key factor that came up as helping establish that they were in fact employees was the control the coach had over scholarships. The text of the NLRB decision can be found at http://espn.go.com/pdf/2014/0326/espn_uniondecision.PDF.

12. Academic disclosure has long been the anchor of the Drake Group's academic integrity plan. How it can work is detailed in the outstanding Wisconsin Law Review article by M. Salzwedel and J. Ericson (2003), "Cleaning Up Buckley: How the Family Educational Rights and Privacy Act Shields Academic Corruption in College Athletics," *Wisconsin Law Review* (6): 1053–114.

CHAPTER 8: MODEL 2—AN ACADEMIC/ATHLETIC COMMERCIALIZED SOLUTION

1. Dr. Gerdy is a longtime scholar and critic of the NCAA. His background and expertise in empirical research on college sports are unsurpassed, and he is the author of several books and articles on intercollegiate athletic reform. He is also a strong advocate for music education in primary and secondary

schools and currently runs an organization called Music for Everyone (http://musicforeveryone.org). Gerdy had a standout career as an All-American basketball player at Davidson College and was drafted by the New Jersey Nets and played professionally in the Continental Basketball Association. After earning an MA in sports administration and PhD in higher education at Ohio University, from 1986 to 1989 he worked at the NCAA as a legislative assistant, before serving six years at the Southeastern Conference as associate commissioner for compliance and academic affairs. See http://www.johngerdy.com.

2. Beebe was a longtime and respected intercollegiate athletics administrator before leaving to form the Dan Beebe Group consulting firm. His stellar career included being a member of the NCAA's enforcement staff and a commissioner for the Ohio Valley Conference and the Big 12 Conference, where he was widely credited with keeping the conference together in 2010, when it appeared that several more schools would leave for other conferences after the departures of Texas A&M, the University of Nebraska, and the University of Colorado.

3. Academic disclosure is a lynchpin of the Drake Group plan and is also applicable to the other models presented here. Salzwedel and Ericson (2003), cited above in the text, is one of the better scholarly articles on academic disclosure, written by Drake Group founder Dr. Jon Ericson, the former provost at Drake University, and Minnesota lawyer Matthew Salzwedel.

4. Matthews was one of the most notable figures in sports broadcasting. He, along with Burke Magnus and others, really drove the expansion of college sports programming at ESPN. I met Matthews and Aresco at a Knight Commission on Intercollegiate Athletics meeting in Washington, DC, in February 2004, where Matthews famously uttered that he was not putting anything on television that the universities were not giving to him: "If you don't want it on ESPN on a Thursday night at 9:00 p.m., don't do it. I only do what you let me do" (quoted from personal notes). Sadly, Matthews passed away in March 2013. Aresco, whose notable accomplishments at CBS included negotiating the contracts for the NCAA men's basketball tournament and the fifteen-year agreement for Southeastern Conference football, moved from the high-pressure world of college sports broadcasting to become commissioner of the Big East Conference in August 2012. Less than a year later, the Big East became a casualty of conference realignment in NCAA Division I football when West Virginia moved to the Big 12 and Louisville and Syracuse moved to the Atlantic Coast Conference, leaving the Big East as a basketball-only conference dominated primarily by private schools. From the remnants of the old Big East and some teams from Conference USA, Aresco joined in creating the American Athletic Conference in August 2013, and has served as its commissioner ever since.

5. Matthews quote from 2001 Knight Commission on Intercollegiate Athletics meeting held in Washington, DC, quoted in Gerdy (2006), 176–77. In 2004, under the leadership of Dr. Myles Brand, the NCAA membership embarked on a historic set of reforms that resulted in the creation of the Academic

Progress Rate (APR), an institutionally based metric designed to incentivize an emphasis on athletes' academic progress. "Each college team in Division I is awarded points when an athlete remains eligible and when the athlete advances academically from semester to semester. A college with programs that fall below a specified point level can lose athletic scholarships in those sports, and since 2008–9 can be kept from postseason play in the sport at issue" (Goldstein 2009). The APR has been assailed by many as not being an effective measure of academic primacy and for punishing lower-resource schools that are not able to pay for athlete-focused academic advisers and other targeted and enhanced academic support.

6. Aresco quote from November 2013 Knight Commission on Intercollegiate Athletics meeting held in Washington, DC, quoted in Gerdy (2006), 177.

7. See http://insider.espn.go.com/nfl/draft/schools/_/id/2344/year/2015/ohio-state.

8. The NCAA twenty-hour rule was instituted in the 1980s in an attempt to limit countable athletically related activities for college athletes so they could ostensibly spend more time being a college student. This has not been a successful endeavor. See the NCAA Division II information packet on "Countable Athletically Related Activities" at http://www.ncaa.org/sites/default/files/20-Hour-Rule-Document.pdf for what counts and what does not as of this writing.

CHAPTER 9: MODEL 3—A "EUROPEAN-TYPE" CLUB SPORTS DEVELOPMENT MODEL OR HYBRID MODEL

1. I am part of working group on multisport participation with several distinguished individuals as an offshoot of Project Play and the Aspen Institute (http://www.aspenprojectplay.org). This group has discussed several research studies that demonstrate the benefits of multisport participation in all aspects of life, including noting that forty-two nongovernmental bodies, professional leagues, and other influential organizations have endorsed multisport play as a means to stop the trend toward early sport specialization. Organizations represented in the group include higher education institutions, the United States Tennis Association, USA Triathlon, US Ski and Snowboard, Major League Soccer, and US Lacrosse.

CHAPTER 10: MODEL 4—A COMPLETE SEPARATION OF COMPETITIVE SPORTS FROM SCHOOLS

1. European countries are obviously smaller and more densely populated. However, the template is there for an integrated sports-club system in America. In the Netherlands alone there are over twenty-seven thousand sports clubs.

2. Information on Ajax and its governance, youth development programs, and structure was gleaned over several years and many visits to the club and is based on my own observations, interviews with personnel, and discussions with students at the Hogeschool van Amsterdam.

3. See Layton (2015) for a great discussion of facts and myths with regard to European health care.

CHAPTER 11: FUNDING AND SUSTAINABILITY OF ALTERNATIVE MODELS OF SPORTS DEVELOPMENT AND DELIVERY IN AMERICA

1. See Eurostat: Statistics Explained for detail on EU expenditures on sport at http://ec.europa.eu/eurostat/statistics-explained/index.php/Government _expenditure_on_recreation,_culture_and_religion#Expenditure_on_ .27recreation.2C_culture_and_religion.27.

2. Kuhlmann (2014) and Bucy (2013) offer good reviews of why primary and secondary schools in the United States have moved to a "pay to play" model for school sports in the past ten to twenty years.

3. See the Ministry of the Interior's web page on Germany's federal sports policy at http://www.bmi.bund.de/DE/Themen/Sport/Sportpolitik/sportpolitik _node.html.

4. The estimate that the NFL is so profitable that it theoretically could survive for more than three years without ever selling a ticket was made by Andy Dolich, former chief operating officer of the San Francisco 49ers, in conversation with the author.

5. Conversation with volunteer club president Gert-Jan Pruijn June 2015 at FC Haarlem in Haarlem, the Netherlands.

6. In contrast to the definition of volunteerism in the United States, volunteers in Germany can theoretically receive a modest income for their efforts, although most do not take advantage of this. For example, a volunteer filling a staff role in a sports club is allowed to earn an annual maximum of €2,100 (approximately $2,400). Anyone earning above that amount will count as paid staff. Breuer and Feiler 2013, 12nn10–11; Wicker and Breuer 2011, 191.

References

American Heart Association News. 2015. "Proposed Legislation Could Increase Funding for Physical Education in Schools." *American Heart Association News* (blog), April 25, 2015. http://blog.heart.org/proposed-legislation -could-increase-funding-for-physical-education-in-schools.

Aspen Institute. 2015. *Sport for All, Play for Life: A Playbook to Get Every Kid in the Game.* Washington, DC: Aspen Institute. https://assets.aspeninstitute .org/content/uploads/2015/01/Aspen-Institute-Project-Play-Report.pdf.

———. 2016. *State of Play 2016.* Washington, DC: Aspen Institute. http: //www.aspenprojectplay.org/sites/default/files/StateofPlay_2016 _FINAL.pdf.

Ballinger, Charles E. 1988. "Rethinking the School Calendar." *Educational Leadership* 45 (5): 57–61. http://ascd.com/ASCD/pdf/journals/ed_lead /el_198802_ballinger.pdf.

———. 1995. *Rethinking the School Calendar.* LaCrosse, WI: Alpine Video.

Barber, Bonnie L., Jacquelynne S. Eccles, and Margaret R. Stone. 2001. "Whatever Happened to the Jock, the Brain, and the Princess? Young Adult Pathways Linked to Adolescent Activity Involvement and Social Identity." *Journal of Adolescent Research* 16 (5): 429–55.

Beebe, Dan. 2014. "New Collegiate Model Would End One-Size-Fits-All Approach." *Sports Business Journal.* October 20. http://www.sportsbusinessdaily .com/Journal/Issues/2014/10/20/Opinion/Dan-Beebe.aspx.

Belkin, Douglas, and Melissa Korn. 2016. "University of Missouri System President Tim Wolfe Resigns. Departure comes amid criticism over handling of racial issues; chancellor also steps down." *Wall Street Journal*, November 9. https://www.wsj.com/articles/university-of-missouri -system-president-tim-wolfe-resigns-1447086505.

Bennett, Brian. 2014. "Northwestern Players Get Union Vote." ESPN.com, March 27. http://espn.go.com/college-football/story/_/id/10677763 /northwestern-wildcats-football-players-win-bid-unionize.

Berkowitz, Steve. 2014. "NCAA's Mark Emmert gets Grilling from Senate Committee." *USA Today*, last updated July 9, 2014. https://www.usatoday.com/story/sports/college/2014/07/09/senate-commerce-committee-ncaa-mark-emmert/12409685/.

Berkowitz, Steve, Jodi Upton, and Erik Brady. 2013. "Most NCAA Division I Athletic Departments Take Subsidies." *USA Today*, last updated July 1, 2013. http://www.usatoday.com/story/sports/college/2013/05/07/ncaa-finances-subsidies/2142443/#.

Bernett, Hajo. 1973. *Untersuchungen zur Zeitgeschichte des Sports*. Schorndorf, Germany: Hofmann.

Branch, Taylor. 2011. "The Shame of College Sports." *Atlantic*, October. http://www.theatlantic.com/magazine/archive/2011/10/the-shame-of-college-sports/308643.

Breuer, Christoph, and Svenja Feiler. 2013. *Sportentwicklungsbericht 2011/2012: Analyse zur Situation der Sportvereine in Deutschland: Kurzfassung*. Bonn: Hausdruckerei des Statistischen Bundesamtes.

Broh, Beckett A. 2002. "Linking Extracurricular Programming to Academic Achievement: Who Benefits and Why?" *Sociology of Education* 75 (1): 69–95.

Brown, Gary T. 1999. "NCAA Answers Call to Reform." *NCAA News*, November 22, A1–A4.

Bryant, Howard. 2015. "Today's Athletes Can Change Tomorrow—But Only If They Choose to Do So." ESPN.com, December 15. http://www.espn.com/college-football/story/_/id/14284755/missouri-football-team-shows-athletes-change-tomorrow-push-it.

Bucy, Micah. 2013. "The Costs of the Pay-to-Play Model in High School Athletics." *University of Maryland Law Journal of Race, Religion, Gender and Class* 13 (2): 278–302.

Bundesministerium für Familie. 2010. Familien Report 2010. https://www.bmfsfj.de/blob/93786/bf2701b4762dfda3a843780c36b62c65/familienreport-2010-data.pdf.

Bundesministerium für Gesundheit. 2014. *Daten des gesundheitswesens 2014*. https://www.bundesgesundheitsministerium.de/fileadmin/Dateien/Publikationen/Gesundheit/Broschueren/140813_DdG_2014_Internet_pdf.pdf.

Bundesregierung Deutschland. 2010. *12. Sportbericht der Bundesregierung* [12th Sports Report of the Federal Government]. Berlin: Deutscher Bundestag.

Byers, Walter. 1995. *Unsportsmanlike Conduct: Exploiting College Athletes*. With Charles Hammer. Ann Arbor: University of Michigan Press.

Carpenter, Linda Jean, and R. Vivian Acosta. 2005. *Title IX*. Champaign, IL: Human Kinetics.

Chapman, Michael, B. David Ridpath, and Matthew Denhart. 2014. "An Examination of Increased NCAA Division I Athletic Department Budgets: A Case Study of Student Perceptions of Fee Allocations for Athletics." *International Journal of Sport Management* 15 (1): 25–48.

Cheslock, John. 2007. *Who's Playing College Sports? Trends in Participation*. East Meadow, NY: Women's Sports Foundation.

Chu, Donald, Jeffrey O. Segrave, and Beverly J. Becker, eds. 1985. *Sport and Higher Education*. Champaign, IL: Human Kinetics.

Coakley, Jay. 2014. *Sports in Society: Issues and Controversies*. 11th ed. Boston: McGraw-Hill Education.

Coleman, James S. 1961. "Athletics in High School". *Annals of the American Academy of Political and Social Science* 338 (1): 33–43.

Collings, Buddy. 2014. "High-School National Bowl Games Are On." *Orlando Sentinel*, September 23. http://www.orlandosentinel.com/sports /highschool/blog/os-hs-national-bowl-series-on-20140923-post.html.

Cornell Law School: Legal Information Institute. 2017. 36 *U.S. Code* § *220501 - Short title and definitions*. https://www.law.cornell.edu/uscode /text/36/220501.

Crowley, Joseph N. 2006. *In the Arena: The NCAA's First Century*. Indianapolis, IN: National Collegiate Athletic Association.

Curry, Timothy John, and Otmar Weiss. 1989. "Sport Identity and Motivation for Sport Participation: A Comparison between American College Athletes and Austrian Student Sport Club Members." *Sociology of Sport Journal* 6 (3): 257–68.

Delany, Jim. 2015. *Education First, Athletics Second: The Time for a National Discussion Is upon Us*. http://i.usatoday.net/sports/college/2015-4-17 -Education First Athletics Second.pdf.

Denhart, Matthew, and Richard Vedder. 2010. "Intercollegiate Athletics Subsidies: A Regressive Tax." Washington, DC: Center for Collegiate Affordability and Productivity. http://centerforcollegeaffordability.org/uploads /ICA_Subsidies_RegressiveTax.pdf.

Der Tagesspiegel. 2014a. "Kleine feine Amerikaner." *Der Tagesspiegel*, February 26. http://www.tagesspiegel.de/weltspiegel/gesundheit-kleine-feine -amerikaner/9543102.html.

———. 2014b. "Dickschiff Deutschland." *Der Tagesspiegel*, November 6. http://www.tagesspiegel.de/wissen/uebergewicht-dickschiff-deutschland /10945438.html.

Deutsche Gesellschaft für Kardiologie. 2014. "Neuer Deutscher Herzbericht— Herzmedizin-Fortschritte: Sterblichkeit nimmt weiter ab, immer bessere Versorgung." January 29. http://dgk.org/pressemitteilungen/neuer -deutscher-herzbericht-herzmedizin-fortschritte-sterblichkeit-nimmt-weiter -ab-immer-bessere-versorgung.

Deutscher Olympischer Sportbund. 2014. *Sportstätten in Deutschland: Ein Überblick*. http://www.dosb.de/fileadmin/fm-dosb/arbeitsfelder/umwelt -sportstaetten/Downloads/Sportstaetten/Sportstaetten_Deutschland _Ansicht.pdf.

Dittmore, Stephen W., Daniel F. Mahony, and Damon P. S. Andrew. 2008. "Financial Resource Allocation in U.S. Olympic Sport: National Governing Body Administrators' Fairness Perceptions." Abstract presented at the 23rd Annual Conference of the North American Society for Sport Management, Toronto, Ontario, May 28–31.

Dosh, Kristi. 2013. *Saturday Millionaires: How Winning Football Builds Winning Colleges*. New York: Wiley.

Duderstadt, James J. 2000. *Intercollegiate Athletics and the American University: A University President's Perspective*. Ann Arbor: University of Michigan Press.

Dure, Beau. 2015. "U.S. College Sports Are a Factory for Olympic Medalists— But for How Much Longer?" *Guardian* (US ed.), December 1. https:// www.theguardian.com/sport/blog/2015/dec/01/us-college-sports-are-a -factory-for-olympic-medalists-but-for-how-much-longer.

ESPN. 2013. "Grambling Players End Boycott." ESPN.com, October 22. http://espn.go.com/college-football/story/_/id/9858903/grambling -state-tigers-players-end-boycott-practicing.

European Commission. 1999. *The European Model of Sport*. Publication of the Directorate-General X for Information, Communication, Culture and Audiovisual Media. http://www.bso.or.at/fileadmin/Inhalte/Dokumente /Internationales/EU_European_Model_Sport.pdf.

———. 2014. *Sport and Physical Activity*. Special Eurobarometer 412, report requested by the Directorate-General for Education and Culture. March. http://ec.europa.eu/public_opinion/archives/ebs/ebs_412_en.pdf.

Eurostat: Statistics Explained. 2017. "Government Expenditure on Recreation, Culture and Religion," last updated February 2017. http://ec.europa.eu /eurostat/statistics-explained/index.php/Government_expenditure_on _recreation,_culture_and_religion#Expenditure_on_.27recreation.2C _culture_and_religion.27.

Expert Group on Sustainable Financing of Sport. 2012. "Strengthening Financial Solidarity Mechanisms within Sport." December. http://ec.europa .eu/sport/library/documents/xg-fin-201211-deliverable.pdf.

Falla, Jack. 1981. *NCAA: The Voice of College Sports*. Mission, KN: National Collegiate Athletic Association.

Farrell, Andrew. 2008. "America's Top 10 Olympic Schools." *Forbes*, August 20. http://www.forbes.com/2008/08/20/olympics-colleges-phelps-biz- sports_cx_af_0820olympics.html.

Farrey, Tom. 2009. *Game On: How the Pressure to Win at All Costs Endangers Youth Sports, and What Parents Can Do about It*. New York: ESPN Books.

———. 2014. "Jeffrey Kessler Files against NCAA." ESPN.com, March 18. http://www.espn.com/college-sports/story/_/id/10620388/anti-trust -claim-filed-jeffrey-kessler-challenges-ncaa-amateur-model.

Fenno, Nathan. 2013. "In Court Filing, NCAA Denies Legal Duty to Protect Athletes." *Washington Times*, December 18. http://www.washingtontimes .com/news/2013/dec/18/court-filing-ncaa-denies-legal-duty-protect -athlet/.

Finkel, Ross, Trevor Martin, and Jonathan Paley. 2013. *Schooled: The Price of College Sports*. New York: Makuhari Media in association with the Slater Group.

Folsom, Jim. 2010. "John Calipari and the 'One and Done' Rule: Are There Any Winners?" *Bleacher Report*, April 1. http://bleacherreport.com/articles /372204-john-calipari-and-the-one-and-done-rule-are-there-any-winners.

Forde, Pat. 2015. "U.S. Olympic Committee 'Candidly Concerned' Non -revenue College Sports Will Be Cut." *Yahoo Sports*, April 1. http://sports .yahoo.com/news/u-s--olympic-committee--candidly-concerned--non -revenue-college-sports-will-be-cut-212917571-ncaab.html.

Fornelli, T. 2015. "LSU Prez: Decision to Keep Les Miles Made at Half-time of Texas A&M Game." CBSsports.com, December 3. http:// www.cbssports.com/college-football/news/lsu-prez-decision-to-keep -les-miles-made-at-halftime-of-texas-am-game.

Fort, Rodney. 2000. "European and North American Sports Differences(?)." *Scottish Journal of Political Economy* 47 (4): 431–55.

Foster, George, Norm O'Reilly, and Antonio Dávila. 2016. *Sports Business Management: Decision Making around the Globe*. New York: Routledge.

Frank, Robert H. 2004. *Challenging the Myth: A Review of the Links among College Athletic Success, Student Quality, and Donations*. N.p.: Knight Commission on Intercollegiate Athletics. http://www.knightcommission.org /images/pdfs/kcia_frank_report_2004.pdf.

Frank, Scott. 2015. Presentation, Ohio State University Sports and Society Initiative. u.osu.edu/sportsandsociety/files/2015/10/SportsandSociety-1pkzj8s .pptx.

Fredricks, Jennifer A, and Jacquelynne S. Eccles. 2006. "Is Extracurricular Participation Associated with Beneficial Outcomes? Concurrent and Longitudinal Relations." *Developmental Psychology* 42 (4): 698–713.

Frei, Carolin. 2015. "The History, Development and Impact of the European Club Sports System Compared to the American Educational Sports Model." Master's thesis, University of Bayreuth.

Funk, Gary D. 1991. *Major Violation: The Unbalanced Priorities in Athletics and Academics*. Champaign, IL: Leisure Press.

Gaul, Gilbert. 2015. *Billion-Dollar Ball: A Journey through the Big-Money Culture of College Football*. New York: Viking.

Gems, Gerald R., and Gertrud Pfister. 2009. *Understanding American Sports*. New York: Routledge.

Gerdy, John R. 2002. *Sports: The All-American Addiction*. Jackson: University Press of Mississippi.

———. 2006. *Air Ball: American Education's Failed Experiment with Elite Athletics*. Jackson: University Press of Mississippi.

———. 2014. *Ball or Bands: Football vs. Music as an Educational and Community Investment*. Bloomington, IN: Archway.

Goldstein, Richard. 2009. "Myles Brand, N.C.A.A. President, Dies at 67." September 16. http://www.nytimes.com/2009/09/17/sports/17brand.html ?_r=0.

Grimes, Paul W., and George A. Chressanthis. 1994. "Alumni Contributions to Academics: The Role of Intercollegiate Sports and NCAA Sanctions." *American Journal of Economics and Sociology* 53 (1): 27–40.

Gurney, Gerald, and Mary Willingham. 2014. "Academic Fraud, Athletes and Faculty Responsibility." InsideHigherEd.com, July 18. www.insidehighered

.com/views/2014/07/18/professors-must-take-academic-fraud-among
-athletes-more-seriously-essay.

Gurney, Gerald, Mary Willingham, Donna Lopiano, Brian Porto, B. David
Ridpath, Allen Sack, and Andrew Zimbalist. 2015. *The Drake Group Position Statement: Freshmen Ineligibility in Intercollegiate Athletics.* April
20. https://drakegroupblog.files.wordpress.com/2015/04/tdg-freshman
-ineligibility-position-paper.pdf.

Gurney, Gerald, Mary Willingham, Donna Lopiano, Brian Porto, B. David
Ridpath, Allen Sack, and Andrew Zimbalist. 2015. *The Drake Group Calls
Upon NCAA, Its Member Institutions and Higher Education Regional
Accreditation Agencies to Fulfill Athlete Academic Protection Responsibilities.* April 16. https://drakegroupblog.files.wordpress.com/2015/04/tdg
-position-protecting-athletes-from-acad-exploitation-final.pdf.

Hartmann-Tews, Ilse. 1996. *Sport für alle? Strukturwandel europäischer Sportsysteme im Vergleich: Bundesrepublik Deutschland, Frankreich, Grossbritannien.* Schorndorf, Germany: Hofmann.

Heinemann, Klaus, and Manfred Schubert. 1999. "Sports Clubs in Germany."
In *Sport Clubs in Various European Countries,* edited by Klaus Heinemann,
143–67. Schorndorf, Germany: Hofmann.

Henry, Ian. 2013. "Athlete Development, Athlete Rights and Athlete Welfare:
A European Union Perspective." *International Journal of the History of
Sport* 30 (4):7 356–73.

Hintsanen, Mirka, Saija Alatupa, Helle Pullmann, Paula Hirstiö-Snellman, and
Liisa Keltikangas-Järvinen, L. 2010. "Associations of Self-Esteem and Temperament Traits to Self- and Teacher-Reported Social Status among Classmates." *Scandinavian Journal of Psychology* 51 (6): 488–94.

Hogan, Kieran, and Kevin Norton. 2000. "The 'Price' of Olympic Gold."
Journal of Science and Medicine in Sport 3 (2): 203–18.

Holt, Richard, and Tony Mason. 2000. *Sport in Britain, 1945–2000.* Oxford:
Blackwell.

Howard-Hamilton, Mary F., and Sherry K. Watt. 2001. "Editors' Notes." In
"Student Services for Athletes," edited by Mary F. Howard-Hamilton and
Sherry K. Watt, special issue, *New Directions for Student Services* 2001 (93):
1–6.

Huma, Ramogi, and Ellen J. Staurowsky. 2012. "The $6 Billion Heist: Robbing College Athletes under the Guise of Amateurism." http://www
.ncpanow.org/news/articles/body/6-Billion-Heist-Study_Full.pdf.

Jütting, Dieter H. 1999. "Sportvereinssysteme in Europa: Nationale Strukturen—europäische Gemeinsamkeiten—vergleichende Bemerkungen." In
Sportvereine in Europa zwischen Staat und Markt, edited by Dieter H. Jütting, 35–60. Münster, Germany: Waxmann.

Kalland, Robby. 2016. "Louisiana Governor: College Football in Jeopardy in Midst of Budget Crisis." CBSsports.com, February 12. http://
www.cbssports.com/collegefootball/eye-on-college-football/25481731
/louisiana-governor-college-football-in-jeopardy-in-midst-of-budget-crisis.

Kohl, Harold W., III, and Heather D. Cook, eds. 2013. *Educating the Student Body: Taking Physical Activity and Physical Education to School.* Washington, DC: National Academies Press.

Krüger, Michael. 1993. *Einführung in die Geschichte der Leibeserziehung und des Sports,* vol. 2, *Leibeserziehung im 19. Jahrhundert: Turnen fürs Vaterland.* Schorndorf, Germany: Hofmann.

———. 2013. "The History of German Sports Clubs: Between Integration and Emigration." *International Journal of the History of Sport* 30 (14): 1586–603.

Kuhlmann, Douglas J. 2014. "Lutheran High School, St. Charles, MO: Student-Athlete Activity Participation Fee 2014–2015." Paper submitted to the National Interscholastic Athletic Administrators Association. http://www.niaaa.org/assets/Budget-and-fundraiser.pdf.

Kurscheidt, Markus, and Angela Deitersen-Wieber. 2011. "Sport Governance in Germany." In *Sports Governance in the World: A Socio-historic Approach,* vol. 1, *The Organization of Sport in Europe: A Patch-Work of Institutions, with Few Shared Points,* edited by Claude Sobry, 259–305. Paris: Le Manuscrit.

Lawrence, Heather J., and Ming Li. 2007. "Intercollegiate Athletic Spending: An Examination of Gender Specific Expenditures." Paper presented at the Girls and Women Rock Conference celebrating the 35th anniversary of Title IX, Cleveland, OH, March 29.

Layton, Roslyn. 2015. "10 Things Bernie Sanders (and Paul Krugman) Should Know about Denmark." *Forbes.* October 23. http://www.forbes.com/sites/roslynlayton/2015/10/23/10-things-bernie-sanders-and-paul-krugman-should-know-about-denmark.

Lederman, Douglas. 1991. "Officials Criticized for Athletes' Low Graduation Rates." *Chronicle of Higher Education,* July 31.

———. 1992. "Academically Deficient Athletes Get Some Help." *Chronicle of Higher Education,* November 4.

Lee, Bruce Y. 2016. "Getting Children More Physically Active Could Save Well Over $50 Billion." Forbes.com, May 17. http://www.forbes.com/sites/brucelee/2016/05/17/getting-children-more-physical-active-could-save-well-over-50-billion/.

Liebeskind, Josh, and Mike Baker. 2015. "Bellevue High's Football Success Aided by 'Diploma Mill.'" *Seattle Times,* August 22. Last updated May 26, 2016. http://www.seattletimes.com/sports/high-school/bellevue-highs-football-success-aided-by-diploma-mill.

Litan, Robert E., Jonathan M. Orszag, and Peter R. Orszag. 2003. *The Empirical Effects of Collegiate Athletics: An Interim Report.* N.p.: Sebago Associates. https://www.ncaa.org/sites/default/files/empirical_effects_of_collegiate_athletics_interim_report.pdf.

Littlefield, Bill. 2015. "Ralph Nader and a Plan to 'Save Sports.'" WBUR.org, February 28. http://www.wbur.org/onlyagame/2015/02/28/sports-culture-america-exercise-youth.

Lopiano, Donna, Gerald Gurney, Brian Porto, B. David Ridpath, Allen Sack, Mary Willingham, and Andrew Zimbalist. 2015. *The Drake Group Position*

Statement: Establishment of a Presidential Commission on Intercollegiate Athletics Reform. March 31. https://drakegroupblog.files.wordpress.com /2015/03/final-presidential-commission-position-paper.pdf.

Lopiano, Donna, Brian Porto, Gerald Gurney, B. David Ridpath, Allen Sack, Mary Willingham, and Andrew Zimbalist. 2015. *The Drake Group Position Statement: Compensation of College Athletes Including Revenues from Commercial Use of Their Names, Likenesses, and Images.* March 24. https://drakegroupblog.files.wordpress.com/2015/03/tdg-position-paper -name-image-likeness-final1.pdf.

Lumpkin, Angela. 2015. "Ethical Issues in Intercollegiate Athletics: Purpose Achieved or Challenged?" In *Introduction to Intercollegiate Athletics,* edited by Eddie Comeaux, 48–58. Baltimore, MD: Johns Hopkins University Press.

MacLean, Malcolm. 2013. "A Gap but Not an Absence: Clubs and Sports Historiography." *The International Journal of the History of Sport* 30 (14): 1687–98.

Mandell, Nina. 2015. "Northwestern Football Players May Not Be Allowed to Unionize, But College Sports Still Need a Change." *USA Today,* August 18. http://ftw.usatoday.com/2015/08/northwestern-football-players-may -not-be-allowed-to-unionize-but-college-sports-still-need-a-change.

Mandell, Richard D. 1984. *Sport: A Cultural History.* New York: Columbia University Press.

Marsh, Herbert W., and Sabina Kleitman. 2002 "Extracurricular School Activities: The Good, the Bad, and the Nonlinear." *Harvard Educational Review* 72 (4): 464–514.

Martinez, Courtney. 2016. "2016 Rio Olympics: Current NCAA Student -Athletes Competing by School." NCAA.com. Last updated August 25. http://www.ncaa.com/news/ncaa/article/2016-07-28/2016-rio-olympics -ncaa-olympic-student-athletes-school.

McMillen, Tom. 1992. *Out of Bounds: How the American Sports Establishment Is Being Driven by Greed and Hypocrisy—and What Needs to Be Done about It.* With Paul Coggins. New York: Simon and Schuster.

Miège, Colin. 2011. The Organization of Sport in Europe: A Patch-Work of Institutions, with Few Shared Points." In *Sports Governance in the World: A Socio-historic Approach,* vol. 1, *The Organization of Sport in Europe: A Patch-Work of Institutions, with Few Shared Points,* edited by Claude Sobry, 17–67. Paris: Le Manuscrit.

Miller, Kathleen E. 2009. "They Light the Christmas Tree in Our Town: Reflections on Identity, Gender, and Adolescent Sports." *International Review for the Sociology of Sport* 44 (4): 363–80.

Miracle, Andrew W., Jr., and C. Roger Rees. 1994. *Lessons of the Locker Room: The Myth of School Sports.* Amherst, NY: Prometheus Books.

Morgan, William J. 2012. "The Academic Reform of Intercollegiate Athletics: The Good, the Problematic, and the Truly Worrisome." *Journal of Intercollegiate Sport* 5 (1): 90–97.

Nagel, Siegfried. 2006. *Sportvereine im Wandel: Akteurtheoretische Analysen zur Entwicklung von Sportvereinen.* Schorndorf, Germany: Hofmann.

Nagel, Siegfried, Achim Conzelmann, and Hartmut Gabler. 2004. *Sportvereine: Auslaufmodell oder Hoffnungsträger? Die WLSB-Vereinsstudie.* Tübingen, Germany: Attempto.

NCAA. 2014. *2014–15 NCAA Division I Manual.* Indianapolis, IN: National Collegiate Athletic Association. http://www.ncaapublications.com/productdownloads/D115.pdf.

———. 2016. "NCAA GOALS Study of the Student-Athlete Experience: Initial Summary of Findings." January. http://www.ncaa.org/sites/default/files/GOALS_2015_summary_jan2016_final_20160627.pdf.

Nixon II, Howard. 2014. *The Athletic Trap: How College Sports Corrupted the Academy.* Baltimore: Johns Hopkins University Press.

Noll, Roger G. 2002. "The Economics of Promotion and Relegation in Sports Leagues: The Case of English Football." *Journal of Sports Economics* 3 (2): 169–203.

Office for Civil Rights, Office of the Secretary, Department of Health, Education, and Welfare. 1979. "A Policy Interpretation: Title IX and Intercollegiate Athletics." 44 Fed. Reg. 239 (Dec. 11).

Ohio State University Sports and Society Initiative. Presentation, u.osu.edu/sportsandsociety/files/2015/10/SportsandSociety-1pkzj8s.pptx.

Opaschowski, H. 1996. *Die Zukunft des Sports: Zwischen Inszenierung und Vermarktung.* Hamburg: BAT Freizeit-Forschungsinstitut.

Orszag, Jonathan M., and Mark Israel. 2009. *The Empirical Effects of Collegiate Athletics: An Update Based on 2004–2007 Data.* N.p.: Compass Lexecon. https://www.soe.vt.edu/highered/files/Perspectives_PolicyNews/04-09/TheEmpiricalEffects.pdf.

Orszag, Jonathan M., and Peter R. Orszag. 2005. *The Empirical Effects of Collegiate Athletics: An Update.* N.p.: Compass. http://www.ncaa.org/sites/default/files/empirical_effects_of_collegiate_athletics_update.pdf.

Park, R. 2007. "Sport, Gender and Society in a Transatlantic Victorian Perspective." *International Journal of the History of Sport* 24 (12): 1570–603.

Petchesky, Barry. 2013. "How Temple Football Pulled Everything Down with It." *Deadspin,* December 6. http://deadspin.com/how-temple-football-pulled-everything-down-with-it-1478147064.

Petry, Karen, and Kirstin Hallmann. 2013. "Germany." In *Comparative Sport Development: Systems, Participation and Public Policy,* edited by Kirstin Hallmann and Karen Petry, 75–86. New York: Springer.

Planos, Josh. 2015. "Does Education Have Any Place in College Sports Programs?" *Pacific Standard,* March 16. http://www.psmag.com/books-and-culture/does-education-have-any-place-in-college-sports-programs.

Pot, Niek, and Ivo van Hilvoorde. 2013. "Generalizing the Effects of School Sports: Comparing the Cultural Contexts of School Sports in the Netherlands and the USA." *Sport in Society: Cultures, Commerce, Media, Politics* 16 (9): 1164–75.

Pound, Richard. 2009. "NCAA's Clearinghouse Rules: Who's Looking Out for the Student-Athlete?" Fastweb.com, April 21. http://www.fastweb.com/student-life/articles/ncaa-s-clearinghouse-rules-who-s-looking-out-for-the-student-athlete?page=2.

Reed, Ken. 2015. *How We Can Save Sports: A Game Plan*. New York: Rowman and Littlefield.

———. 2014, September 17. "Is it Time for a National Sports Commission?" http://www.huffingtonpost.com/ken-reed/is-it-time-for-a-national_b_5600613.html.

Ridpath, B. David. 2002. "NCAA Division I Student-Athlete Characteristics as Indicators of Academic Achievement and Graduation from College." PhD diss., West Virginia University. Available from ProQuest Dissertations and Theses database (UMI No. 3055939).

———. 2007. *Confessions of a former wrestling coach regarding the application of Title IX and the sport of wrestling*. Paper presented at the meeting of the Girls and Women Rock Symposium celebrating the 35th Anniversary of Title IX, Cleveland, OH, April.

Ridpath, B. David, Gerald Gurney, and Eric Snyder. 2015. "NCAA Academic Fraud Cases and Historical Consistency: A Comparative Content Analysis." *Journal of Legal Aspects of Sport* 25 (2): 75–103.

Ridpath, B. David, Brian Porto, Gerald Gurney, Donna Lopiano, Allen Sack, Mary Willingham, and Andrew Zimbalist. 2015. *The Drake Group Position Statement: Student Fee and Institutional Subsidy Allocations to Fund Intercollegiate Athletics*. March 2. https://drakegroupblog.files.wordpress.com/2015/04/position-statement-student-fees-final-3-2-15.pdf.

Ridpath, B. David, Athena Yiamouyiannis, Heather Lawrence, and Kristen Galles. 2008. "Changing Sides: The Failure of the Wrestling Community's Challenges to Title IX and New Strategies for Saving NCAA Sport Teams." *Journal of Intercollegiate Sport* 1 (2): 255–83.

Rosen, Linda. 2013. "The Truth Hurts: The STEM Crisis Is Not a Myth." *Huffington Post*. Last updated November 11, 2013. http://www.huffingtonpost.com/linda-rosen/the-truth-hurts-the-stem-_b_3900575.html.

Rosenwald, Michael S. 2015. "Are Parents Ruining Youth Sports? Fewer Kids Play amid Pressure." *Washington Post*, October 4. https://www.washingtonpost.com/local/are-parents-ruining-youth-sports-fewer-kids-play-amid-pressure/2015/10/04/eb1460dc-686e-11e5-9ef3-fde182507eac_story.html.

Ryan, Frank J. 1989. "Participation in Intercollegiate Athletics: Affective Outcomes." *Journal of College Student Development* 30 (2): 122–28.

Sabo, Don, and Marj Snyder. 2013. *Progress and Promise: Title IX at 40*. Ann Arbor, MI: SHARP Center for Women and Girls.

Sack, Allen L., and Ellen J. Staurowsky. 1998. *College Athletes for Hire: The Evolution and Legacy of the NCAA's Amateur Myth*. Westport, CT: Praeger.

Sack, Allen L., and Andrew Zimbalist. 2013. "Drake Group Report: O'Bannon, Amateurism, and the Viability of College Sport." http://thedrakegroup

.org/2013/04/10/drake-group-report-obannon-amateurism-and-the
-viability-of-college-sport.

Salzwedel, Matthew R., and Jon Ericson. 2003. "Cleaning Up Buckley: How
the Family Educational Rights and Privacy Act Shields Academic Corruption in College Athletics." *Wisconsin Law Review* 2003 (6): 1053–114.

Sawyer, Thomas H., Kimberly J. Bodey, and Lawrence W. Judge. 2008. *Sport
Governance and Policy Development: An Ethical Approach to Managing
Sport in the 21st Century.* Champaign, IL: Sagamore.

Scarbinsky, Kevin. 2014. "Former UAB Football Players Concerned the Program May Be Shut Down." AL.com, November 5. http://www.al.com
/sports/index.ssf/2014/11/former_uab_football_players_co.html.

Scheerder, Jeroen, Hanne Vandermeerschen, Charlotte Van Tuyckom, Remco
Hoekman, Koen Breedveld, and Steven Vos. 2011. *Understanding the
Game: Sport Participation in Europe: Facts, Reflections and Recommenda-
tions.* Leuven, Belgium: Katholieke Universiteit Leuven.

Schlicht, Wolfgang, and Ralf Brand. 2007. *Körperliche Aktivität, Sport und
Gesundheit: Eine interdisziplinäre Einführung.* Weinheim, Germany: Beltz
Juventa.

Shulman, James L., and William G. Bowen. 2001. *The Game of Life: College
Sports and Educational Values.* Princeton, NJ: Princeton University Press.

Smolianov, Peter, Dwight H. Zakus, and Joseph Gallo. 2015. *Sport Development in the United States: High Performance and Mass Participation.* New
York: Routledge.

Sobry, Claude, ed. 2011. *Sports Governance in the World: A Socio-historic Approach,* vol. 1, *The Organization of Sport in Europe: A Patch-Work of Institutions, with Few Shared Points.* Paris: Le Manuscrit.

Sparvero, Emily, Laurence Chalip, and B. Christine Green. 2008. "United
States." In *Comparative Elite Sport Development: Systems, Structures and
Public Policy,* edited by Barrie Houlihan and Mick Green, 242–70. Oxford:
Butterworth-Heinemann.

Sperber, Murray A. 1990. *College Sports, Inc.: The Athletic Department vs. the
University.* New York: Henry Holt.

Splitt, Frank G. 2003. *Reclaiming Academic Primacy in Higher Education:
A Brief: Working for Reform in Intercollegiate Athletics and Engineering
Education.* Chicago: IEC Publications. https://drakegroupblog.files
.wordpress.com/2012/12/splitt_reclaiming_academic_primacy.pdf.

Staurowsky, Ellen J., and Robertha Abney. 2011. "Intercollegiate Athletics."
In *Contemporary Sport Management,* 4th ed., edited by Paul M. Pedersen,
Janet B. Parks, Jerome Quarterman, and Lucie Thibault, 142–63. Cham-
paign, IL: Human Kinetics.

Stiegelmayr, Judith. 2015. "The Funding, Marketing, and Sponsorship Apparatus
of the European Club Sports System." Master's thesis, University of Bayreuth.

Stokvis, Ruud. 2009. "Social Functions of High School Athletics in the United
States: A Historical and Comparative Analysis." *Sport in Society* 12 (9):
1236–49.

Strauss, Ben. 2014. "Colleges' Shift on Four-Year Scholarships Reflects Players' Growing Power." *New York Times*, October 28.

Taks, Marijke. 2011. "Sport Clubs, the 'Sport for All Movement,' and the Recession in Western Europe." In *Contemporary Sport Management*, 4th ed., edited by Paul M. Pedersen, Janet B. Parks, Jerome Quarterman, and Lucie Thibault, 24–25. Champaign, IL: Human Kinetics.

Talty, John. 2015. "3 Key Reasons Why UAB Erred in Dropping Sports, According to OSKR Report." AL.com, April 23. http://www.al.com/sports/index.ssf/2015/04/3_key_points_from_oskrs_report.html.

Thelin, John R. 1994. *Games Colleges Play: Scandal and Reform in Intercollegiate Athletics*. Baltimore: Johns Hopkins University Press.

———. 2000. "Good Sports? Historical Perspective on the Political Economy of Intercollegiate Athletics in the Era of Title IX, 1972–1997." *Journal of Higher Education* 71 (4): 391–410.

Thiel, Ansgar, and Jochen Mayer. 2009. "Characteristics of Voluntary Sports Clubs Management: A Sociological Perspective." *European Sport Management Quarterly* 9 (1): 81–98.

Thoma, James E., and Laurence Chalip. 2003. *Sport Governance in the Global Community*. Morgantown, WV: Fitness Information Technology.

Thomas, Robert McG. 1985. "Olympics to Allow Pros in 3 Sports." *New York Times*, March 1. http://www.nytimes.com/1985/03/01/sports/olympics-to-allow-pros-in-3-sports.html.

van Hilvoorde, Ivo, Jan Vorstenbosch, and Ignaas Devisch. 2010. "Philosophy of Sport in Belgium and the Netherlands: History and Characteristics." *Journal of the Philosophy of Sport* 37 (2): 225–36.

Wagaman, Michael. 2014. "O'Bannon Trial: Survey Says Public Doesn't Want College Athletes to Be Paid." *USA Today*, last updated June 25, 2014. http://www.usatoday.com/story/sports/college/2014/06/24/ed-obannon-antitrust-case-vs-ncaa-day-12/11312913.

Watt, Sherry K., and James L. Moore III. 2001. "Who Are Student-Athletes?" In "Student Services for Athletes," edited by Mary F. Howard-Hamilton and Sherry K. Watt, special issue, *New Directions for Student Services* 2001 (93): 7–18.

Wegener, Ger J. 1992. *Sport in the Member States of the European Community*. Arnhem, Netherlands: Netherlands Sports Confederation.

Wicker, Pamela, and Christoph Breuer. 2011. "Scarcity of Resources in German Non-profit Sport Clubs." *Sport Management Review* 14 (2): 188–201.

Wilson, Kenneth L., and Jerry Brondfield. 1967. *The Big Ten*. Englewood Cliffs, NJ: Prentice-Hall.

Windhorst, Brian. 2012. "Decade Later, LBJ-Melo Still Goin' Strong" ESPN.com, February 23. http://espn.go.com/nba/truehoop/miamiheat/story/_/id/7605201/lebron-james-vs-carmelo-anthony-10-years-ago.

Wise, Mike. 2003. "Basketball: LeBron James Is Ruled Ineligible after Taking Gifts." *New York Times*. February 1. http://www.nytimes.com/2003/02/01/sports/basketball-lebron-james-is-ruled-ineligible-after-taking-gifts.html.

Wolken, Dan. 2014. "NCAA: Mo'ne Davis Won't Lose Amateur Status from Ad." October 22. http://www.usatoday.com/story/sports/college/2014/10/22/mone-davis-ncaa-amateur-status-eligibility-chevrolet-commercial-uconn-huskies-llws/17702519.

Wolverton, Brad. 2007. "The Athletics Department of the Future." *Chronicle of Higher Education* 53 (46): A28.

———. 2015. "NCAA Says It's Investigating Academic Fraud at 20 Colleges." *Chronicle of Higher Education*, January 21. http://chronicle.com/article/NCAA-Says-It-s-Investigating/151315.

Zimbalist, Andrew. 1999. *Unpaid Professionals: Commercialism and Conflict in Big-Time College Sports*. Princeton, NJ: Princeton University Press.

Zimmer, Annette. 2013. "Auslaufmodell Verein? Vom Veralten eines ge-sellschaftlichen Strukturmoments." *Theorie und Praxis der sozialen Arbeit* 64 (6): 447–55.

Znidar, Mark. 2007. "Running on Empty." *Columbus Dispatch*, May 3. Last updated November 9, 2007. http://www.dispatch.com/content/stories/sports/2007/05/03/ou_track.ART_ART_05-03-07_C1_JV6IUI9.html.

Index